Rotarian Flavors of the World Cookbook

A collection of 400 recipes from Rotary Districts in over 100 Countries throughout the world

END POLIO NOW

A World Wide Fundraising project for the Eradication of Polio

Appreciation

The Rotary Club of Long Grove, would like to thank all Rotary Districts throughout the world, their friends and acquaintances that submitted recipes for publication in this unique cookbook. Every cookbook purchased contributes to the Polio Plus eradication fund and takes us one step closer to the elimination of polio. A special 'thank you' to the volunteers who dedicated their time and talents to compiling this International Cookbook. Let us all work together to make this world polio free and a better place.

Copyright © 2011
Morris Press Cookbooks
All rights reserved. Reproduction in whole or
in part without written permission is prohibited.

Printed in the U.S.A. by

Morris Press Cookbooks

P.O. Box 2110 • Kearney, NE 68848
800-445-6621 • www.morriscookbooks.com

What is Rotary

Rotary is a worldwide volunteer organization of more than 1.2 million business professionals and community leaders united worldwide to provide humanitarian service and help build goodwill and peace. More than 34,000 Rotary clubs in more than 200 countries conduct projects to address today's challenges, including illiteracy, disease, hunger, poverty, lack of clean water, and environmental concerns, while encouraging high ethical standards in all vocations.

Polio Plus is Rotary's flagship program. By the time Polio is eradicated, Rotary club members will have contributed over $1 billion and countless volunteer hours to immunize more than two billion children in 122 countries. Rotary is a spearheading partner in the Global Polio Eradication Initiative, along with the World Health Organization, UNICEF, and the U.S Centers for Disease Control and Prevention.

Founded in Chicago in 1905 as the world's first volunteer service organization, Rotary quickly expanded around the globe. Today, club members meet weekly to plan service projects, discuss community and international issues, and enjoy fellowship. Clubs are nonpolitical and open to every race, culture and creed.

Object of Rotary

The Object of Rotary is to encourage and foster the ideal of service as a basis of worthy enterprise and, in particular, to encourage and foster:

FIRST: The development of acquaintance as an opportunity for service;

SECOND: High ethical standards in business and professions, the recognition of the worthiness of all useful occupations, and the dignifying of each Rotarian's occupation as an opportunity to serve society;

THIRD: The application of the ideal of service in each Rotarian's personal, business, and community life.

FOURTH: The advancement of international understanding, goodwill, and peace through a world fellowship of business and professional persons united in the ideal of service.

The Rotary 4 Way Test

The test, which has been translated into more than 100 languages, asks the following questions: Of the things we think, say or do

Is it the **TRUTH**?

Is it **FAIR to all concerned**?

Will it build **GOODWILL and BETTER FRIENDSHIPS**?

Will it be BENEFICIAL to all concerned?

∞∞

Disclaimer: The recipes herein are submitted by members of various Rotary Districts, their friends and acquaintances. Rotary International does not endorse any recipe herein. Neither Rotary International, nor any of its directors, officers, members, districts and clubs, or affiliates shall be responsible for the authenticity, preparation, and/or results of the recipes herein.

The Rotary Foundation

Through Foundation grants and programs, Rotarians and other contributors can help change the world. They can finance a well for a village that lacks clean water, improve the environment, or provide scholarships to educate the next generation. The grants and programs available to Rotarians allow them to realize Rotary's humanitarian mission throughout the world, including its number-one goal of eradicating polio.

Polio Plus: To eradicate polio, Rotarians are working to ensure that children are immunized against this disease. Since the Polio Plus program's inception, more than two billion children have received the oral polio vaccine.

Humanitarian Grants Program:
1. **Disaster Recovery** - Allows Rotarians to donate money in response to specific disasters. Funds are distributed to local committees to support recovery efforts.
2. **District simplified Grants** - Support the service activities of districts locally and abroad.
3. **Health, Hunger and Humanity (3-H) Grants** - Fund large-scale, two-to four- year projects that improve health, alleviate hunger, or promote human development.
4. **Matching Grants** - Provide matching funds for the international service projects of Rotary clubs and districts.

Educational Programs:
1. **Youth Exchange:** As a Student, you'll spend up to a year living with a few host families and attending school in a different country. Age: 14-19 years old.
2. **Ambassadorial Scholarships** -The program sponsors several types of scholarships for undergraduate and graduate students. Scholars serve as goodwill ambassadors to the host country. Age: 18-30 years old.
3. **Group Study Exchange** - an activity that enables paired districts in different countries to send teams of five young business and professional men and women for a six-week period of study and exploration. Age: 25-40.
4. **Rotary World Peace Fellowships** - Sponsorship of a scholar to study at one of the seven Rotary Centers for International Studies in peace and conflict resolution for a master's level degree.

Table of Contents

Appetizers & Beverages   1

Soups & Salads. 29

Vegetables & Side Dishes 63

Main Dishes. 95

Desserts 147

Ten Minute Meals 189

Index 197

Appetizers & Beverages

Helpful Hints

- Add flavor to tea by dissolving old-fashioned lemon drops or hard mint candies in it. They melt quickly and keep the tea brisk.

- Make your own spiced tea or cider. Place orange peels, whole cloves, and cinnamon sticks in a 6-inch square piece of cheesecloth. Gather the corners and tie with a string. Steep in hot cider or tea for 10 minutes; steep longer if you want a stronger flavor.

- Always chill juices or sodas before adding them to beverage recipes.

- Calorie-free club soda adds sparkle to iced fruit juices and reduces calories per portion.

- To cool your punch, float an ice ring made from the punch rather than using ice cubes. It appears more decorative, prevents diluting, and does not melt as quickly.

- Place fresh or dried mint in the bottom of a cup of hot chocolate for a cool and refreshing taste.

- When making fresh lemonade or orange juice, one lemon yields about ¼ cup juice, while one orange yields about ⅓ cup juice.

- Never boil coffee; it brings out acids and causes a bitter taste. Store ground coffee in the refrigerator or freezer to keep it fresh.

- Always use cold water for electric drip coffee makers. Use 1–2 tablespoons ground coffee for each cup of water.

- How many appetizers should you prepare? Allow 4–6 appetizers per guest if a meal quickly follows. If a late meal is planned, allow 6–8 appetizers per guest. If no meal follows, allow 8–10 pieces per guest.

- If serving appetizers buffet-style or seating is limited, consider no-mess finger foods that don't require utensils to eat.

- Think "outside the bowl." Choose brightly-colored bowls to set off dips or get creative with hollowed-out loaves of bread, bell peppers, heads of cabbage, or winter squash.

- Cheeses should be served at room temperature – approximately 70°.

- To keep appetizers hot, make sure you have enough oven space and warming plates to maintain their temperature.

- To keep appetizers cold, set bowls on top of ice or rotate bowls of dips from the fridge every hour or as needed.

APPETIZERS & BEVERAGES

SKEWERS WITH CASHEW NUT SATAY

From the region of District 9350
Namibia

1 crocodile filet or 2 lg. chicken breasts, cut into thin strips
½ tsp. salt to taste
½ tsp. fresh ground pepper to taste
2 garlic cloves, crushed
2 T. soy sauce
Juice of 1 lemon
3 T. olive oil
4 T. crunchy peanut butter
6 oz. unsalted cashews, crushed
Juice of 1 lemon
6 oz. thick coconut milk
1 fresh green chile, chopped to taste
1 T. soy sauce to season
Dash of palm sugar according to taste
8-12 bamboo skewers or 8-12 cocktail sticks, soaked in water for assembling

Season the crocodile or chicken generously with salt and freshly ground black pepper. Cut into strips about 3 inches long and ½ inch wide. Mix together the marinade ingredients of lemon juice, olive oil, garlic and soy sauce and marinate the crocodile or chicken strips for an hour. **To make the satay sauce:** Combine peanut butter, cashews, lemon juice, coconut milk, chile, soy sauce and sugar together in a small pan, adding just enough soy sauce to season. Simmer very gently for five minutes. Preheat a barbecue, grill or griddle pan until very hot. Thread two or three strips of marinated crocodile or chicken meat onto each skewer and place on the barbecue grill. Cook for a few minutes on each side until cooked through and golden. Serve the skewers with the hot satay sauce for dipping.

STUFFED PRUNES WITH BACON

From the region of District 1170-1220
England

48 dried pitted prunes
48 walnut halves
1½ c. ruby port
½ c. water
24 slices bacon

(continued)

Stuff each prune with walnut half. Mix port and water; pour over prunes in bowl. Let stand, stirring occasionally, until prunes are plump, about 2 hours. Cut bacon slices into halves. Wrap bacon around prunes. Arrange on rack in broiler pan. Set oven to broil or 500°F. Broil for 10 minutes until bacon seems crisp and done.

SKEWERED CANADIAN BACON

From the region of District 5020, 5040
Canada

32 slices Canadian bacon
1 lb. mozzarella cheese
16 slices French bread (the long narrow kind)
16 slices raw tomato
$\frac{2}{3}$ c. salad oil

2 cans tomato sauce (approx. 8 oz. each)
2 c. grated Parmesan cheese
1 tsp. paprika
$\frac{1}{2}$ c. salad oil
4 skewers, 12 inches long

Cut the French bread into ½-inch pieces. The raw tomato is also cut into ½-inch slices. You'll need 32 pieces of cheese to equal the number of slices of bacon. Cut the cheese into 1-inch squares about ¼ inch thick. Wrap the slice of bacon around the cheese. Press the bacon firmly to hold the cheese in place. Cut each piece of tomato and each piece of bread in half. Heat the ⅔ cup of oil in a large skillet. Brown bread on both sides. Be prepared to turn bread quickly to avoid burning. It should be merely light brown. On each skewer, thread alternate pieces of bacon wrapped cheese, bread and tomato. Begin and end with the cheese. Place each skewer in a shallow baking pan. Be sure the folded top of each piece of bacon is up. Pour tomato sauce over each skewer. Sprinkle generously with Parmesan cheese. Sprinkle lightly with paprika and additional salad oil. Preheat the oven to 400°F. Bake the skewers until brown on top. Serve immediately while still warm.

SEVEN LAYER DIP FOR TORTILLA CHIPS

From the region of District 5170
USA

1 (16-oz.) can refried beans
1 c. thick 'n chunky salsa
2 c. guacamole
2 c. sour cream
1 c. chopped green onions
2 tomatoes, cut into ½-inch cubes

2 sm. (3⅘-oz.) cans sliced black olives
8 oz. Cheddar or Mexican mix cheese

(continued)

Stir refried beans and salsa together. Spread them on the bottom of your square or rectangular serving dish, then layer the rest of the ingredients, finishing with the cheese. Chill for several hours. Serve with tortilla chips.

TONGAN OTAI (Fruit Drink)

From the region of District 9920
Tonga

½ watermelon, skinned and flesh removed
2 c. chopped apples
2 c. chopped pineapple

2 c. coconut milk
Cold water
Sugar to taste

Mix watermelon, apples and pineapple in a processor and then pour in coconut milk or cream, mixing. Add cold water. Sweeten with sugar and refrigerate.

FISH HOUSE PUNCH

From the region of District 6440
USA

36 oz. dark rum
24 oz. lemon juice
25 oz. brandy

4 oz. peach brandy
¾ lb. superfine sugar
40 oz. water

Dissolve sugar in some of the water. Add juice and the rest of the water and stir. Add liquor 2-3 hours before serving and refrigerate. Serve in a punch bowl with ice.

TADAM MIMLI (Stuffed Tomatoes)

From the region of District 2110
Malta

8 lg. tomatoes
1 lg. c. fine bread crumbs
1 T. capers
8 anchovy fillets

1 T. mint
2 T. olive oil
1 T. wine vinegar
Salt and pepper to taste

Halve tomatoes horizontally, peel and de-seed. Chop capers, anchovies and mint and mix well with bread crumbs, adding oil, and dash of vinegar to moisten. Knead well using hands and fork, adding salt and pepper to taste. Fill tomatoes and let stay in the refrigerator. Usually tastes better the next day.

TONKATSU (Breaded Pork on Skewers)

From the region of District 2500-2840
Japan

6 pork loin cutlets, about ½ inch thick
Salt and pepper to season
1 ½ c. flour

2 c. Japanese dried bread crumbs (panko)
2 eggs, lightly beaten
Bamboo skewers

Sauce:

½ c. tomato sauce
2 T. Worcestershire sauce

2 T. soy sauce
2 T. white wine

Cut pork into even-sized thin narrow strips. Insert meat into bamboo skewers. Sprinkle with salt and pepper on both sides. Dip each pork skewer into the flour, then the egg and then coat with the panko bread crumbs. Press the bread crumbs lightly into the meat. Lay the breaded skewer in a single layer and refrigerate for half an hour so the coating adheres well. Heat enough oil to cover the meat. Slide 3-4 skewers of breaded pork and fry until the underside turns golden brown, then turn over. Do not fry too many pieces together at one time. Drain on a rack or paper towels. Serve on top or next to a bed of well drained shredded cabbage. Mix all the ingredients for the sauce and use as a dip for the skewers.

TOLTOTT PAPRIKA (Stuffed Peppers)

From the region of District 1911
Hungary

6 lg. bell peppers
½ c. uncooked rice, soaked in water for 20 minutes
½ c. finely chopped onion
¼ lb. ground pork
½ lb. ground beef
3 cloves garlic, minced

¼ c. chopped parsley
1 T. Hungarian paprika
Salt and pepper to season
2 eggs well beaten
1 c. tomato sauce
½ tsp. sugar

Prepare the bell peppers by cutting off the stem and discarding it. Cut about ⅛ off the top of the peppers so that the opening is pretty wide. Scoop out the membrane from the inside and discard. Chop the top of the pepper that has been cut off. Add the chopped pepper tops to a large bowl, along with the beef, pork, rice, onions, garlic, parsley, paprika, salt, pepper and eggs. Mix together well. Stuff each pepper with some of the meat mixture. Let it be a very loose filled pepper. Leave a little room for the stuffing to grow as the rice will swell as it cooks. Preheat oven

(continued)

to 350°F. Grease a casserole dish large enough to hold the peppers standing up. Mix together the tomato sauce and sugar and pour it over the peppers. Cover the casserole tightly with aluminum foil and place in the oven. Bake for 45 minutes to an hour or until the stuffing is cooked through. Serve pepper with a dollop of sour cream.

HOT DEVIL DAIQUIRI

From the region of District 6450
USA

1½ c. hot water
¼ c. sugar
2 sticks cinnamon
8 whole cloves

6 oz. frozen lemonade concentrate
6 oz. frozen limeade concentrate
½ c. light rum

In 2-quart microproof casserole, combine hot water, sugar, spices and condensed juices. Stir, then cook on high 5-6 minutes or until mixture boils. Heat rum in microproof container on high for 30 seconds. Ignite and pour over hot beverage. Ladle into punch cups for serving.

CRAB PANCAKES

From the region of District 3330-3360
Thailand

200g cooked crab meat
⅓ c. self-rising flour
⅔ c. thick coconut milk
2 T. milk
1 egg yolk

2 tsp. fish sauce
1½ tsp. green curry paste
500g lg. uncooked prawns, shelled, chopped finely
½ c. (60ml) peanut oil

Salsa:

2 med. mangoes (430g), chopped finely
3 lg. tomatoes, seeded and chopped finely
2 green onions, chopped finely
1 T. sweet chili sauce

2 tsp. balsamic vinegar
2 tsp. lime juice
2 T. chopped fresh coriander leaves
1 hot green pepper, chopped finely

Squeeze excess moisture from crab. Place flour in medium bowl; gradually stir in combined milks, egg yolk, sauce and paste; beat until smooth. Stir in crab and prawns. Heat oil in large frying pan, drop rounded tablespoons of prawn mixture into pan; spread to 7-centimeter rounds. Cook until bubbles appear, turn pancakes, cook until browned on other side and cooked through. Cover pancakes to keep warm. You
(continued)

will need 12 pancakes for this recipe. Just before serving, top pancakes with Spicy Salsa. **Spicy Salsa:** Combine ingredients in medium bowl.

COURGETTES IN YOGHURT

From the region of District 2482
Bulgaria

4 courgettes (zucchini), thinly sliced
Salt
Plain flour for coating

Oil for shallow frying
2 c. thick natural yoghurt
3 garlic cloves, crushed
2 T. freshly chopped dill

Place the sliced courgettes in a pan, sprinkle with salt and leave for 10 minutes. Dry the courgette slices on kitchen paper, then coat with flour on all sides. Heat the oil in a large frying pan until very hot, then add the courgette slices and fry on both sides until golden brown. Pat dry. Place the yoghurt, garlic and dill in a mixing bowl and mix well. Place the yoghurt in a wide shallow serving dish and top with the drained courgettes. Chill in the refrigerator for 2 hours before serving.

DRUNKIN BOURBON

From the region of District 5300
USA

9 c. water
2-3 c. bourbon
1 (12-oz.) can frozen orange juice concentrate, thawed and undiluted
1 (12-oz.) can frozen lemonade concentrate, thawed and undiluted

1 ¼ c. sugar
1 T. instant tea
3 (16-oz.) bottles lemon-lime carbonated beverage

Combine first 6 ingredients; stir well. Freeze overnight or until firm. Remove from freezer 30 minutes before serving (mixture should be slushy); combine with lemon-lime beverage, stirring well. Makes 1 gallon.

FRUIT CHEESE SPREAD

From the region of District 5360
Canada

½ c. chopped mixed dried fruits
2 T. port or orange juice
250g pkt. cream cheese

½ c. grated cheddar cheese
Grated rind of 1 orange

Combine fruits in bowl. Add port (or orange juice), cover, stand 1-2 hours. Beat softened cream cheese and cheddar cheese together in electric mixer, stir in orange rind and fruit mixture. Spoon into a small serving dish and serve with crackers. For maximum flavor, prepare a day in advance. It will keep for 4 days.

FLAPJACKS

From the region of District 1280
Isle of Man

½ c. unsalted butter
4 oz. cheddar cheese, finely grated

¼ c. honey
2 c. porridge oats
1 pinch salt and pepper

Put butter, cheese and honey into a saucepan over low heat; stir until melted. Add oats and blend thoroughly. Press mixture into well greased square pan. Bake in 350°F oven, or gas mark 4, for 30 minutes or until golden brown. Cut into fingers while still warm. Allow to cool before removing from baking tin. Store in airtight container.

FRUIT DIP

From the region of District 7040
USA

1 (8 oz.) cream cheese, softened
1 c. Cool Whip
¾ c. brown sugar

⅓ c. Kahlua
1 c. sour cream

Mix cream cheese and Cool Whip; set aside. On low heat, mix Kahlua and brown sugar until blended (about 2 minutes). Mix the two together and add sour cream, beat until creamy. Refrigerate for 2 days. Serve with sliced fruit for dipping. A big hit for summer barbecues or any time.

GROMPEREKICHELCHER (Potato Fritters)

From the region of District 1630
Luxembourg

1 ¼ kg potatoes
3 onions
2 shallots
Parsley
6 eggs

3 T. flour
Salt
Pepper
Oil for frying

Wash, peel and coarsely grate the potatoes. Put them in a cloth and press them. Chop the parsley, shallots and onions and mix them in. Add the beaten eggs. Salt and pepper to taste. Mix in the flour. Heat the oven in a pan until very hot. Form flat cakes out of the potato mixture and fry them in the oil until golden brown on both sides.

APPLE CIDER DRINK

From the region of District 6440
USA

2 sticks cinnamon
1 tsp. whole cloves
1 tsp. whole allspice

2 qt. apple cider
½ c. brown sugar, packed
1 orange, sliced

Place cinnamon, cloves and allspice in a double thickness of cheesecloth; bring up corners of cloth and tie with a string to form a bag. Place cider and brown sugar in a slow cooker; stir until sugar dissolves. Add spice bag. Place orange slices on top. Cover and cook on low for 2-5 hours. Remove spice bag before serving.

HOT ARTICHOKE & SPINACH DIP

From the region of District 6000
USA

1 c. coarsely chopped artichokes
½ c. frozen spinach, thawed
8 oz. cream cheese
½ c. Parmesan cheese

½ tsp. crushed red pepper flakes
¼ tsp. salt
⅛ tsp. garlic powder
Dash of pepper

Boil spinach and artichoke 10 minutes until tender. Drain very well. Heat cream cheese for 1 minute in microwave, combine everything. Bake in ovenproof dish at 350°F until bubbly hot (approximately 30 minutes). Serve hot with bread or crackers.

HUMMUS

From the region of District 2490
Israel

2 c. canned chickpeas
1 c. tahini
½ c. lemon juice
3 cloves garlic, peeled
1 tsp. salt
Pepper to taste
½ tsp. ground cumin

3 T. olive oil
3 T. pine nuts
Dash of paprika
3 T. fresh parsley, chopped
Raw vegetables, a selection of your choice
Pita bread

Drain the chickpeas from the can and reserve the liquid. In a food processor, process the chickpeas with the tahini, lemon juice, garlic, salt, pepper, cumin and ½ cup of the reserved chickpea liquid. If hummus is too thick, add more liquid. Heat 1 tablespoon olive oil in a frying pan and brown pine nuts. Put hummus in a large bowl, make a small dent in the center. Pour the remaining olive oil over the top and sprinkle with pine nuts, paprika and parsley. Serve with raw vegetables and warm pita wedges.

TUNA TARTAR (Cham Chi Hwe)

From the region of District 3590-3750
Korea

½ lb. fresh tuna
1 Korean pear
1 ½ T. sugar
½ tsp. soy sauce

1 T. lemon juice
⅛ tsp. garlic juice
⅛ tsp. sesame oil

Thinly slice the tuna. Put in a dish, cover and refrigerate. Peel the pear and slice thinly. Soak pear in cold salt water to preserve color, then drain. In a bowl, mix the sugar, soy sauce, lemon juice, garlic juice and sesame oil well. Place a couple of pear slices on a plate with a slice of tuna over it. Drizzle lemon and garlic mixture on top of tuna and serve. Makes several appetizer bites.

LAMB KEBABS WITH FETA SAUCE

From the region of District 7190
USA

For the Kebabs:

½ c. extra-virgin olive oil
½ tsp. finely grated lemon zest, plus ⅓ c. fresh lemon juice, plus 1 lemon, cut into 8 wedges
3 garlic cloves, minced

2 T. fresh oregano or mint
½ boneless leg of lamb (3½ lbs.), cut into 1½-inch cubes
Coarse salt and freshly ground pepper

For the Feta Sauce:

3 oz. feta cheese, crumbled (½ c.)
4 oz. Greek yogurt (½ c.)

2 garlic cloves, minced
2 T. extra-virgin olive oil
1 T. fresh lemon juice

Make the kebabs: Combine oil, zest and juice, garlic, oregano and lamb in a non-reactive dish; refrigerate for 30 minutes. **Meanwhile, make the feta sauce:** Pulse all the ingredients in a food processor until very smooth. Refrigerate. Heat grill to medium-high. Thread lamb onto 8 metal skewers; finish each with a lemon wedge. Season with salt and pepper. Grill 10-12 minutes for medium-rare, flipping halfway through. Serve with sauce. Serves 4.

DERAILER

From the region of District 6450
USA

½ c. triple sec
1 c. vodka
1 c. gin
1 c. sloe gin
1 c. rum
1 c. peach schnapps

1 c. amaretto almond liqueur
½ c. grenadine
½ gal. cranberry juice
6 oz. grapefruit juice
½ bottle Sprite

Mix all the alcohol, then add juices. Add the Sprite just before serving.

MUSTARD VEGETABLE DIP

From the region of District 6420
USA

2 tsp. oil
2 tsp. garlic powder
½ c. sugar

4 tsp. yellow mustard
1 c. Miracle Whip

Mix together and chill. Serve with raw vegetables.

MINI FRATAS

From the region of District 7190
USA

½ (10-oz.) pkg. frozen chopped spinach
1 c. ricotta cheese
¾ c. Parmesan cheese
⅔ c. chopped mushrooms (4-oz. can)

½ tsp. oregano
1 egg
24 slices pepperoni

Thaw spinach and squeeze dry. Mix all ingredients, except pepperoni. Lightly grease small size muffin tins (tea cakes). Put one slice of pepperoni in each tin; spoon mixture over pepperoni. Bake at 375°F for 25 minutes or until golden brown. Cool 10 minutes and remove from pan. Serve warm or cold. May be frozen, then baked at 375°F. Makes 24. You may also use entire package of spinach and double the recipe. Makes 48.

MOCHA CREAM

From the region of District 7870
USA

½ c. med. to coarsely ground Colombian coffee
4½ c. cold water
About 3 T. chocolate syrup

About ½ c. creme de cacao
Sweetened whipped cream
Grated chocolate

Brew coffee and water in a drip coffee maker or percolator. (Use medium grind for drip coffee maker, coarse grind for percolator.) Pour brewed coffee into 6-ounce coffee cups. Add 1 teaspoon chocolate syrup and 1 tablespoon creme de cacao to each serving with whipped cream and sprinkled with grated chocolate. Serve immediately. Yield: 4½ cups.

BA-THEETH (Date Crumbles)

From the region of District 2450
United Arab Emirates

3 c. sticky dates, seeded and pulled apart
1¼ c. toasted sesame seeds
3½ c. flour (prefer wheat flour)

½ tsp. cardamom
¾ c. clarified butter or Samen (oil)

In a large bowl, sprinkle dates with cardamom and sesame seeds and set aside. Brown the flour in a skillet. When reddish brown, add this to the dates together with the clarified butter and mix the ingredients together with your fingertips. When well mixed, mixture should resemble chunks of large crumbs. When cool, store in an airtight container up to a week. Serve with Arabic coffee.

ONION CRESCENTS

From the region of District 7130
USA

1 (3-oz.) pkg. cream cheese, softened
½ c. crumbled Gorgonzola cheese (2 oz.)
1 (8-oz.) can Pillsbury refrigerated crescent dinner rolls or 1 (8-oz.) can Pillsbury crescent recipe creations refrigerated seamless dough sheet

⅓ c. Fisher Chef's Naturals chopped pecans
1 tsp. Crisco, 100% extra virgin or pure olive oil
⅓ c. finely chopped red onion
1 T. balsamic vinegar
¼ c. Smucker's apricot preserves
⅛ to ¼ tsp. dried thyme leaves

Heat oven to 375°F. In small bowl, mix cream cheese and Gorgonzola cheese with fork until blended. Unroll dough; separate or cut into two rectangles, each about 11 inches long. Place one rectangle on cutting board; if using crescent dough, press perforations together to seal. Spread half of the cheese mixture over dough to within ½ inch of long sides; sprinkle half of the pecans evenly over the cheese. Starting at one long side, roll up; press seam to seal. Cut roll into 16 (about ¾-inch) slices with serrated knife; place cut sides down on ungreased large cookie sheet. Repeat with remaining dough, cheese and pecans. Bake 14-17 minutes or until golden brown. Meanwhile, in 8-inch nonstick skillet, heat oil over medium heat. Add onion; cook 3-5 minutes, stirring frequently, until soft and lightly brown. Remove from heat. Stir in vinegar, preserves (breaking up large pieces of fruit if necessary) and thyme; set aside. After removing rolls from oven, immediately press back of a

(continued)

teaspoon into center of each roll to make small indentation. Spoon slightly less than ½ teaspoon onion jam into each indentation. Remove from cookie sheet. Serve warm. Makes 32.

OYSTER PÂTÉ

From the region of District 5020
USA

4 env. unflavored gelatin
1 c. water
2 (8-oz.) pkgs. cream cheese
2 c. mayonnaise
4 (3.6-oz.) cans smoked oysters, drained and minced
¼ c. chopped fresh parsley

2 T. Worcestershire sauce
1 tsp. garlic powder
Dash of hot sauce
Cranberries (opt.)
Fresh parsley sprigs (opt.)
Spiced crabapples (opt.)

Soften gelatin in water; set aside. Combine cream cheese and mayonnaise in a heavy saucepan. Cook over low heat, stirring until cream cheese melts and mixture is smooth. Add gelatin mixture and next 5 ingredients to saucepan; stir until smooth. Pour mixture into a well-oiled 6-cup mold. Cover and refrigerate several hours or until set. Garnish with cranberries, parsley and crabapples, if desired. Serve with crackers. Yield: 6 cups.

PHYLLO SHELLS WITH SAUSAGE STUFFING

From the region of District 6840
USA

1 lb. mild ground pork sausage
1 ¼ c. (5 oz.) shredded Monterey Jack cheese
1 ¼ c. shredded cheddar cheese
1 (8-oz.) bottle Ranch-style dressing

1 (4 ¼-oz.) can chopped ripe olives, drained
1 tsp. ground red pepper
5 (2.1-oz.) pkgs. frozen mini phyllo shells

Cook sausage in a large skillet, stirring until it crumbles and is no longer pink; drain. Combine sausage, Monterey Jack cheese, cheddar cheese, Ranch dressing, olives and red pepper in a large bowl. Fill each phyllo shell with a heaping teaspoonful of sausage mixture and place on ungreased baking sheets. Bake at 350°F for 8-10 minutes or until cheese melts. Serve warm.

AVOCADO SALSA (Guatemala Appetizer)

From the region of District 4250
Guatemala

2 mangoes, peeled and chopped
1 red pepper, diced
2 tomatoes, diced
3 avocados, peeled and chopped

½ c. red onion, diced
Dash of garlic
Dash of salt

Combine all ingredients in a medium-size bowl. Cover and chill for 20-30 minutes. Serve with tortilla or bread chips. Enjoy!

AMERICAN-MEXICAN TACO DIP

From the region of District 6000
USA

Spread on large serving plate/platter in layers:

1st Layer:

2 reg. cans refried beans (low-fat is fine)

2nd Layer:

1 c. prepared avocado dip (add more if you like avocados)

Or make your own:

Meat of 1 avocado, mashed
2 T. lemon juice

½ tsp. salt
¼ tsp. pepper

3rd Layer (blend):

1 c. sour cream

½ c. mayonnaise

Sprinkle on top ¼ to ½ package taco seasoning (the amount depends on your taste). Top with your preferred toppings: shredded lettuce, finely chopped onions, diced tomatoes, sliced ripe olives and finely shredded cheese of your choice. Eat with tortilla chips of your choice. Don't be surprised if none is left!

NEGRONI

From the region of District 6450
USA

1½ oz. Bombay sapphire gin
1½ oz. Campari
1½ oz. sweet vermouth

2 c. crushed ice
1 lg. orange slice

Pour gin, Campari and sweet vermouth into a cocktail shaker filled with 1 cup of crushed ice. Shake vigorously for 23 seconds. Pour the above contents through a cocktail strainer into an old fashion cocktail glass filled with crushed ice. Garnish with the slice of an orange. Alternatively, pour the above chilled contents through a cocktail strainer into a chilled classical martini glass. Garnish with the slice of an orange. Yield: 1 serving.

ARTICHOKE SPINACH BAKE

From the region of District 7710-7730
USA

2 (6-oz.) jars marinated artichoke hearts (other vegetable could replace)
3 (10-oz.) pkgs. frozen, chopped spinach, thawed
1 (8-oz.) pkg. cream cheese

4 T. butter or margarine, softened
6 T. milk
Pepper
⅓ c. grated Parmesan cheese

Drain marinade from artichokes, saving it for other uses. Reserving a few for garnish, distribute remaining artichokes over the bottom of a shallow 1½-quart casserole or 9-inch square baking dish. Squeeze out as much moisture as possible from spinach and arrange evenly over artichokes. With a mixer, beat cream cheese and butter until smooth. Gradually blend in milk (it can be mixed and fluff up by hand). Spread mixture over spinach. Sprinkle lightly with pepper, then sprinkle cheese. You may refrigerate until next day. Bake, uncovered, at 375°F for 40-50 minutes.

BABA GHANOUSH

From the region of District 2450
Bahrain

1 very lg. eggplant
3 sm. cloves garlic
2 T. sesame paste (tahini)
¼ tsp. salt
2 T. lemon juice

½ c. yogurt
3 T. olive oil
5 black seedless olives, coarsely chopped

Bake eggplant on a baking dish for about 1 hour 15 minutes at 250°F until the skin is crisp and the inside pulp is soft and mushy. Scoop out the inside pulp into a food processor or a blender. Add yogurt, sesame paste, lemon juice, garlic and salt. Purée until creamy. Spoon onto serving dish and spoon over the olive oil and chopped olives. Serve cold or warm with sliced pita bread for dipping.

ROCKET PUNCH

From the region of District 6440
USA

1 bottle champagne
2 L. white wine
½ bottle vodka

½ bottle gin
½ L. pineapple juice
1 L. orange juice

Mix all together in a 10-liter punch bowl.

CONCH FRITTERS

From the region of District 7020
Turks & Caicos Island

1½ lbs. prepared conch meat, chopped in a food processor
1 green pepper, seeded
2 stalks celery
4 cloves garlic
1 carrot
1 tsp. salt

1 white onion
2 eggs, beaten
1 c. flour
1 tsp. baking powder
¼ c. milk
2 T. jerk sauce

Dipping Sauce (mix together):

1 c. mayonnaise
1 c. sour cream

1 c. chilled tomatoes

(continued)

Transfer the chopped conch meat to large bowl and stir in the eggs and set aside. Place the garlic, green pepper, onion, carrot and celery stalks through food processor until finely chopped. Drain the vegetables with cheesecloth until they are really dry, then add to the conch in the mixing bowl. Stir to combine the ingredients. Stir the flour and baking powder together, then mix in with the other ingredients. Add the salt, milk and jerk sauce. Fold everything together to form a thick dough. Cover and refrigerate at least 2 hours. Remove the dough and let it stand for 15-20 minutes. Preheat deep-fryer. Drop dough by the teaspoonful into hot oil and fry until golden brown. Drain the fritters on paper towels and serve immediately. Garnish with fresh lemon and dipping sauce. Serves 8 people.

CREMA DE CABRALES

(Blue Cheese, Apple and Walnut Spread)

From the region of District 2203, 2202
Spain

½ lb. blue cheese (the Spanish variety is Cabrales, but Gorgonzola or Roquefort may be used)
2 tsp. raisins

1 T. white grape juice or cider
2 T. cream
½ c. finely chopped apples
½ c. finely chopped walnuts
⅛ tsp. dried thyme

Soak the raisins in the fruit juice for 20 minutes. Using a spoon, remove the raisins from the juice and set aside. Bring cheese to room temperature. Place it in a small mixing bowl. Add the cream and fruit juice. Using a fork or wooden spoon, combine ingredients until smooth. Stir in raisins, apple, walnuts and thyme. Serve with crackers.

CELEBRATION PUNCH

From the region of District 5280
USA

4 (6-oz.) cans frozen lemonade concentrate, thawed and undiluted
4 (6-oz.) cans frozen pineapple juice concentrate, thawed and undiluted

6 c. water
Ice cubes or ice ring
2 (33.8-oz.) bottles ginger ale
1 (28-oz.) bottle tonic water
1 (25.4-oz.) bottle champagne

Combine first 3 ingredients; chill well. **To serve:** Pour the juice mixture over ice in a large punch bowl. Gently stir in ginger ale, tonic water and champagne. Yield: 1½ gallons.

MUSHROOM CROSTINI

From the region of District 6950
USA

½ c. dried porcini mushrooms
6-8 slices Italian bread
5 T. olive oil
½ to ¾ c. sliced mushrooms
1 egg
⅓ c. plus 1 T. milk
1 T. grated Grana Padano or Parmesan
1 T. minced parsley (1 tsp. and rest)
2 garlic cloves, minced
12 sage leaves (4 minced and 8 whole)
8 slices fontina

Soak porcini in cool water, covered, for 1-2 hours, strain and rinse and chop. Preheat oven to 450°F. Place bread on baking sheet and brush with olive oil. Bake until golden brown about 5 minutes, remove and set aside. In a bowl, beat egg with milk, cheese, 1 teaspoon parsley, salt and pepper. Heat remaining olive oil in pan over medium-low heat. Add garlic, porcini mushrooms, sliced mushrooms, minced sage and remaining parsley. Cook about 5 minutes. Add egg mixture and remove from heat. Distribute mushroom-egg mixture over bread and top with fontina cheese. Preheat broiler and place bread under broiler until cheese forms a light crust, 3 minutes. Serve immediately before they cool!

CEVICHE DE OSTRAS (Guatemalan Oyster Ceviche)

From the region of District 4250
Guatemala

50 oysters, shucked
¾ c. fresh lime juice
¾ c. fresh lemon juice
3 tomatoes, peeled, seeded and chopped
1½ c. chopped onion
1 T. hot pepper sauce (more or less to taste)
3 T. finely chopped fresh mint
½ tsp. salt
½ tsp. freshly ground black pepper
Lettuce leaves, fresh mint sprigs and tomato wedges for garnish

Using a ceramic bowl, marinate oysters in lime and lemon juice for 12 hours. Drain the oysters and reserve ¼ cup of the juice. Add the chopped onion, tomatoes, pepper sauce, mint and salt to the oysters, along with the reserved juice and toss the mixture gently. Line salad plates with the lettuce leaves, arrange oysters on top of the lettuce and garnish with fresh mint and tomato wedges. Serves approximately 6.

CALENTITA

From the region of District 0037
Gibraltar

250g chickpea flour
3 c. water (more if it is too thick)
4 T. olive oil

1 egg
Pinch of cumin
Salt and pepper to taste

Mix chickpea flour, cumin, egg, water, salt and pepper in a bowl. Leave to stand. Preheat oven to 175°C/350°F. In a cake pan or oven dish, put enough oil to cover the bottom. Heat in oven. When hot, spread oil over the sides of pan with a pastry brush or by tilting. Stir chickpea mixture, pour immediately into pan, then put it back in the oven for about one hour (until it is set in the middle). Will serve two or three people. Use it like a bread.

CRAB WON TONS

From the region of District 7620
USA

1 (8-oz.) can Pillsbury refrigerated crescent dinner rolls or 1 (8-oz.) can Pillsbury crescent recipe creations refrigerated seamless dough sheet
1 (3-oz.) pkg. cream cheese, softened

¾ c. chopped cooked crab meat
1 T. chopped green onion (1 med.)
⅛ to ¼ tsp. ground red pepper (cayenne)
1 egg white, beaten

Heat oven to 375°F. Spray cookie sheet with cooking spray. Unroll dough on work surface (if using crescent rolls, pinch seams to seal); cut into six rows by four rows to make 24 squares. In small bowl, mix cream cheese, crab meat, onion and red pepper. Spoon about 1 teaspoon crab mixture ½ inch from one corner of one square. Starting with same corner, fold dough over filling and tuck end tightly underneath filling; continue rolling to within ½ inch of opposite corner. Lightly brush exposed corner with egg white. Roll moistened corner of dough over roll; press to seal. Place on cookie sheet. Brush with egg white. Repeat with remaining squares and filling. Bake 10-15 minutes or until golden brown. Remove from cookie sheet. Serve warm. Makes 24 won tons.

CHIPOTLE CHILE PEPPER GUACAMOLE

From the region of District 4150
Mexico

3 chopped chipotle peppers in Adobo sauce
3 avocados
4 lemons, juice only

3 T. chopped cilantro
1 chopped onion
Salt and pepper to taste

Mix all the ingredients in a bowl. Stir well and serve.

POTATO PANCAKES/TORTILLAS WITH TUNA

From the region of District 4150
Mexico

1 lb. potatoes, cooked
1 whole egg
1 can tuna, crumbled
1 head chopped lettuce

Bread crumbs
Juice of 1 lemon
Oil for frying

Once the potatoes are cooked, mash them and let them cool. Add the egg, a tablespoon of flour and the crumbled tuna. Season with salt and pepper. Mix it all together well. Form pancakes. Dip them in the bread crumbs and fry them on low heat until browned on all sides. Serve with chopped lettuce and season with lemon.

CRAB CAKES WITH SHRIMP SAUCE

From the region of District 7020
British Virgin Island

1 c. green, red or yellow bell peppers or a combination, diced
6 T. butter, divided
3 eggs, separated
2 c. soft bread crumbs

8-10 oz. cooked crab meat
1 T. Caribbean seasoning
Flour for dusting
Worcestershire and Tabasco sauces
Salt and pepper to taste

Sauce:

4 chopped garlic cloves
3 chopped shallots
6 oz. raw shrimp, shells removed and reserved
2 T. vegetable oil

1 tsp. paprika
¼ c. dry sherry
¼ c. heavy cream
Salt and pepper to taste

(continued)

In a small skillet, sauté the peppers in 3 tablespoons butter until they are soft. Beat the egg whites until soft peaks form. Put the bread crumbs and crab meat in a bowl. Add the yolks and the seasonings. Fold in the egg whites. Form the mixture into 3-inch cakes; dust them in the flour and fry them in the remaining 3 tablespoons butter, turning them once, until they are golden brown. In a small saucepan, sauté the garlic, shallots and shrimp shells in the oil until the shells turn red. Add the paprika and sherry and cook over medium heat until the sherry has been reduced to half. Strain the sherry and discard the shells and return the sherry to the pan. Dice the peeled shrimp and add it with the heavy cream to the saucepan. Cook and reduce the sauce until it coats the back of a spoon. Season with salt and pepper and keep the sauce warm. Serve the crab cakes with the warm shrimp sauce.

REUBEN DIP

From the region of District 6000
USA

½ lb. corned beef, chopped
1 c. chopped sauerkraut, drained
¼ chopped onion (microwave with 1 tsp. butter)

1½ c. shredded cheese
4 oz. cream cheese
2 T. catsup
2 tsp. Dijon mustard
¼ tsp. pepper

Microwave everything, except beef and sauerkraut, for 2½ minutes, then add other two ingredients. Serve with toasted rye bread wedges.

SCOTCH EGGS

From the region of District 1170-1220
England

6 med. eggs, room temp.
1 lb. seasoned pork sausage
1 c. all-purpose flour, seasoned with salt and freshly ground pepper

2 eggs, lightly beaten
2 c. fine, dry bread crumbs
Oil (for deep-frying)

Boil eggs and peel. Set aside. Divide the sausage meat into six equal pieces and roll each out on a lightly floured surface into a 5- to 6-inch circle. Cover each egg with the sausage circle. Compress the meat with the palm of your hand so all air bubbles escape. In one bowl, mix the flour with the salt and pepper. In the second bowl, put the beaten egg and bread crumbs in the third bowl. Dip the meat covered eggs into the flour mixture, then into the egg mixture and then into the bread

(continued)

crumb mixture. Deep-fry each egg. When done, remove and set aside on a paper towel. Slice the egg in half. Place on a serving bowl and serve with English mustard.

BUUZ (Mongolian Dumplings)

From the region of District 3450
Mangolia

1 lb. ground beef or mutton
1 lg. onion, minced
Salt
¼ tsp. ground pepper

3 garlic cloves
Chopped herbs (opt.)
5 spices (opt.)

Dough:

¾ lb. wheat flour
Pinch of salt

1½ c. lukewarm water

Dissolve a pinch of salt in lukewarm water; mix in flour and knead into smooth soft dough. Leave the dough to rest for ½ hour. Knead again and cut into small pieces. Roll the pieces into balls the size of a walnut and leave them to rest in a bowl. Sprinkle with flour to avoid from sticking together. **For the meat filling:** Combine the meat in a bowl with minced onion, crushed garlic, herbs (optional) and other seasonings like salt and pepper and spices (optional). Add some water to make the filling wet. Roll out the rested dough ball into circles by leaving the center thicker than the edges. Put the meat filling in the center of the circle and start sealing the edges with your fingers. Sealing requires agility and skillfulness from your fingers. Steam the filled dumplings until done and serve with ketchup.

SEASONED PRETZELS

From the region of District 5950
USA

1 (16-oz.) bottle Orville Redenbacher popcorn oil
2½ T. Hidden Valley Ranch salad dressing (powder form)

1¼ T. dill weed
2 lbs. pretzels

Mix above ingredients and pour over 2 pounds of mini twist pretzels. Put in a large pan in a 150°F oven for 45-60 minutes, stirring every 15 minutes. (Best if you bake until oil is baked in.)

SIMIT (Sesame Rings)

From the region of District 2420-2440
Turkey

½ lb. flour
½ tsp. salt
4 T. (½ stick) margarine, melted
1 T. olive oil

1 T. milk, plus extra
1 T. water
2 eggs, beaten
Sesame seeds

Mix flour with salt. Place the flour and salt in a large bowl and make a hole in the middle. Into this hole pour the margarine, olive oil, milk, water and beaten egg. Stirring from the outside into the middle, gradually mix all the liquids into the flour until you have a dough. It will feel a bit oily and sticky. With floured hands, shape the dough into rings about 4 inches in diameter. Brush them over with milk and sprinkle the sesame seeds on top. Bake them for about 30 minutes at 400°F or until they are nicely browned. Serve as a snack.

SHRIMP ON TOSTONES

From the region of District 6000
USA

1 lg. green plantain
Vegetable oil for frying
2 oz. cilantro
6 sprigs parsley
½ lemon
8 oz. shrimp, cleaned and deveined

1 med. tomato, chopped
½ med. onion, chopped
Hot sauce
Salt
Pepper

Heat 1 inch of oil in a large skillet. Under water, remove the outer skin of the plantain. Cut the plantain at an angle into ½-inch slices. Fry until each cut side is slightly brown. Flatten to the thickness of a pancake and re-fry until light brown. Remove and place on paper towel. Lightly salt the plantains when still hot. Sauté onions until transparent. Add tomatoes, cilantro, shrimp and squeezed lemon juice. Cook for an additional 5 minutes. Add salt, pepper and hot sauce to taste. Scoop mixture of shrimp onto plantains and serve. Top with parsley for color.

PUNCH SLUSH

From the region of District 6440
USA

9 c. water
3 (3-oz.) boxes strawberry Jello or flavor of choice
4 c. water
4 c. sugar

2 (46-oz.) cans pineapple juice
1 (8-oz.) bottle lemon juice
2 (2-L.) bottles ginger ale, chilled

Bring 9 cups water to a boil. Mix in the boxes of Jello, stir to dissolve and set aside to cool. Bring to boil 4 cups water and sugar; remove from heat and cool. Add Jello water and juice. Mix well and freeze. Set out 2 hours before serving. When ready to serve, add the ginger ale to the slush. May add sherbet of choice to punch. **Tip:** Freeze some of the liquid in a container and float as a large ice chunk in the punch. It keeps it cold and doesn't dilute the punch.

PICTIONARY PUNCH

From the region of District 6440
USA

1 c. sugar
1 c. water
3 c. grapefruit juice
3 c. orange juice

3 c. pineapple juice
½ c. lemon juice
½ c. lime juice
2 L. chilled ginger ale

In a saucepan, bring sugar and water to a boil; cook and stir for 2 minutes. Remove from the heat; cool. Pour into a large bowl; add juices. Cover and refrigerate. Stir in ginger ale just before serving. Yield: 5 servings.

BAKED MUSHROOMS WITH CHEESE

From the region of District 1912
Slovania

1 ctn. mushrooms (approx. 8-10 oz.)

¼ lb. Muenster cheese

Preheat oven to 300°F. Wash the mushroom caps and remove the stems. Dry well. Cut the cheese into squares to fit between two mushroom caps. Make a sandwich of two mushroom caps with one square of sliced cheese between them. Secure this with a toothpick and place in a cookie pan or baking dish and bake for 10 minutes until

(continued)

cheese melts. Serve warm or at room temperature. Makes about 20 snacks (depending on the number of mushrooms in the package).

SPICY STRAWBERRY SALSA

From the region of District 5110
USA

1 fresh serrano or jalapeño chili
1 c. finely chopped strawberries
¼ c. finely chopped white onion
2 T. finely chopped fresh coriander

½ tsp. fresh lime juice
¼ tsp. salt
½ tsp. sugar if desired
2 firm, ripe avocados, cubed

Wearing rubber gloves, remove stems, seeds and ribs from chili and chop fine. In a bowl, stir together chili and remaining salsa ingredients. Salsa may be made several hours ahead and chilled, covered. Serve with large tortilla chips.

SPINACH BALLS

From the region of District 6040-6080
USA

¾ lb. butter
6 eggs
4 c. Parmesan cheese

2 pkgs. Stove Top seasoned stuffing
2 pkgs. frozen, chopped spinach

Cook and drain spinach. Beat eggs and add melted butter. Add stuffing, spinach and cheese. Make into little balls. Place on ungreased cookie sheet and bake in 350°F oven for 10 minutes.

SMOKED FISH PÂTÉ

From the region of District 6220
USA

2 smoked mackerel, skinned and boned or other smoked fish
3 oz. cream cheese spread

Juice of ½ lemon
10 oz. (1 ¼ c.) butter, melted
Salt
Pepper

Purée mackerel in a blender or mash well with a fork. Gradually add the remaining ingredients and blend until smooth or mash the mackerel with the cream cheese and then add the other ingredients. Turn into small ramekins and chill before serving. Serves 6.

CRUNCHY SHRIMP DIP

From the region of District 6950
USA

1 pkg. Knox gelatin
¼ c. water
1 can tomato soup
8 oz. cream cheese
4 cans shrimp (very sm.)
 (2-3 large cans will do)

¾ c. chopped celery
¾ c. chopped onions
1 c. mayonnaise

Add gelatin and water, then boil. Add tomato soup and boil a few minutes. Beat cream cheese and add tomato soup mixture. Beat until smooth. Add shrimp, celery, onions and mayonnaise. Pour into oiled mold and refrigerate. Unmold and serve with crackers.

CHEESE PUFFS

From the region of District 6220
USA

2 (8-oz.) pkgs. cream cheese
1 c. mayonnaise
1 T. minced onion
¼ c. minced chives
4 oz. blue cheese crumbles

½ tsp. cayenne pepper
1 whole loaf, thinly sliced wheat
 bread
Paprika

Mix cream cheese and mayonnaise in a bowl. Stir in onions, chives, blue cheese and cayenne pepper. Set aside. Using a 1½- to 2-inch round cookie cutter, cut bread slices into rounds. Spread 1 tablespoon of cheese mixture on each round. Place puffs on a baking sheet and freeze. When ready to serve, preheat oven to 350°F. Remove baking sheet from freezer. Bake 15 minutes. Sprinkle with paprika. Serve immediately.

KAPPUNATA (Caponata)

From the region of District 2110
Malta

2 lg. aubergines
4 lg. tomatoes
2 lg. onions
4 cloves garlic
4 T. capers
2 tsp. sugar

1 T. oregano
6 green peppers
1 T. stoned olives
4 T. oil
Salt and pepper

Peel and chop all vegetables. In a large saucepan, heat the oil and fry all the vegetables together. Add the herbs and seasonings. Cover and simmer gently until vegetables are tender. Add capers and olives. Stir well. Serve hot or cold with crackers or crisp bread.

Recipe Favorites

Soups & Salads

Helpful Hints

- If the soup is not intended as the main course, count on 1 quart to serve 6. As the main dish, plan on 1 quart to serve 2.

- After cooking vegetables, pour any water and leftover vegetable pieces into a freezer container. When full, add tomato juice and seasoning to create a money-saving "free soup."

- Instant potatoes help thicken soups and stews.

- A leaf of lettuce dropped in a pot of soup absorbs grease from the top – remove the lettuce and serve. You can also make soup the day before, chill, and scrape off the hardened fat that rises to the top.

- To cut down on odors when cooking cabbage or cauliflower, add a little vinegar to the water and don't overcook.

- Three large stalks of celery, chopped and added to about two cups of beans (navy, brown, pinto, etc.), make the dish easier to digest.

- Fresh is best, but to reduce time in the kitchen, use canned or frozen broths or bouillon bases. Canned or frozen vegetables, such as peas, green beans, and corn, also work well.

- Ideally, cold soups should be served in chilled bowls.

- Perk up soggy lettuce by spritzing it with a mixture of lemon juice and cold water.

- You can easily remove egg shells from hard-boiled eggs if you quickly rinse the eggs in cold water after they are boiled. Add a drop of food coloring to help distinguish cooked eggs from raw ones.

- Your fruit salads will look better when you use an egg slicer to make perfect slices of strawberries, kiwis, or bananas.

- The ratio for a vinaigrette is typically 3 parts oil to 1 part vinegar.

- For salads, cook pasta al dente (slightly chewy to the bite). This allows the pasta to absorb some of the dressing and not become mushy.

- Fresh vegetables require little seasoning or cooking. If the vegetable is old, dress it up with sauces or seasoning.

- Chill the serving plates to keep the salad crisp.

- Fruit juices, such as pineapple and orange, can be used as salad dressing by adding a little olive oil, nutmeg, and honey.

SOUPS & SALADS

AVOCADO SOUP

From the region of District 9100
Côte d'Ivoire

4 ripe avocados, peeled and pitted
8 c. cold chicken or vegetable stock, 2 (14-oz.) cans
4 T. lime juice
3 T. plain yogurt
2 dashes Tabasco sauce or to taste
Salt and pepper
8 lime slices for garnish

Add the avocado flesh to a blender and purée. Add the stock and continue blending until smooth. Blend in the Tabasco sauce, lime juice, yogurt and salt and pepper. Refrigerate for at least 1 hour. When ready to serve, spoon into bowls and top each with a slice of lime. Serves 8.

AZTEC SOUP OR TORTILLA SOUP

From the region of District 4150
Mexico

10 refrigerated tortillas
8 tomatoes
2 garlic cloves
1 pinch oregano
1 pinch of pepper
Knorr chicken flavor bouillon to taste
Salt
Oil
Avocado
Chihuahua cheese
Guajillo chile to taste

Set the tomatoes in water to boil. Once cooked, empty them into the blender and add garlic, oregano, Knorr bouillon, salt and a little water. Blend and set aside. Cut the tortillas into small strips. Then fry them in oil until they are nice and crunchy. Set aside. Empty the tomato mixture into a pot and let it boil with the Guajillo chile. Serve the soup. Add the tortilla strips. Adorn with avocado strips and Chichuahua cheese.

BUTTERNUT SOUP (A firm South African winter favorite)

From the region of District 9320
South Africa

2 med. butternuts
1 apple
2 med. onions
50g butter or margarine (4 T.)
7ml med. curry powder (1 ¼ tsp.)
40g cake flour (4 T.)

Pinch of ground nutmeg
2 chicken stock cubes
750ml boiling water (3 c.)
500ml milk (2 c.)
7ml salt (1 ½ tsp.)

Peel, seed and dice the butternuts. Peel, core and chop the apple. Peel the onions and chop roughly in a large saucepan. Sauté the chopped onions in the butter or margarine. Add the curry powder and fry the mixture lightly. Add the butternut and apple and sauté the mixture for a while. Add the flour and nutmeg and stir-fry lightly. Dissolve the chicken stock cubes in the boiling water. Add the stock, together with the milk and salt to the butternut mixture. Boil with the lid on, over moderate heat until the butternut pieces are soft. Stir the mixture occasionally. Purée or blend until smooth. The color of the soup should be deep yellow and the texture creamy. Serve the soup hot. Each bowl of soup may be garnished with a teaspoon of cream and a little finely chopped parsley. **For an interesting variation:** Replace the nutmeg with a little fine grated orange rind and few shreds of orange rind to garnish.

BLACK BREAD SOUP WITH FRUIT (Leivasupp)

From the region of District 1420
Estonia

¾ c. raisins
½ c. plum brandy
½ c. sugar
5 c. water
6 slices black sourdough bread, crusts removed, toasted
2 sm. tart apples, peeled, halved and sliced

¾ c. fresh cranberries
¾ c. pitted dried prunes
¾ c. cranberry juice
1 piece (inch) cinnamon stick
3 cloves, whole
Zest of 1 lemon
Whipped cream for garnish

Soak the raisins in the brandy for 20-30 minutes. In a soup pot, bring the water and sugar to a boil over high heat. Add the bread and then reduce the heat to low and simmer until the bread just begins to dissolve. You may remove the bread with a slotted spoon and push it through a sieve. Or use a food processor for a pulse or two. The bread should not be puréed, but grainy. Put the bread back into the pot. Add the raisins with their soaking liquid, cranberries, cranberry juice, apples,

(continued)

prunes, cinnamon stick, lemon zest and cloves. Bring to a boil and then reduce the heat and simmer, covered, until the fruits are tender. Taste the soup and add more sugar, if desired. Cool, then refrigerate for at least 2 hours. Remove the cinnamon stick and cloves before eating. Serve the soup into serving bowl with whipped cream.

BROCCOLI RAISIN SALAD

From the region of District 6420
USA

1 head raw broccoli, washed and cut into sm. flowerets
10 slices bacon, cooked and crumbled

1 sm. red onion, chopped
½ to ¾ c. raisins
½ c. sunflower seeds or sliced almonds

Dressing:

1 c. mayonnaise
¼ c. sugar

2 T. tarragon vinegar

Mix broccoli, bacon, onion, raisins and seeds or almonds together in large size bowl and set aside. Mix dressing ingredients, pour over mixed salad ingredients. Stir until well mixed and refrigerate.

BELGIAN SOUP

From the region of District 1620, 1630
Belgium

¾ lb. Brussels sprouts
4 green onions, chopped
2 c. rich chicken stock
½ tsp. salt
¼ tsp. white pepper
¼ tsp. tarragon

¼ c. nonfat dry milk
3 T. low fat yogurt
1 T. chopped parsley
Yogurt or chopped parsley for garnish

Cook sprouts and onions in chicken stock with salt, pepper and tarragon until tender, about 12 minutes. Purée in a blender with dry milk, parsley and yogurt. Reheat until hot through. Garnish with a dollop of yogurt and parsley.

BUTTERNUT SQUASH SOUP

From the region of District 6440
USA

1 (2-lb.) butternut squash, halved lengthwise
Vegetable oil
½ c. olive oil
½ c. (¼ inch) diced onion
¼ c. (¼ inch) diced celery
¼ c. (¼ inch) diced carrots
4 c. chicken stock, either homemade or store-bought
Pinch of grated nutmeg
Salt and freshly ground black pepper

Preheat oven to 375°. Grease a 13 x 9 x 2-inch baking dish with vegetable oil. Place butternut squash, cut side up in prepared dish. Pierce each square half several times with toothpick or skewer. Bake until squash is tender, about 45 minutes. Heat the olive oil in a large saucepan over medium heat until hot. Add the onion, celery, carrots and sauté until soft, but not brown, about 10 minutes. Season with salt and pepper. Add the chicken stock and bring to a boil. Simmer for several minutes until soft. When the squash is done cooking, using a large spoon, remove seeds, scrape squash into the pot and discard peel. Add 3½ cups chicken stock and nutmeg and purée in blender or food processor until smooth. Add additional stock to reach desired consistency. Stir soup over medium heat until heated through. Season to taste with salt and pepper. Ladle soup into bowls. (The soup can be made ahead to this point, cooled, covered and refrigerated for several days or frozen for about 1 month. It will thicken as it cools and may need thinning with stock or water when reheating.) Hope you enjoy!

COCONUT BEAN SOUP

From the region of District 9200
Tanzania

½ c. onions, chopped
2 T. oil
½ c. green peppers, chopped
1½ tsp. curry powder
1 tsp. salt
¼ tsp. pepper
4 T. butter or margarine, softened
1½ c. fresh tomato, seeded and cut into chunks
2½ c. canned kidney beans with liquid
2 c. coconut milk
3 c. water
½ c. cooked rice
1 c. shredded coconut

Heat the oil and sauté the onions until softened. Add green peppers, curry powder, salt, pepper, butter or margarine and tomato and simmer for 2 minutes. Add the kidney beans with their liquid, the coconut milk and water. Simmer gently for 10 minutes. Stir in the cooked rice and

(continued)

heat for about 2 minutes. Ladle into bowls. Top each serving with 1 tablespoon of shredded coconut and serve. Makes approximately 8 servings.

CALLALOO SOUP

From the region of District 7020
Saint Martin

1 ½ lbs. fresh kale
½ lb. callaloo or fresh spinach
10 okra pods
¼ lb. salt pork, cut into thin strips
½ lb. fresh lean pork, cubed
2 onions, thinly sliced
Freshly ground black pepper to taste
1 hot pepper, seeds removed, sliced
2 tsp. chopped fresh thyme
6 c. chicken stock

Pull all stems from kale and callaloo. Discard stems and roughly chop the leaves. Wash leaves thoroughly. Roughly chop the kale. Place salt pork in a large, heavy soup kettle and cook over medium heat for 10 minutes, rendering fat. Discard all but 2 tablespoons of fat. Add pork cubes and onions to pan. Sauté over medium heat until cubes are brown and onions are translucent, about 7 minutes. Add kale, callaloo, okra, black pepper and hot pepper. Add thyme and stock. Cover and simmer 3 hours. Remove salt pork before serving. Makes 6-8 servings.

CAPRESE SALAD

From the region of District 2030-2120
Italy

2 lbs. fresh mozzarella, sliced ¼-inch thick
3 lbs. ripe tomatoes, sliced ¼-inch thick
6 T. extra-virgin olive oil
10 fresh basil leaves, chopped or torn apart
Salt and pepper to taste

Arrange tomato slices on a platter. Top each tomato with a slice of mozzarella. Drizzle extra virgin olive oil over the tomato and mozzarella. Sprinkle the chopped basil leaves on top. Season with salt and pepper and serve.

CHICKEN SALAD (Kyllingsalat)

From the region of District 1440-1480
Denmark

8 oz. cream cheese
2 T. milk
1 lb. cooked chicken, diced or sliced

3 T. butter
6 oz. split blanched almonds
12-oz. can asparagus
Salt and pepper

Mix cream cheese with milk until soft and well blended, then stir in pieces of chicken. Drain asparagus and cut into 1-inch pieces. Melt butter in frying pan and fry almonds until golden. Stir almonds into chicken and cream cheese mixture. Season with salt and pepper. Garnish with asparagus.

CABBAGE SALAD (Curtido Salvadoreno)

From the region of District 4240
El Salvador

1 head cabbage, sliced thin
2 carrots, grated
2 sm. onions, sliced
½ tsp. dry red pepper
½ tsp. oregano

2 tsp. extra virgin olive oil
1 tsp. salt
1 tsp. brown sugar
¼ c. vinegar
½ c. water

Put the cabbage in boiling water for 1 minute; drain. Throw away the water. Place the cabbage in a large bowl and add in grated carrots, red pepper, sliced onion, oregano, extra virgin olive oil, brown sugar, vinegar, water and salt. Place in the refrigerator for at least 2 hours before serving. Serve with Pupusas.

CREAM OF CARROT SOUP (Porkkanasosekeitto)

From the region of District 1380-1430
Finland

1 lb. carrots, peeled
1 c. beef broth
4 T. brandy
3 T. butter
3 T. flour

4 c. milk
1 T. sugar
1 dash of pepper
4 T. fresh parsley, chopped
2 tsp. ground nutmeg

Cook peeled carrots in beef broth and brandy until tender, adding additional brandy if necessary. Drain carrots, reserving the stock. Mash the carrots to make a smooth purée. You may use the food processor.

(continued)

Heat the butter in a saucepan, add the flour and stir until blended. Add the milk gradually, stirring constantly. Heat to the boiling point and simmer for 10 minutes. Add reserved stock, carrot purée, sugar and pepper. Garnish each serving with parsley and a dash of nutmeg.

CRANBERRY APPLE SALAD

From the region of District 7910
USA

1 (3 oz.) raspberry Jello
½ c. boiling water

1 can whole cranberry sauce
3-4 med. Granny Smith apples

Dissolve Jello in boiling water. Peel, core and shred apples. Mix into cranberry sauce. Add dissolved Jello. Pour in a Jello mold.

CUCUMBER SALAD

From the region of District 6560
USA

1½ lg. English hothouse cucumbers, cut into ½-inch pieces
3 c. (½-inch cubes) seeded watermelon
3½ T. fresh lime juice

3 T. hoisin sauce
¼ c. chopped fresh cilantro
2 T. chopped fresh mint
⅓ c. coarsely chopped, lightly salted dry roasted peanuts

Combine cucumbers and watermelon in medium bowl. Cover with plastic wrap and refrigerate at least 15 minutes and up to 4 hours. Drain; discard liquid. Whisk lime juice and hoisin sauce in small bowl to blend. Pour dressing over cucumber-watermelon mixture and toss gently. Season salad to taste with pepper. Sprinkle salad with cilantro, mint and then peanuts. Serve immediately.

CAULIFLOWER SALAD

From the region of District 5610-5650
USA

4 c. thinly sliced cauliflower
1 c. sliced ripe olives
⅔ c. chopped green pepper
1 (4-oz.) jar diced pimiento, drained
½ c. chopped onion

½ c. vegetable oil
3 T. wine vinegar
3 T. lemon juice
1 tsp. sugar
½ tsp. salt
¼ tsp. pepper

Combine first 5 ingredients in a salad bowl; toss gently. Combine remaining ingredients in a jar. Cover tightly and shake vigorously. Pour dressing over vegetables, tossing gently. Cover salad and chill 8 hours or overnight, stirring occasionally. Yield: 6-8 servings.

CRUNCHY MIXED SALAD

From the region of District 6650
USA

1 onion, chopped up
1 c. celery, chopped up
2 carrots, grated
1 green pepper, cut up

1 can peas
1 can French-cut green beans
1 can white corn
1 jar pimento

Assemble in a large bowl.

1 c. sugar
¾ c. vinegar

½ c. oil
Salt and pepper

Mix well and pour over the vegetables. Let stand overnight. Good for weeks.

CABBAGE SALAD

From the region of District 9350
Angola

1 med. cabbage, shredded
1 lb. (16-oz. can) sweet corn, drained
1 c. dill, finely chopped

2 tsp. salt
2 tsp. sugar
2 T. olive oil

Shred the cabbage, add 1 tablespoon of salt and sugar. Mix manually and press a bit. Leave to rest for half an hour so that cabbage lets juices out. Add corn, chopped dill, oil and remaining salt; mix well. Serve.

CHICKPEA AND NOODLE SALAD

From the region of District 3330-3360
Thailand

200g rice vermicelli noodles
500g broccoli
500g snow peas
4 med. carrots

2 cans chickpeas, rinsed and drained
2 T. finely chopped coriander leaves

Dressing:

¾ c. lime juice
½ c. brown sugar
2 stems fresh lemon grass, sliced thinly

1 tsp. Sambal Oelek

Place noodles in large heatproof bowl, cover with boiling water, stand only until just tender; drain. Boil, steam or microwave broccoli and snow peas, separately until just tender; cool. Cut carrots into thin strips. Combine broccoli, snow peas, carrot, noodles, chickpeas and coriander in large bowl; mix well. Just before serving, drizzle with dressing; toss gently. **Dressing:** Combine ingredients in jar; shake well.

CRAB SOUP

From the region of District 9220
Seychelles

3 common crabs
4 c. water
2 T. soy sauce
3 stalks lemon grass, chopped
2 tsp. grated ginger
2 chili peppers, chopped

2 limes, grated and zested
2 sweet potatoes, cooked and sliced
2 tsp. chopped fresh mint plus a few whole leaves for garnish

Boil crabs for 6 minutes. Remove and cut into quarters and sauté in hot oil. Put the crabs back into the water and bring to a boil. Simmer for a few minutes, skimming the surface. Remove crab and set aside. Strain the broth. Put broth in a saucepan and heat for 6 more minutes. Now add the chili, lime zest, soy sauce, ginger and lemon grass. Cook for another 2 minutes and then add the crab to it and simmer for 2 minutes. **To serve:** Put sliced sweet potato in individual serving bowls, sprinkle with fresh mint and crab and then pour broth over. This soup should be served hot.

CHICKEN AND MANGO SALAD

From the region of District 9150
Burundi

1 lb. boneless, skinless chicken breasts, grilled and cut up into sm. chunks
1 lg. can black beans, drained and rinsed
1 (10-oz.) pkg. frozen corn, thawed
2 c. chopped ripe mangoes
½ c. sweet green peppers, chopped
⅓ c. sweet onions, chopped

½ c. chopped fresh cilantro
¼ c. lime juice
⅓ c. balsamic vinegar
2 T. honey
4 T. orange marmalade
¼ c. extra virgin olive oil
1 tsp. garlic powder
1 T. soy sauce
1 tsp. black pepper
½ tsp. ground red pepper

Toss all ingredients in large bowl. Refrigerate. Serve with baked tortilla crisps if desired.

CUCUMBER SOUP-COLD

From the region of District 1470
Denmark

2 cucumbers
6dl yogurt
Chives
½ onion

2 pinches crushed dry chili seeds
Lemon juice
Salt & pepper

Add cucumbers, yogurt, chives, onion and chili together in a blender. Cool it for a couple of hours. Taste with lemon, salt and pepper. Can be served with fried tandoori shrimp and fresh mint or some toast. Serves 4 pairs.

CAULIFLOWER SOUP

From the region of District 5360
Canada

½ sm. cauliflower
15g (½ oz.) butter
1 sm. onion

2 c. chicken stock
Salt and pepper
2 T. cream

(continued)

Spinach Soup:

250g pkg. frozen chopped spinach
1 T. pine nuts
15g (½ oz.) butter
1 T. water
1 clove garlic

1 sm. onion
2 c. chicken stock
Few sprigs parsley
3 tsp. cornstarch
1 T. water
Salt and pepper

Cauliflower Soup: Cut cauliflower into small flowerets. Melt butter in pan, add peeled and chopped onion, cook until transparent. Add cauliflower, mix well, cook 2 minutes; stir to prevent browning. Add stock, bring to boil, reduce heat, simmer, covered, 20 minutes. Purée soup in blender in batches, push through sieve. Return soup to pan, season with salt and pepper; when soup reboils, add cream. Heat through without boiling. **Spinach Soup:** Place pine nuts in pan, stir over low heat until light golden brown; remove from pan immediately. Add butter, crushed garlic and peeled and chopped onion to pan; cook until onion is transparent. Add unthawed spinach and stock, bring to boil, reduce heat, simmer gently, covered, 15 minutes, stirring occasionally. Pour soup into blender, add pine nuts and parsley, blend until puréed. Push mixture through sieve. Return to pan, add combined cornstarch and water. Stir over medium heat until soup boils, season with salt and pepper. Pour soups into two separate jugs. With one jug in each hand, pour soup into individual bowls at the same time, then swirl soups gently with handle of spoon.

DOVGA (Pea and Sorrel Soup with Meatballs)

From the region of District 2430
Azerbaijan

1 lb. ground lamb
1 c. onions, grated
1 c. dried peas, soaked in water overnight
2 c. vegetable stock
1½ c. matsoni (sour cream)
¼ lb. rice

¼ lb. sorrel
4 T. mixed herbs (i.e. coriander, dill, mint, parsley)
Salt and black pepper to taste
Nutmeg, paprika and ground cloves to taste

Mix the lamb and onions, salt and pepper in a bowl. Mix well before shaping into small balls. Cook the peas in the vegetable stock for 45 minutes until tender. To this, add the rice, sorrel, herbs, matsoni and meatballs. Season with the salt, black pepper and spices. Gently bring the mixture to a boil and cook until the meatballs are done for about 30 minutes. Ladle into warmed soup bowls and serve.

EGG LEMON SOUP (Soup Fidhe)

From the region of District 2090
Albania

10 c. chicken broth
1 c. vermicelli
Salt and pepper to taste

Juice of 1 lemon
4 eggs, beaten

Bring broth to a boil. Add vermicelli and simmer for 15-20 minutes or until tender. Season with salt and pepper. Add lemon juice to the beaten eggs. Slowly stir some of hot soup into egg mixture. Stir egg mixture into the soup. Remove from heat and let stand for 5 minutes to thicken. Serve at once. Add 1 tablespoon of water to beaten eggs to prevent curdling. Serves 6.

FIDDLEHEAD SOUP

From the region of District 7810
Canada

1 ½ lbs. Fiddlehead fern, cleaned well (may substitute asparagus)
1 lg. onion, chopped
3 chopped garlic cloves

3 c. vegetable stock
1 tsp. chopped parsley
1 tsp. chopped basil
½ tsp. chopped oregano
1 c. evaporated milk

Place the Fiddleheads, onions, celery, garlic and a little of the stock in a food processor and process to a purée. Transfer to a large soup pot together with all the remaining ingredients, except the evaporated milk, bring to simmering point, then partially cover and simmer for 20 minutes. Add the evaporated milk and continue to simmer for a further 10 minutes. Serve hot.

FROZEN YOGURT SALAD

From the region of District 6270
USA

2 (8-oz.) ctn. yogurt
1 (1-lb.) can fruit
½ c. sugar

⅓ c. coarsely chopped nuts (walnuts)

Cut up fruit. Combine ingredients. Freeze.

FRUITY SLAW

From the region of District 9830
Australia

5 med. Kohlrabi bulbs, peeled and grated
1 c. cabbage, shredded
2 sm. red onion, diced
2 Red Delicious apples, cored and diced

½ c. currants
½ c. seedless grapes
2 tsp. olive oil
¼ c. apple cider

Combine the first 6 ingredients in a large bowl. Lightly drizzle the oil and cider over the top. Gently toss and refrigerate for several hours to let the flavors mellow. Toss and serve.

FASOLADA (Greek Bean Soup)

From the region of District 2470
Greece

1 lb. dried beans
Water
½ c. olive oil
½ tsp. ground black pepper
2 T. tomato paste
1 c. diced tomato

2 carrots, diced
1 med. potato, diced
2-3 stalks celery with leaves, diced
1 sm. hot red peppers
½ tsp. sea salt

Soak the beans in warm water and leave them overnight. The next morning, drain and rinse the beans. Add more water and bring them to boil in a large pot. Boil for 5 minutes and drain them. Then move them into a clean pot and cover them with water. Put the potatoes and carrots in the beans. Now add the oil, black pepper, celery, hot pepper and tomatoes to the pot. Reduce heat and cover the pot. Simmer for about an hour and a half. You'll know when the fasolada is ready by simply checking the beans; if they are soft, the soup is ready. Add salt and remove from heat. Serve into soup bowls.

GERMAN POTATO SALAD

From the region of District 6270
USA

⅓ lb. bacon, diced
2 T. chopped onion
2 T. flour
2 T. sugar
1 tsp. salt

½ tsp. white pepper
½ c. vinegar
½ c. water
¾ qt. sliced, cooked potatoes
Parsley

Fry bacon until delicately brown, drain, reserving at least ¼ cup bacon drippings in skillet. Add onion and sauté about 3 minutes. Add flour, sugar, seasonings and blend well. Add vinegar and water gradually and cook until thickened (about 5 minutes), stirring constantly. Pour over potatoes and toss. Add parsley flakes. Yield: 6 servings.

GADO GADO (Indonesian Salad)

From the region of District 3400
Indonesia

1 c. blanched moong bean
2 carrots, sliced round and blanched
1½ c. green beans, cut into strips and blanched
3 potatoes, cooked, peeled, cubed
2 c. shredded romaine lettuce

Some outer romaine leaves
1 cucumber, seeded and sliced into half moons
3 tomatoes, sliced
3 hard-boiled eggs, sliced
12 shrimp crackers (krupuk crackers)

Peanut Sauce:

1 c. peanut butter
½ c. water
¼ c. coconut milk
¾ c. soy sauce
1 tsp. chili paste or chopped chilies

3 tsp. brown sugar
1 T. turmeric
¼ tsp. salt

Lay the outer whole leaves of the romaine lettuce on a large platter to form a base. Spread the shredded lettuce over the base. Layer the blanched, drained vegetables over the shredded lettuce. Garnish the platter with the eggs, cucumber wedges, tomatoes and crackers. Mix all the ingredients for the peanut sauce and blend well. Pour the sambal kacang or peanut sauce over the vegetables and serve.

HONDURAN CONCH SOUP (Soupa de caracol)

From the region of District 4250
Honduras

1 lb. conch, peeled and chopped
2 c. coconut milk
2 lg. onions, chopped
3 green bananas, cubed
2 garlic cloves, chopped
3 carrots, cubed

2 lbs. yellow yucca, cubed
2 green peppers, cubed
2 c. fish or vegetable stock
1 c. coriander leaves, chopped
⅛ c. margarine

Sauté in margarine, onions, garlic, green peppers and all vegetables, except bananas. Add the stock and the coriander. Add the coconut milk to the fried vegetables. Let it simmer for 20 minutes. Add the bananas and simmer for another 5 minutes or until the bananas are soft. Add the conch and simmer for another 5 minutes. Serve warm.

HUBOVA POLIEVKA (Mushroom Potato Soup)

From the region of District 2240
Slovakia

½ kg fresh mushrooms
½ kg potatoes
6 whole black peppers
3 L. cold water
7 juniper berries
2 c. milk

3 tsp. flour
1 spoon oil
Pinch of salt
½ tsp. sugar
½ tsp. vinegar

Wash the mushrooms and chop them into very fine pieces. Mix together water, mushrooms, black pepper and juniper berries. Cook until the mushrooms are tender, approximately 20 minutes. Just before they are cooked, add oil together with peeled and cubed potatoes. When the potatoes are cooked, thicken the soup with a mixture of milk and flour mixed together, creating a smooth paste. Bring to the boil and add salt, sugar and vinegar according to taste, achieving the sweet and sour flavor. Serve warm.

IRISH CREAM OF TURNIP SOUP

From the region of District 1160
Ireland

¼ lb. turnip
¼ lb. leek
¼ lb. celery
¼ lb. onion
¼ lb. butter
3 T. flour

8 c. chicken stock or vegetable stock for totally vegetarian
½ to 1 pt. fresh cream, depending on how creamy you like your soup

Sauté the celery, onion and leeks in butter. When vegetables are done, add flour and stir well. Add the chicken stock, slowly mixing well. Now, add the turnip. Simmer for about 15 minutes until the turnip is tender. Remove from the heat. Blend in the blender until smooth. Pass through a sieve to catch any remaining lumps. Reheat for 5 minutes. Add the cream and salt and pepper to taste. Stir well. Serve with slices of wheat bread.

ICEBERG SALAD

From the region of District 5010
USA

2 c. vegetable oil
¾ c. cider vinegar
⅓ c. lemon juice
½ c. chopped fresh parsley
2-3 cloves garlic, minced

½ tsp. salt
½ tsp. pepper
2 c. (8 oz.) freshly grated Romano cheese
3 heads iceberg lettuce, torn

Combine first 7 ingredients in a large jar. Cover tightly and shake vigorously until blended; stir in cheese. Toss dressing as needed with lettuce; store remaining dressing in refrigerator. Yield: 18 servings.

KRAUTSALAT

From the region of District 1800-1900
Germany

1 lg. white cabbage
½ c. oil
1 tsp. caraway seeds
½ c. white vinegar

1½ c. warm water
1 tsp. salt
½ tsp. pepper
60g cooked ham, diced (¼ lb.)

Slice the cabbage very thin and soak in salt water for about ½ hour. Drain and pour ½ cup oil over it and let it rest for another ½ hour. Mix

(continued)

together the white vinegar, warm water, salt, pepper and the chopped caraway. Now pour the vinegar dressing over cabbage and let it rest for about one hour. Garnish cabbage salad with ham before serving.

LASOPY (Madagascar Vegetable Soup)

From the region of District 9220
Madagascar

4 lbs. veal bones
3 qt. water

2 T. salt

Add:

2 sm. turnips, peeled and cut in chunks
8 scallions, cut in lg. pieces
4 carrots, peeled and cut into 2-inch pieces

1 c. string beans
1 c. tomatoes, cut in chunks
½ tsp. black pepper

In a 5-quart pot, simmer the veal bones, water and salt for one hour with the pot closed. Now add the turnips, scallions, carrots, string beans, tomato and black pepper. Simmer for about 1 hour or until vegetables are tender. Remove the veal bones. Purée the vegetables. Serve thick and hot from the pot to the soup bowls. Serve with crackers. Serves 8.

LEMON PINEAPPLE SALAD

From the region of District 5000
USA

1 (6-oz.) pkg. lime-flavored gelatin
1 c. boiling water
1 c. cold water
1 (3-oz.) pkg. cream cheese, softened
1 c. whipping cream, whipped
1 c. miniature marshmallows

1 (8-oz.) can crushed pineapple, drained
1 c. chopped pecans
Fresh parsley sprigs (opt.)
Crabapples (opt.)
Orange cups (opt.)
Cranberries (opt.)

Dissolve gelatin in boiling water; stir in cold water. Beat cream cheese until smooth. Gradually add gelatin; beat well. Chill until the consistency of unbeaten egg white. Fold in next 4 ingredients. Pour mixture into a shallow 6-cup mold; cover and chill. Unmold and garnish with parsley, crabapples and orange cups filled with cranberries if desired. Yield: 12 servings.

LENTIL AND SWEET POTATO SOUP

From the region of District 3280
Bangladesh

2 c. water for soaking
2 c. water
½ lb. red lentils (masoor dahl)
1 tsp. ground turmeric
1 sweet potato, peeled and cut into cubes
3 T. vegetable oil, divided
½ c. onion, finely chopped
1 c. diced tomato

2 fresh green chilies, seeded and finely chopped (add 1 more for a spicy soup)
Salt and freshly ground black pepper to taste
¾ c. chopped fresh coriander for garnish
¾ c. chopped spring onion for garnish

Soak lentils in 2 cups water for 30 minutes and drain. Boil lentils in 2 cups water and turmeric for 15 minutes or tender. Boil sweet potato and mash it into the dahl, water and all. You may purée it in the food processor. Put everything into the soup pot. Heat the oil in a frying pan over medium heat and cook the onion until lightly browned. Stir in chilies, tomatoes, salt and pepper and continue cooking another 3-5 minutes. Add this to the lentils and potatoes in the pot and mix together over medium heat. Stir in additional water as needed to attain your desired consistency for soup. Serve warm with coriander or spring onions. Serves 6.

MARINATED GREEN PAPAYA

From the region of District 2750
Micronesia

1 med. papaya, firm, but not ripe as yet
1 tsp. ground black pepper
1½ c. distilled white vinegar

¼ tsp. salt
1 c. water
2 T. sugar
3 Boonie peppers

Peel the papaya and cut into matchstick-size pieces. Place the papaya sticks upright in a clean Mason jar. Add salt, pepper, sugar and peppers to the jar. Fill the jar with approximately equal amounts of vinegar and water to cover the papaya. Cover the jar tightly with its lid. Store the jar in the refrigerator for a week, shaking the jar at least once a day to mix the spices.

MOE'S FAVORITE POTATO SALAD

From the region of District 5950
USA

¼ c. vinegar
¼ c. water
¼ c. sugar
¼ tsp. salt
Dash of pepper
1 tsp. prepared mustard

2 eggs, well beaten
½ c. Ranch salad dressing
4 hard-cooked eggs, chopped
1 T. minced onion
4 c. cooked potatoes, cubed

Combine vinegar, water, sugar, salt, pepper and mustard and bring to a boil, reduce heat and gradually beat in 2 well beaten eggs. Continue cooking, stirring constantly, about 5 minutes, until slightly thickened. Beat in ½ cup of salad dressing. Toss together with 4 hard-cooked eggs, 1 tablespoon minced onion and 4 cups cubed, cooked potatoes. Makes 6 servings. (Triple recipe for 5 pounds of potatoes.)

TOMATO AND WATERMELON SALAD

From the region of District 6000
USA

8 c. seedless watermelon, cut into 1¼-inch chunks
3 lbs. (about 6 c.) tomatoes, cut into 1¼ inch
1 tsp. kosher salt
4 T. olive oil, divided

1½ T. red wine vinegar
3 T. total chopped basil and mint
¾ c. crumbled feta cheese
½ c. sliced almonds, slightly toasted

Combine melon and tomatoes. Sprinkle with salt and let it stand for about 10-15 minutes. Add olive oil, vinegar and herbs. Sprinkle with feta cheese and toasted almonds and serve. Makes 6-8 servings.

MANGO JICAMA SLAW

From the region of District 4270, 4280, 4290
Colombia

2 mangoes, julienned
1 lb. jicama, peeled, julienned
¾ c. carrots, julienned
2 red bell peppers, seeded, julienned

½ c. fresh lime juice
½ c. chopped fresh cilantro
Salt to taste
Freshly ground black pepper to taste

Mix all ingredients and let it rest for 10 minutes. Serve cold.

MARIE'S WEST SIDE SEAFOOD SALAD

From the region of District 7890
USA

2 lbs. lg. shrimp, peeled and deveined
2 lbs. sea scallops, cleaned
3 lbs. thawed frozen calamari (squid), cleaned and cut into rings and sm. tentacles
2 (6-oz.) cans lg. black olives, drained
1 bunch celery hearts
2-3 (24-oz.) bottles Zesty Italian salad dressing
Juice of 5 med. lemons
1 T. crushed red pepper seeds, more to taste
2 tsp. salt
2 tsp. dried oregano

Boil separately shrimp, scallions and calamari until just cooked (do not overcook); drain well. Place all seafood into an extra-large container or bowl. Add 2 bottles salad dressing, lemon juice, salt, oregano and red pepper; mix well. If seafood is not completely covered, add additional dressing. Marinate at least 8 hours or overnight in refrigerator. Remove from refrigerator; add olives. Slice celery into ¼-inch pieces; add to salad. Mix well and serve still chilled with slotted spoon. Serves 10-12.

MUSHROOM SOUP

From the region of District 7350
USA

6 c. boiling water
1 lb. mushrooms, chopped or sliced
3 T. chicken bouillon
1 lg. potato, diced
2 carrots, diced
2 sticks celery, cut fine
1 lg. onion, diced
¾ stick margarine
½ c. pearl barley
2 pinches dry dill

Melt butter or margarine. Add vegetables and sauté lightly. Add water and rest of ingredients. Simmer 2 to 2½ hours.

MONTSERRAT SALAD

From the region of District 7030
Montserrat

½ green cabbage, shredded
½ red cabbage, shredded
2 lg. tomatoes, diced and set aside
1 green bell pepper, finely chopped
2 red bell peppers, finely chopped
3 shallots, minced
½ c. roasted sunflower seeds (opt.)

2 T. The Spice House buttermilk dressing
1 T. ground ginger
1 tsp. freshly ground black pepper
1 T. sugar
½ tsp. salt
¼ c. Miracle Whip
Sm. ctn. vanilla yogurt

Put all the vegetables in a bowl and mix well. Mix the spices, buttermilk, sugar, Miracle Whip and yogurt together to make the dressing. Add dressing to the chopped cabbage mixture. Mix thoroughly. Then add tomato as a topping along with optional sunflower seeds. Let sit for an hour before serving. Serves 4.

NEW ENGLAND CLAM CHOWDER

From the region of District 7780, 7790
USA

1 c. cooked and crumbled bacon
½ c. chopped onion
4 potatoes, peeled and cubed
2 T. olive oil
1 T. all-purpose flour

1 c. bottled clam juice
1 c. half-and-half
2 (6-oz.) cans minced clams
Salt and pepper to taste
½ c. heavy cream (opt.)
2 T. chopped fresh parsley

Sauté the onion and potatoes in the olive oil for 3-5 minutes. Sprinkle with the flour and stir well to coat. Pour in the clam juice, bring to a boil, reduce heat to low and simmer for about 15 minutes or until potatoes are tender. Add the half-and-half and minced clams and season with salt and pepper to taste. Allow to heat through, about 5 minutes. (If adding cream, whisk it in and do not boil.) Garnish with the parsley and crumbled bacon. Do not boil if adding cream.

NUTTY ORZO SALAD

From the region of District 5440
USA

1 lb. orzo
3 T. fresh lemon juice
½ c. olive oil

½ c. pine nuts, toasted
1¼ c. feta, crumbled
1 c. thinly sliced scallion greens

Cook orzo until tender, then drain. Whisk lemon juice, oil, salt and pepper to taste in a large bowl, then add hot orzo and toss. Cool orzo, then toss with pine nuts, feta and scallion greens. Season with additional salt and pepper if necessary.

OKRA SOUP

From the region of District 1910
Bosnia & Herzegovinia

½ kg veal, cubed sm.
1½ c. fresh okra, sliced
2 T. butter
2 T. sour cream
2 T. flour

1 c. carrots, diced
1 c. onions, diced
1 T. flat-leaf parsley, chopped
2 egg yolks
Lemon slices for garnish

In a saucepan, melt the butter and fry the veal until browned all over. Now add the onions and carrots and continue cooking for about 10 minutes. Mix in the flour and let it combine with the meat, carrots and onions. Transfer the mixture to a larger saucepan, then stir in 3 cups of water along with the okra. Season to taste, then bring the mixture to a boil. Whisk together the egg yolks and sour cream in a bowl. Add this slowly to the soup, whisking constantly. Take the soup off the heat and stir in the parsley. Ladle into soup bowls and serve with a slice of lemon on top.

PLOUGHMAN'S SOUP

From the region of District 1170-1220
England

1 c. finely chopped onions
3 T. butter
¼ c. whole wheat flour
3 c. chicken stock
1 c. light ale (do not substitute beer)

1 tsp. Worcestershire sauce
2 c. crumbled Cheshire cheese
Salt and pepper, to taste
Slices of scallion for garnish

(continued)

Sauté the onions in butter until golden. Stir in the flour and cook for 1 minute. Remove from the heat, then gradually whisk in the stock and ale, a little at a time. Return to the heat and bring to a boil. Simmer 5 minutes or until thickened. Stir in the Worcestershire sauce. Stir in 1½ cups cheese, a little at a time (keeping the heat low), until the cheese is all melted. Season with salt and pepper. Garnish each bowl with the reserved cheese and the scallion. Serves 4.

POTATO SALAD

From the region of District 7020
Haiti

8 potatoes, peeled and cubed
2 carrots, peeled and coarsely chopped
6 tsp. salt
2 beets
4 eggs

1 c. sweet peas
1 onion, minced
⅔ c. red bell pepper, diced
⅔ c. green bell pepper, diced
4 T. mayonnaise
½ tsp. black pepper

Boil potatoes and carrots in water with 2 teaspoons salt for 10 minutes or until tender. Boil beets separately in water with 2 teaspoons salt until tender. Peel and coarsely chop. Boil eggs separately in water with 2 teaspoons salt until hard. In a bowl, place cubed potatoes and carrots, chopped beets, sweet peas, onion, red and green bell peppers and mix with mayonnaise. Add black pepper. Serve on a platter or over a bed of lettuce.

POLYNESIAN DRESSING

From the region of District 9920
French Polynesia

1½ c. prepared Italian dressing or French dressing
1½ c. prepared Thousand Island dressing

½ c. crushed pineapple, drained
½ tsp. celery seed

Combine all ingredients in a jar and shake well to combine.

RAUGINTU KOPŪSTAI SRIUBA

(Lithuanian Sauerkraut Soup)

From the region of District 1460
Lithuania

¾ lb. smoked ribs or other smoked meat
3 qt. water
2 med. onions, quartered
2 bay leaves, cracked in half

10 black peppercorns
2 lbs. rinsed and drained sauerkraut
½ head cabbage, shredded

In a large Dutch oven, place smoked meat, water, onion, bay leaf and peppercorns. Bring to a boil, reduce heat and let simmer partially covered 1 hour. Remove meat, bay leaves and peppercorns. Add sauerkraut, bring back to the boil, reduce heat and simmer 30 minutes. Add cabbage and cook until tender. Adjust seasonings. Remove fat and bones from meat, chop and return to the soup. Allow soup to cool completely, skim off any fat that rises to the surface, reheat and serve. Serves 8.

RADISH SALAD

From the region of District 2241
Moldova

3 bunches radishes (approx. 2 c. sliced)
3 hard-boiled eggs
4 chives

1 bunch dill
½ c. sour cream
Salt

Wash and thinly slice the radishes. Mix in chopped chives and dill. Separate the yolk and whites from the boiled eggs. Chop the yolk and mix with sour cream; pour onto the radishes. Add thinly sliced egg white, salt and mix well.

REJESALAT (Shrimp Salad)

From the region of District 1440-1480
Denmark

½ c. mayonnaise
½ c. sour cream
2 T. cocktail sauce
4 T. sherry
Dash of white pepper

1 ½ lbs. cooked shrimp
¾ lb. fresh mushrooms, sliced
8-oz. can cut asparagus
Canned sliced pineapple
Lemon slices for garnish

(continued)

Stir together mayonnaise and sour cream. Mix in the sherry and cocktail sauce. Mix well. Fold in cooked shrimp, sliced mushrooms and asparagus. Serve on slices of pineapple on leaf lettuce. Garnish with lemon slices.

RAGU JUHA (Ragu Soup)

From the region of District 1913
Croatia

500g chicken meat, washed
½ c. each: vegetables for soup (carrots, celery, parsley, parsnips)
2 T. butter

1 T. flour
½ c. peas
½ c. rice
1 sm. onion
Salt and pepper

Place washed meat and rice into cold water; add salt and cook it. In separate pot, melt butter, fry onions and add remainder of vegetables. When vegetables are semi-tender, mix in flour, stir and allow to fry. Pour the soup in which meat was cooked over it. Separate meat from bones, cut into pieces and add to soup.

TACO SOUP FROM DALLAS VANHEYINGENS RESTAURANT

From the region of District 7190
USA

1 lb. ground beef
½ c. chopped onion
1 c. chopped green pepper
2 (16-oz.) cans kidney beans or black beans

2 (16-oz.) cans diced tomatoes and 2 cans water
2 c. canned tomato purée
1 env. taco seasoning mix
2 c. corn

Brown beef, onion and green pepper together. Drain off fat. Add kidney beans, tomatoes, water, purée and taco seasoning mix and simmer 30 minutes. Add corn and simmer for 15 minutes.

Toppings:

1 avocado, diced
Shredded cheese
Corn chips

Sour cream
Chopped black olives
Chopped green onion

TAMARIND BEEF SOUP

From the region of District 9550
Timor

1 kg top round beef, in 1 piece
1 tsp. dried shrimp paste, toasted
1 T. palm sugar, chopped
2 red chilies, de-seeded and sliced in fine strips
2 spring onions (scallions), cut in 2.5cm lengths

5 shallots, peeled and sliced
3 garlic cloves, peeled and sliced
1 tsp. sweet soy sauce
2 T. tamarind juice
Cooking oil
Water
Salt to taste

In a wok or pan, add enough water to cover the beef and bring water to a boil, then put in the beef and let simmer until half cooked, reserving the stock. When cool, cut beef into 2 centimeter cubes, then sauté them in 2 tablespoons of oil and set aside. Grind the shallots, garlic, shrimp paste and palm sugar. Sauté the mixture in 1 tablespoon of oil for 2 minutes. Add the beef and sweet soy sauce and sauté for another minute or so, then pour in the reserved beef stock, tamarind juice and salt. Allow to simmer until beef is tender. Garnish with chilies and spring onions.

TOMATOES SALAD

From the region of District 9140
Nigeria

½ c. parsley
½ c. lettuce
½ c. onion

1 c. tomatoes, chopped
4 T. mixed tomato ketchup
½ c. mayonnaise

Slice parsley, lettuce, onions and tomatoes and mix together with the mixed ketchup and mayonnaise. Serves 2.

TUNA AND CHOW MEIN NOODLE SALAD

From the region of District 5170
USA

1 head iceberg lettuce
2 med. size tomatoes, cut into ½-inch cubes
½ cucumber, diced
¼ c. chopped cilantro (opt.)
1 (7-oz.) can tuna (198g)

1-2 T. grated Parmesan cheese
Juice of 1 lemon
⅓ c. mayonnaise
¼ tsp. garlic salt or to taste
1 c. chow mein noodles

Cut lettuce into bite-sized pieces, dice tomatoes and cucumber. Drain tuna. Stir all ingredients together. Noodles can be served in separate bowl.

TRINI CORN SOUP

From the region of District 7030
Trinidad & Tobago

2 T. vegetable oil
2 onions, chopped
3 cloves garlic, minced
1 lb. English potatoes, peeled and quartered
2 diced carrots
⅓ c. chopped chives
¼ c. chopped celery
⅓ c. fresh thyme, chopped
2 pimento peppers, seeded and chopped
¾ c. yellow split peas, washed and picked over

8 c. beef or vegetable stock
1 Congo or hot pepper, left whole
½ c. coconut milk (opt.)
6 ears corn, cut into 2-inch pieces
1 quantity of dumplings (see recipe below)
½ c. chopped chadon beni (cilantro)

Heat the oil in a large soup pot or Dutch oven. Add the onions and garlic and sauté until fragrant. Add the potatoes, carrots, chives, celery, thyme and pimento peppers and cook for another 5 minutes. Add peas, stock, peppers, and coconut milk. Boil till peas are done and then puree. Add corn, dumplings and cilantro and serve. Serves 6-8.

Dumplings:

2 c. flour
1 tsp. butter

2 tsp. baking powder
½ tsp. salt

Mix all into stiff dough and form a rope. Cut in 2-inch pieces and put in boiling water till they float on top.

VEGETABLE BACON CHOWDER

From the region of District 7280
USA

2 c. diced potatoes
½ c. sliced carrots
½ c. sliced celery
½ c. chopped onion
1½ tsp. salt
½ tsp. pepper
2 c. boiling water

¼ c. butter
¼ c. flour
2 c. milk
2½ c. (10 oz.) shredded sharp Cheddar cheese
10 slices bacon, crisply cooked and crumbled

Combine potatoes, carrots, celery, onion, salt and pepper in 2 cups boiling water. Cover and simmer 10 minutes. **Do not drain.** In another saucepan, melt butter and add flour; cook slowly over low flame, stirring constantly, until mixture bubbles and foams (about 3 minutes). The mixture should be golden; do not brown. Add milk, stirring rapidly. Cook over medium heat, again stirring until mixture bubbles. Cook 1 minute more. Add cheese; stir until melted. Add bacon and undrained veggies. Heat; do not boil. Add a little milk if too thick.

STILTON SOUP

From the region of District 1130-1140
England

¼ c. butter
¾ c. finely chopped onion
½ c. finely chopped carrot
1 bay leaf
¼ c. all-purpose flour

¼ tsp. white pepper
2½ c. chicken broth
1½ c. half-and-half
1½ c. crumbled Stilton cheese
Chives

Sauté the onions, carrots and bay leaf in butter until carrots and onions are cooked. Stir in flour and white pepper. Cook over low heat, stirring constantly until smooth and bubbly. Remove from heat and cool. Stir in broth and half-and-half. Heat to boiling over medium heat, stirring constantly; boil and stir 1 minute. Reduce heat to low. Stir in cheese; heat over low heat, stirring constantly, just until cheese is melted. Remove bay leaf; sprinkle soup with chives.

XORIATIKI (Greek Village Salad)

From the region of District 2470, 2481
Greece

1 onion
1 green bell pepper
5 ripe tomatoes
1 cucumber
2 T. sliced olives

2 T. capers
1 T. fresh chopped oregano
⅓ lb. feta cheese, crumbled
½ c. olive oil
Salt

Cut the vegetables into slices and mix in a salad bowl. Top with the olives, capers and oregano and cover with crumbled feta cheese. Pour the olive oil evenly over the top. Serves 6.

ZAMA DE PASOLE VERDE (Green String Bean Soup)

From the region of District 2241
Romania

1½ lbs. string beans, cut
2 lbs. spring chicken, cut up
2 T. butter
½ T. flour
1 lg. onion, chopped

1 tsp. red pepper
2 garlic cloves
1 c. onion, sm., minced
Parsley and dill, chopped fine
3 qt. water

Place lard, onion and flour in a pot. Sauté. Add red pepper, water, chicken and cook. Cook cut-up green beans, garlic and onion in 4 ounces water separately for a half hour, then add to chicken pot and cook for 45 minutes or more. Add parsley and dill last.

ZESTY BEAN SALAD

From the region of District 6270
USA

2 (14.5-oz.) cans cut green beans
1 (14.5-oz.) can yellow beans
1 (14.5-oz.) can red kidney beans

1 (14.5-oz.) can garbanzo beans
1 c. diced celery
1 sm. onion, chopped

Dressing:

¼ c. cider vinegar
¼ c. oil
¼ c. sugar

1 tsp. black pepper
1 T. Italian herb seasoning

(continued)

Combine all dressing ingredients; stir and mix well. Pour over beans, celery and onions. Refrigerate. Stir again before serving.

SEAWEED AND EGG SOUP

From the region of District 3460-3520
Taiwan

3 eggs
2 sheets of nori (dried seaweed)
2 c. chicken stock
2 c. water
1 tsp. corn flour
4 sprigs spring onion
½ tsp. sesame oil
Salt and pepper to taste

Boil the water, oil and chicken broth in a saucepan. Mix the corn flour with a little water and pour into boiling soup to thicken. Break up the nori seaweed sheets into small pieces and put into the soup mixture. Beat the eggs and slowly pour the egg mixture into the soup, stirring. Add salt and pepper to taste and sprinkle with thinly sliced spring onions.

SUAASAT

From the region of District 1470
Greenland

1 kg reindeer meat, cubed
8 c. water
3 onions, chopped
300g wild mushrooms
1 c. carrots, sliced
¼ kg cherries, dried
1 tsp. each: rosemary, thyme
   and sage, chopped
1 c. pearl barley
1 lemon, zest only
Sea salt and black pepper

Pour the water into a large pot and add the cubed meat. Add the onions, mushrooms, carrots, cherries, herbs of rosemary, thyme and sage and the salt and pepper to taste, simmering on medium heat until tender, about 1 hour. Add barley and the lemon zest. Check and correct the seasoning and cook until the soup is thick, about 30 minutes.

SOPA DE PALMITO (Heart of Palm Soup)

From the region of District 4310
Brazil

1 stick unsalted butter
1 onion, chopped
2 garlic cloves, minced
1 leek, chopped
2 (10-oz.) cans hearts of palm
4 c. chicken stock (low-sodium is best for you)
1 potato, peeled and sliced
2 c. heavy cream
3 T. chives or scallions
Salt and pepper to taste

Sauté the onion and garlic in the butter in a soup pot. Add the leek. Cook for 4 minutes. Add the sliced potato and chicken stock. Bring to a boil and reduce the heat so that the soup can simmer for about 20 minutes. Add the palm of heart when potatoes are half cooked. Blend soup well. Use a hand processor if necessary. Let the soup cool off. Stir in the heavy cream and refrigerate for a couple hours. Serve cold with chives or scallions on the top.

SALADE COTE CAP VERTE (Chopped Egg Salad)

From the region of District 9100
Senegal

3 c. greens as lettuce, spinach, watercress or romaine, cut in coarse chunks
5 hard-boiled eggs, chopped
1 c. salad oil
½ c. tarragon vinegar
2 tsp. garlic powder
1 tsp. salt
1 tsp. freshly ground pepper
2 T. salad herbs
2 T. honey

Combine the greens and arrange in mounds on individual salad plates. Chop hard-boiled eggs finely. Sprinkle eggs heavily over the mound of greens. In a jar, combine salad oil, tarragon vinegar, garlic powder, salt, freshly ground pepper, salad herbs and honey. Shake thoroughly. Serve dressing separately to pour over greens as individually desired.

SOUTHWEST SALAD

From the region of District 5500
USA

1 ½ c. cooked fresh or drained, canned corn
1 c. cooked black beans, drained and canned

1 red bell pepper, diced
1 green bell pepper, diced
2 green onions, minced

Dressing:

2 T. olive oil
2 T. fresh lime juice

2 T. finely minced fresh cilantro
Salt and pepper to taste

Mix the dressing ingredients and add to the vegetables. Toss and serve.

SHOURABIT SILQ BI LABAN (Chard and Yogurt Soup)

From the region of District 2450
Lebanon

1 c. bulgur
1 lb. fresh greens (chard or spinach)
7 c. water
1 (15-oz.) can chickpeas

1 tsp. salt
2 ½ c. (20 oz.) plain yogurt, room temp.
1 egg, room temp.
Fresh or dried mint to garnish

Rinse the bulgur under cold water and drain. Wash greens well and drain. Remove any hard stems. In a large pot, bring 2 cups water to a boil over high heat. Add greens and return to a boil. Cover and cook about 3 minutes or until leaves are thoroughly wilted. Remove greens with a slotted spoon, place in a bowl and set aside to cool. Save cooking water and add bulgur, chickpeas and 5 cups more water to kettle. Return to a boil. Lower heat, cover and simmer for 2 hours. While soup is cooking, chop greens finely with a sharp knife. In a medium bowl, beat together salt, yogurt and egg. Add chopped greens and about 1 cup of the soup to yogurt mixture. Stir well in same direction to prevent curdling. Remove soup from heat. Gradually add yogurt mixture, stirring constantly. Sprinkle each serving with mint and serve immediately. Do not reheat or soup will curdle.

SOPPA TA 'L-ARMLA (Widow's Soup)

From the region of District 2110
Malta

3 sm. onions
1 med. cabbage
1 lettuce
1 endive
Sm. cauliflower
¾ lb. peas

1 stick celery
4 gbejniet or Rikotta (fresh cheeselets)
3 T. margarine
4 eggs

Chop all the vegetables and sauté in margarine. Add enough water to cover vegetables and simmer gently until the vegetables are well done. Slowly add the eggs, one by one, and the gbejniet and cook for 5 minutes or until well heated. When serving, first place an egg, gbejna or a bit of ricotta in each soup plate and then ladle on the soup.

SWEET CORN SOUP (Mielieroomsop)

From the region of District 9250
Botswana

1 c. onion, finely chopped
2 T. butter
3 tsp. corn flour
2 c. warm milk
2 c. chicken broth
1 can cream-style sweet corn (about 1 c.)

Celery salt
Pepper
¼ c. cream
¼ c. brandy

Fry onions for 5 minutes in butter. Add flour and cook for a minute or two over low heat. Stir frequently. Remove pot from stove and add warm milk while stirring the mixture. Now add all other ingredients, except the cream and brandy. Keep stirring until it starts boiling. Lower the heat and add the cream. Stir once. Just before serving, add the brandy.

SWEDISH CHICKEN SALAD

From the region of District 2320-2410
Sweden

1 shredded roasted chicken meat (about 3 c.)
½ lb. long-grain rice
1 c. thinly sliced green apple
1 c. thinly sliced red apple
2 bananas, sliced thickly
Lemon juice

½ c. double cream
1 c. mayonnaise
½ tsp. curry powder
Salt and freshly ground black pepper to taste
Watercress to garnish

Bring a pan of lightly salted water to a boil; add the rice and cook for about 12 minutes or until the rice is tender. Drain and set aside to cool. Sprinkle the apple and banana slices with lemon juice to prevent discoloration and set aside. Now whip the cream to the same consistency as the mayonnaise, then fold into the mayonnaise to combine. Add the curry powder and stir to mix. Fold in the chicken along with the fruit, then add more lemon juice to taste and adjust the seasonings. Pile the mixture on a bed of rice. Garnish with the watercress and serve.

SALADE DE ZAALOUK (Salad of Cooked Vegetables)

From the region of District 9010
Tunisia

5 T. olive oil
1 onion, chopped
4 courgettes (zucchini), blanched and cubed
3 sm. aubergines (eggplants), blanched and cubed
4 garlic cloves, crushed
4 red bell peppers, blanched and cubed

2 fresh red chilies, finely chopped
4 tomatoes, peeled and chopped not too fine
Salt and black pepper to taste
Chopped coriander to garnish

Heat the oil in a large frying pan and add the onion, courgettes, aubergines and garlic. Cook gently for about 10 minutes, stirring frequently, then add the remaining ingredients, except the coriander, and season liberally with black pepper. Continue cooking gently until the vegetables are completely tender and any liquid in the pan has evaporated. Transfer the contents of the pan to a bowl and set aside the bowl. Cover and refrigerate overnight to allow the flavors to blend. Serve garnished with chopped coriander.

Vegetables & Side Dishes

Helpful Hints

- When preparing a casserole, make an additional batch to freeze for when you're short on time. Use within 2 months.
- To keep hot oil from splattering, sprinkle a little salt or flour in the pan before frying.
- To prevent pasta from boiling over, place a wooden spoon or fork across the top of the pot while the pasta is boiling.
- Boil all vegetables that grow above ground without a cover.
- Never soak vegetables after slicing; they will lose much of their nutritional value.
- Green pepper may change the flavor of frozen casseroles. Clove, garlic, and pepper flavors get stronger when frozen, while sage, onion, and salt become more mild.
- For an easy no-mess side dish, grill vegetables along with your meat.
- Store dried pasta, rice (except brown rice), and whole grains in tightly covered containers in a cool, dry place. Refrigerate brown rice and freeze grains if you will not use them within 5 months.
- A few drops of lemon juice added to simmering rice will keep the grains separated.
- When cooking greens, add a teaspoon of sugar to the water to help vegetables retain their fresh colors.
- To dress up buttered, cooked vegetables, sprinkle them with toasted sesame seeds, toasted chopped nuts, canned french-fried onions, grated cheese, or slightly crushed seasoned croutons.
- Soufflé dishes are designed with straight sides to help your soufflé rise. Ramekins work well for single-serve casseroles.
- A little vinegar or lemon juice added to potatoes before draining will make them extra white when mashed.
- To avoid toughened beans or corn, add salt midway through cooking.
- If your pasta sauce seems a little dry, add a few tablespoons of the pasta's cooking water.
- To prevent cheese from sticking to a grater, spray the grater with cooking spray before beginning.

VEGETABLES & SIDE DISHES

GRAVCHE TAVCHE

From the region of District 2481
Macedonia

½ kg white beans
1 ½ onion, chopped
1 red paprika chile
½ c. cooking oil

3 pieces red dry capsicum
Pepper, salt, plain flour, parsley and mint

Soak the beans in water overnight. After that, cook them until it starts boiling, drain the beans and put them in another pot of hot water. Then add ½ the chopped onion and capsicum. Continue to cook it until the beans are cooked, but still firm. If there is too much water left, drain the beans. Fry the remaining chopped onion and paprika and one spoon of plain flour in cooking oil and then add this to the beans. Put everything in a pottery saucepan and then pour some parsley, mint, pepper and salt on it. Put the saucepan in the oven and cook for a while. The beans should not be too dry. Serve warm.

HERBED KIDNEY BEANS (Lobio Mtsvanilit)

From the region of District 2450
Georgia

2 c. canned kidney beans
¼ c. extra-virgin olive oil
¼ c. red wine vinegar
1 ½ tsp. coriander powder
¼ c. fresh cilantro, fresh and chopped
⅛ c. fresh parsley, fresh and chopped

⅛ c. fresh basil, fresh and chopped
¼ c. fresh dill, fresh and chopped
⅛ c. fresh tarragon, fresh and chopped
Black pepper
Salt

Warm the kidney beans. Let cool. Drain out the liquid. Stir in all other ingredients, adding salt and pepper to taste. Allow the beans to cool to room temperature before serving.

ICELAND VEGETABLES

From the region of District 1360
Iceland

½ lb. Iceland frozen peas
½ lb. Iceland cut green beans
¾ lb. Iceland broad beans

Juice of 1 lemon
Rind of 1 lemon
Freshly ground black pepper

Cook peas in hot boiling water for 2 minutes. Cook green beans in hot boiling water for 4 minutes. Cook broad beans in hot boiling water for 6 minutes. Drain vegetables and mix in bowl. Add the lemon rind and lemon juice and black pepper. Mix thoroughly and serve immediately.

ITALIAN SKILLET FRITTATA

From the region of District 2030-2120
Italy

2 ½ c. shredded potato or hash browns
3 T. oil
1 c. chopped fresh spinach

6 eggs, lightly beaten
2 ½ T. milk or water
1 c. grated Parmesan cheese, divided

Heat oil in large nonstick skillet. Sauté the potatoes until brown and almost cooked, for about 5 minutes. Stir constantly. Now add the spinach and sauté for another 5 minutes until the leaves are wilted. In a bowl, mix the milk, eggs and ½ cup of the cheese. Pour egg mixture evenly over potatoes and spinach. Cover and reduce heat to medium-low. Cook for 12 minutes or until eggs are set. Sprinkle with remaining ½ cup cheese; cover. Let stand 5 minutes. Cut into wedges and serve.

KAK MAZ MAGGI SQUARE

From the region of District 3310
Malaysia

4 pkt. Maggi instant noodles (any instant noodles, chicken or vegetable flavor)
2 eggs, beaten

3 stalks spring onions, finely chopped
Oil for deep-frying

Boil instant noodles with the packet flavor until soft. Drain and press the noodles gently into a baking tin to pack into a compressed block. Leave it to cool and cut into squares. Mix the eggs and spring onions. Dip the noodle squares into the egg mixture and deep-fry until golden brown. Serve hot with chili, tomato sauce and sour sauce. Serves 6.

KARTOFLIANKI

From the region of District 2410
Latvia

¾ kg potatoes
50g starch
2 eggs
20g fat

Flour to shape balls
300g sour cream
20g butter
Salt

Boil potatoes, peel and grate finely. Combine mashed potatoes with starch, butter, egg, salt and pepper. Knead and shape small balls. Use a little flour if needed and put on a baking sheet greased with butter. Bake in a preheated oven for 20 minutes. Stew in sour cream for 5 minutes. Serve hot. Garnish with chopped scallion and dill.

CHAKALAKA (South African Vegetable Dish)

From the region of District 9320
Lesotho

½ c. ground nut oil
2 med. onions, finely diced
6 lg. tomatoes, finely chopped
3 green bell peppers, finely diced

4 lg. carrots, peeled and grated
1-lb. can baked beans
4 tsp. hot curry powder
2 hot chilies, very finely diced
½ tsp. salt

Sauté the onions and green peppers until soft. Add the carrots, tomatoes, chilies and baked beans. Mix thoroughly and allow the mixture to simmer gently for 2 minutes, stirring occasionally. Squash the ingredients against the side of the pan so that the mixture becomes smooth. Add all the remaining ingredients and cook for a further 15 minutes. Serve warm.

DONGO-DONGO

From the region of District 9150
Congo

3 T. oil to sauté
3 sm. onions, finely chopped
2 hot chile peppers, finely chopped
25 okra, ends removed, chopped

3 cloves garlic, minced
2 soup cubes
½ lb. dried, salted or smoked fish, rinsed
1 can tomato paste

(continued)

Sauté onions and garlic in oil for a few minutes. Add soup cube, okra and peppers. Cook for 5 minutes. Add enough water to cover. Bring to a boil, then reduce heat and add fish. Add the tomato paste. Simmer until the okra and fish are tender. Dong-Dongo is usually served with a starch, such as Fufu or rice.

EGGPLANT PIZZA

From the region of District 5170
USA

Sauce:

1 c. tomato sauce
1 tsp. salt
¼ tsp. pepper
1 T. oregano

Stir ingredients together and set aside while you prepare the eggplant.

2 med. sized eggplants
1 c. shredded mozzarella and cheddar cheese or a commercial pizza blend cheese

Slice eggplants crosswise, ½ inch thick. Place slices on paper towels and salt generously. After 15 minutes, turn the eggplant slices over and salt the other side. After another 15 minutes, wipe salt off eggplant and arrange slices in cake pans or cookie sheets with sides that have been lined with aluminum foil. Spoon about 1 tablespoon of the sauce on each eggplant slice. Top with cheese. Bake at 400°F for 25-30 minutes.

VEGETARIAN DELIGHT

From the region of District 3271
Pakistan

¼ kg ladyfingers (okra)
2 lg. onions
2 tomatoes, chopped
¾ tsp. salt
1 tsp. chili powder

¼ tsp. turmeric
½ tsp. garlic
½ tsp. cumin seeds, whole
½ tsp. coriander seeds, whole

Cut ladyfingers vertically or in rounds. Fry ladyfingers and take them out. In the same oil, fry onions (half done). Add fried ladyfingers, tomatoes, salt, chili powder, turmeric and garlic. Cook on low flame. Roast and pound cumin seeds and coriander seeds and sprinkle over the cooked ladyfingers. Yield: 3-4 servings.

FETTAT ADIS (Vegetable over Crisp Bread)

From the region of District 2450
Sudan

1 lb. split red lentils
4 c. vegetable stock
1 lg. carrot
1 chopped, peeled potato
2 med. onions, roughly chopped
2 med. tomatoes, chopped
2 T. finely chopped onion

2 T. olive oil
2 T. lemon juice
2 tsp. cumin
Pinch of cinnamon
Pinch of cardamom
Salt and black pepper to taste

Add the stock to a large pot and bring to a boil. Place the roughly chopped onions, carrot, tomato and lentils in the stock, bring to a boil, then reduce the heat and simmer for about 30 minutes or until the lentils are soft. Add more water if dish becomes too dry and the lentils are not cooked. Allow to cool, then purée the mixture in a food processor or blender, then return to the pot and allow to heat through. Fry the finely chopped onion in the olive oil until they are golden brown, then add the mixture along with the lemon juice, cumin, salt, pepper, cardamom and cinnamon. Stir slowly on low heat for about 3 minutes, then pour over crisp bread pieces so that the bread is all soaked.

KOREAN POTATOES

From the region of District 3590-3750
Korea

2 med. sized potatoes (any kind will do)
2 T. soy sauce
2 tsp. sugar

1 tsp. garlic, minced well
2 tsp. sesame seeds
1-2 tsp. sesame oil
4 T. scallion, minced

Peel potatoes and slice into matchstick pieces, placing in cold water to prevent browning. Drain and place in saucepan with just enough water to barley cover potatoes. Bring to boil and cook just until tender, 3-4 minutes. Meanwhile, in a bowl, combine soy sauce, sugar, garlic, sesame seeds, sesame oil and scallion. Drain cooked potatoes well and add to soy sauce mixture, tossing well.

LAYERED LENTIL RICE

From the region of District 2450
Egypt

1 ¾ c. uncooked brown or white rice
1 lb. lentils
4 T. vegetable oil, divided
2 T. crushed garlic

2 (16-oz.) cans tomato sauce
½ c. water
¼ c. vinegar
2 med. onions

Cook rice according to directions and keep aside. Rinse lentils and put them in a pot, covering them with water and bring to a boil. Simmer on low heat until almost all water is absorbed and lentils are well cooked. Add extra water if longer time is needed. **To make the sauce:** First sauté the garlic in 2 tablespoons of oil until golden. Add both cans of tomato sauce and simmer 10-15 minutes. Then add water and vinegar and bring to a boil. Remove from heat immediately and add salt to taste. Finally, slice onion in thin, small pieces and sauté in remaining 2 tablespoons oil until brown and crispy. This dish should be arranged as a layer of lentils (on the bottom), followed by a layer of rice, then another layer of lentils and another layer of rice. Finish with the onions and sauce on top layer. Serves 6.

MONTENEGRIN AUBERGINES

From the region of District 2483
Montenegro

5 whole aubergines (eggplant)
¾ c. olive oil
3 onions, sliced thinly
8 garlic cloves, chopped

¾ lb. ripe tomatoes, chopped
Salt and freshly ground black pepper to taste

Bring the water to a boil with salt. Halve the aubergines lengthways and add to the pan. Return to a boil and cook for about 20 minutes or until tender. Add oil to a pan and sauté the onions and garlic until transparent. Add the tomatoes and cook for a further 20 minutes or until you have a smooth sauce. Drain the aubergines, return to the pan, then pour the tomato and onion sauce over the top. Season to taste with salt and black pepper, then simmer for 10 minutes, until heated through. Serve immediately.

MANGO SALSA FOR VEGETABLES & FISH

From the region of District 9220
Mauritius

3 green mangoes, peeled and grated
2 very lg. carrots, peeled and grated
2 cucumbers, peeled, seeded and grated
2 onions, finely sliced
2 chilies, chopped
2 tsp. vinegar
4 T. salad oil
Salt and black pepper to taste

Mix all the ingredients in a bowl. Let sit for one hour. Serve with any main dish.

MUSHROOM CASSEROLE

From the region of District 6440
USA

6 slices buttered white bread, cubed
½ c. butter
1 qt. fresh mushrooms, sliced
½ c. chopped onions
½ c. diced celery
½ c. chopped green pepper
½ c. mayonnaise
1 c. cream of mushroom soup
1 c. milk
2 eggs
1½ c. grated cheddar cheese

1st Layer: Place 3 slices of buttered and cubed white bread (do not remove crust) in a buttered 8 x 10-inch baking dish. **2nd Layer:** Sauté in ½ cup butter the following: mushrooms, onions, celery and green peppers. When tender, turn off heat and mix in mayonnaise. **3rd Layer:** Same as the first layer. **4th Layer:** Mix soup, eggs and milk well. Pour over casserole and bake in a 325°F oven for 1 hour. Sprinkle with cheddar cheese the last 15 minutes or cooking time.

MATOKI (GREEN BANANA) BURGERS

From the region of District 9150
Rwanda

For the Burgers:

- 8 sm. green bananas, boiled with the skins on (but pierced) until tender
- 240g white chickpeas, drained and washed (Kabuli channa)
- 1 lg. onion, minced
- 2 lg. cloves garlic, minced
- 4 green chilies (or to taste), minced
- 1 T. extra virgin olive oil
- 2 tsp. sesame seeds
- Juice and zest of one lemon
- ½ c. coriander, chopped finely
- 4 T. sour cream (or plain yogurt)
- 1 tsp. white pepper
- Salt to taste

In a small pan, heat the olive oil and gently sauté the onion, garlic, chilies and sesame seeds until aromatic. Don't let it brown. Set aside. Mash together the peeled green bananas and chickpeas. You could use a food processor, but be sure to pulse it briefly because we want some texture in there. Add in all of the other ingredients for the burgers, including the sautéed onions, garlic, sesame seeds and chilies and combine thoroughly. Using your hands, mold the mixture into burger shapes avoiding any cracks. Lightly coat each burger in semolina and set aside. Grill the burgers on both sides until golden. **Hint:** You can also oven bake these or cook them on a grill. Serve with all the trimmings!

DAHI VADAS (Lentil Puffs)

From the region of District 3040
India

- 8 oz. black dhal (urad)
- 1 pt. oil or 1 lb. ghee
- 6 green chilies
- 1 tsp. mustard seeds
- 4 dry red chilies
- 1 c. grated coconut
- 1 sprig curry leaves
- 2 pt. buttermilk
- Salt to taste

Grind the grated coconut to a fine paste with 4 green chilies and some salt and mix with the buttermilk. Put a pan on the fire containing about a tablespoon of oil. When hot, add the mustard seeds and red chilies. When the mustard begins to sputter, remove the pan from the heat. Add the buttermilk and keep on one side. Remove the black skin of the gram dhal if necessary and soak in water for about 2 hours; drain. Add salt to taste and grind dhal to a fine paste without too much water. Chop the remaining green chilies and curry leaves and mix with the dhal

(continued)

paste. Put a pan on the fire with the remaining oil. When hot, make the paste into small balls, each about the size of a lemon and fry. Remove and put them in the prepared buttermilk. Keep for about 2-3 hours until they are well soaked and soft.

MALAYSIAN VEGETABLE PICKLE (Acar)

From the region of District 3300, 3310
Malaysia

6 lg. cucumbers
½ lb. long beans
½ lb. French beans
½ lb. cabbage
½ lb. cauliflower
3 carrots
20 shallots, peeled
4 fresh red and green chilies
20 garlic cloves, peeled
5 tsp. salt

2 stalks lemon grass
2-inch piece galangal (ginger)
40 dried chilies
6 candlenuts
4cm piece belacan, roasted
   (shrimp paste)
5 T. sugar
½ tsp. salt
600ml vinegar

Cut cucumber, long beans and French beans into lengths. Cut the cauliflower and cabbage into small bite-size pieces. Remove seeds from chilies and sliced thin. Add salt to mixed vegetables and dry in sun for half a day. Soak dried chilies until soft and drain. In a blender, process the chilies, adding lemon grass, galangal, candlenuts and belacan. Heat oil in wok and fry paste until fragrant. Season with salt and sugar and set aside. When vegetables are dried in the sun, boil vinegar in a pot and blanch the vegetables. Add garlic and shallots. Remove and discard vinegar. Mix vegetables with spice paste thoroughly. Set aside in large bowl, keep for 2 days in an airtight container in refrigerator before serving. Serve as a pickle with any main dish.

MATOKE

From the region of District 9200
Kenya

½ c. onion, finely chopped
1 tsp. cumin seeds
1 tsp. mustard seeds
3 garlic cloves, minced
1 T. canola oil
4 red chili peppers, seeded and finely chopped
2 tsp. grated fresh gingerroot
1 tsp. ground cumin
1½ tsp. ground coriander

1 tsp. salt
¾ tsp. ground turmeric
5 med. tomatoes, peeled and chopped
4 plantains, cut into ½-inch slices
1¾ c. water
¾ c. finely ground peanuts
2 T. minced fresh cilantro

In a large skillet, sauté the onion, cumin seeds and mustard seeds in oil until onion is tender. Add garlic and sauté for 2 minutes. Stir in the peppers, ginger, ground cumin, coriander, salt, turmeric and tomatoes. Bring to a boil. Reduce heat; simmer, uncovered, for 5-7 minutes or until slightly thickened (you may need to add a little water so that it does not burn and get too dry). Add plantains and water. Bring to a boil. Reduce heat; simmer, uncovered, for 20 minutes or until plantains are tender, stirring occasionally. Stir in peanuts. Sprinkle with cilantro. Serves 8.

NSHIMA

From the region of District 9210
Zambia

6 c. cornmeal, corn flour or ground maize (1 c. per serving is sufficient)

2 c. water for every c. of cornmeal

Over high heat, bring the water to a boil. After a few minutes, slowly add about half the cornmeal to the water one spoonful at a time, stirring continuously with a sturdy wooden spoon. Continue cooking (and stirring) until the mixture begins to boil and bubble. Reduce heat to medium and cook for 5 minutes. Add remaining cornmeal, as before, sprinkling it spoonful by spoonful as you continue to stir. It is essential to keep stirring. The nshima should be very thick (no liquid remaining) and smooth (no lumps). It may reach this point before all of the remaining cornmeal is added to the pot or it may be necessary to add even more cornmeal than the recipe indicates. Once the desired consistency is reached, turn off heat, cover the pot and allow the nshima to stand for a few minutes before serving. Serve nshima immediately, hot, with the ndiwo of your choice. Serves 4.

ONION TART (Zwiebelkuchen)

From the region of District 1930-1950
Germany

0.4 oz. yeast
¼ c. lukewarm milk
1 ½ c. flour
3 oz. butter
1 tsp. sugar
Pinch of salt
1 egg

2 lbs. onions
2 T. butter
2 oz. flour
½ c. sour cream
4 eggs, separated
Pinch of salt
Caraway seeds

Mix the yeast with the lukewarm milk and sugar. Set aside. Melt the butter and mix in the beaten egg. Set aside. Put the flour in a mixing bowl. Stir in a pinch of salt. Make a well in the center and pour in the yeast mixture and the butter mixture. Knead well. The dough will be a little sticky. If it is too sticky, incorporate a little more flour into it. Oil another mixing bowl, place the kneaded dough into it and let it rise in a warm place until doubled in size. Usually about one and half hours. Make the topping by chopping the onion and frying in butter until it is translucent. Mix the flour with the sour cream, mix in the egg yolks, salt, caraway seeds and cooled onions. Lastly, fold in the egg whites. Grease a baking dish. Punch down the risen dough. Roll out the yeast dough, place in the dish, pulling up the edges slightly. Spread the onion mixture over the dough. Bake onion tart in oven at 350°F until the dough edge is slightly brown and the filling is set. Serve warm.

POTATO SALAD-COLD

From the region of District 1470
Denmark

1 kg firm potatoes

Marinade:

½dl good oil
2 tsp. vinegar

2-3 cloves crushed garlic
Salt and pepper

Salad Sauce:

200g crème fraiche
150g yogurt
Crushed garlic

Salt and pepper
2-3 finely chopped tomatoes
Chives

Cook the potatoes, peel, chill and slice them into a bowl. Whip the marinade together and pour it over the potatoes. Mix. Mix the ingredients to the salad sauce, add salt, pepper and garlic to taste. Pour it over

(continued)

the potatoes and stir carefully. Arrange in a nice bowl and decorate with the chopped tomatoes and the chopped chives. This potato salad goes fine with fried meat and a green salad. Serves 4-6.

PAPA'S CHORREADAS

From the region of District 4270, 4280, 4290
Colombia

1 lb. sm. red potatoes
3 med. tomatoes
¼ tsp. chili powder
¼ tsp. cumin
½ c. heavy cream

Bunch of cilantro
Bunch of scallions/onions
½ c. white cheese, like mozzarella
Table salt to taste

Peel the potatoes (papas) partially leaving some skin on. Boil the papas until tender. Slice in half. Chop onions, cilantro and tomato into fine small pieces. Shred about ½ cup of white cheese. Stir fry the onions, cilantro, tomato, chili powder and cumin in a frying pan. Add the cream, cheese and salt to taste. Turn heat to low and let it simmer until it thickens. Spread potatoes on a serving platter and pour sauce over. Garnish with chopped scallions and serve warm.

POTATO VARENYKY (Potato Dumplings)

From the region of District 2230
Ukrain

2¼ c. flour
2 eggs
1 tsp. salt
3½ c. instant mashed potatoes, prepared

1 c. cheddar or processed cheese, shredded
Salt and pepper to taste

In a large mixing bowl, combine flour, egg and salt. Mix in a little water at a time until dough is stiff. Roll out dough on floured surface, about ¼ inch thick. Cut out circles with the rim of a glass or cookie cutter. **For the filling:** Prepare instant potatoes according to package directions. Add cheese and mix well. Set aside. Fill each circle of dough with about 1 tablespoon of the potato-cheese mixture. Fold over and seal edges. **To cook:** Bring a large pot of water to a boil and drop in the varenyky one at a time. They are done when they float to the top. Serves 6.

PAN DE MAIZ

From the region of District 4060
Dominican Republic

1 ¼ c. yellow corn meal
1 ¼ c. all-purpose flour
1 ½ T. baking powder
½ tsp. salt
4 oz. unsalted butter
1 c. grated fresh coconut, grated fine

¼ tsp. anise seed (opt.)
¼ c. evaporated milk
¼ c. fresh coconut milk
2 lg. eggs, whisked well

Combine cornmeal, flour, baking powder and salt. Cream the butter until it is light and fluffy and gradually add it to the flour mixture. Add the grated coconut and mix well. In a different bowl, gently combine the evaporated milk, coconut milk and the well whisked eggs and add this to the flour mixture. Mix thoroughly, beating for two minutes. Grease two (9 x 5-inch) loaf pans and fill with the mixture. The mixture should be very soft, like a thicker batter. Bake in the center of a preheated oven at 350°F for about 30 minutes or until the center is dry.

ALOO DAM BENGALI

From the region of District 3060
India

1 lb. baby potatoes, boiled and peeled
1 tomato, cut into 8 pieces
1 x 2 inch ginger paste
Pinch of hing (asafodada)
1 tsp. pach foron (mi of mustard, kalangi, methi (fenugreek), jeery (cumin), bori soop

3 cardamom
3 cloves
Cinnamon
2 tsp. melted butter (ghee)
⅛ tsp. chili powder
½ tsp. turmeric powder

Heat melted butter, cardamom, cloves and cinnamon. Fry 1 minute, then add pach foron. When it starts cracking, put in pinch of asafodada, tomato and ginger paste. If needed, add little water, cook 2 minutes to make thick gravy. Add potatoes and cook 5 minutes, make nice gravy, semi thick. Serve with chapati (Indian home-made bread), Puri, Porotha.

ARTICHOKES IN WINE (Topinambours en Daube)

From the region of District 1510, 1520
France

1 ⅕ lbs. Jerusalem artichokes, peeled and thickly sliced
1 onion, finely chopped
1 garlic clove, crushed
2 oz. butter
3 T. olive oil
¼ c. white wine

1 ¼ c. water
1 bouquet garni
Salt
Pepper
2 T. tomato paste
¼ tsp. sugar

Heat the butter and oil in a saucepan. Add the onion and garlic, cover and cook gently until soft and transparent, not browned. Raise the heat, add the artichoke and brown quickly on all sides. Add the wine, water, salt, pepper and bouquet garni. Bring to the boil, then reduce the heat, cover and simmer for 20 minutes. Stir in the tomato paste and sugar and continue to cook, uncovered, for a further 10 minutes over a medium heat to reduce the liquid. Serve hot.

AKKARA

From the region of District 9150
Cameroon

3 c. dried cowpeas (black-eyed peas)
1 onion, finely chopped
½ tsp. salt
2 sm. hot chili peppers, finely chopped

Pinch of cayenne pepper powder
½ tsp. fresh gingerroot, peeled and minced
2 c. peanut oil

Soak the peas in water overnight. Rinse to wash away the skins and any other debris and drain. Crush, grind or mash the black-eyed peas into a thick paste. Add enough water to form a smooth, thick paste of a batter that will cling to a spoon. Add all other ingredients, except oil. Heat oil in a deep skillet. Make fritters by scooping up a spoonful of batter and using another spoon to quickly push it into the hot oil. Deep-fry the fritters until they are golden brown. Serve with an African hot sauce as a snack. This is a spicy dish.

GRANDMA'S PULUT HITAM (Black Rice Pudding)

From the region of District 3310
Malaysia/Brunei

200g gula melaka or palm sugar
500ml water
300g black glutinous rice, soaked overnight and drained
100g white glutinous rice, washed and drained
150g dried longan, washed
½ c. thick coconut milk from 1 coconut
½ tsp. salt

Bring palm sugar or gula melaka and water to a boil and strain for thick syrup. Set aside. Place black glutinous rice in a pot with enough cold water to cover 3 centimeters above the rice. Boil on low heat. Stir in some hot water if the rice becomes too dry. Stir again when the grains burst and the rice is cooked. Add white glutinous rice and continue to cook until the grain softens. Stir occasionally. Add longan and the palm sugar or gula melaka syrup. Add more hot water if the consistency is too thick. Remove from heat and serve with coconut milk. Serves 6-8.

BAKED BANANAS

From the region of District 9150
Gabon

6 bananas
1 egg
2 T. orange juice
100g bread crumbs
¼ c. vegetable oil
2 c. sour cream
½ c. brown sugar

Beat the egg with the orange juice and dip the bananas in this before rolling in the bread crumbs. Heat the vegetable oil in a frying pan and fry the bananas in this until they begin to brown lightly. Transfer to a baking sheet and place in an oven preheated to 170° Celsius for 5 minutes. Serve banana topped with a generous scoop of sour cream and sprinkled with brown sugar.

BASIL PESTO

From the region of District 6950
USA

2 c. fresh basil leaves (tear lg. and med. leaves)
½ c. extra virgin olive oil
2 T. pine nuts (walnuts can be substituted)

2 cloves garlic, crushed
Pinch of salt
½ c. freshly grated Parmesan cheese
2 T. butter, softened (opt.)

Put basil, olive oil, pine nuts, garlic cloves and salt in food processor (can use blender). Mix at high speed. When evenly blended, pour into bowl. Beat in cheese by hand. When well blended, beat in butter. Before adding pesto to pasta, add a tablespoon or so of the hot water pasta cooked in to the pesto and mix.

CORNHUSKER'S CASSEROLE

From the region of District 5650
USA

2½ c. canned corn, drained and patted dry
14 oz. yellow or white hominy, drained and patted dry
1½ c. shredded sharp cheddar cheese

4 lg. eggs, beaten
1¾ c. milk
2 T. flour
1 clove garlic, minced
Salt and ground red pepper to taste

Preheat oven to 350°F. Combine hominy and corn in a greased 2-quart casserole dish. Top with cheese. In a mixing bowl, whisk eggs, milk, flour and garlic. Season with salt and red pepper. Pour mixture over hominy and corn mixture. Bake 50-55 minutes or until inserted knife comes out clean. Let stand 10 minutes before serving. Makes 6-8 servings.

CANADIAN BAKED BEANS

From the region of District 7010, 7040
Canada

10 c. water
2¾ c. dried white beans
6 slices bacon, chopped
¾ c. maple syrup
¾ c. rum

1 c. onion, chopped
1 tsp. salt
¾ tsp. mustard powder
4 T. dark brown sugar
3 T. melted butter

(continued)

Wash beans and soak in boiling water for 5 minutes. Return to the heat and simmer for an hour. Drain beans and reserve 4 cups of the liquid. Set aside. Put bacon in the bottom of an ovenproof casserole. Cover with cooked beans. Mix together mustard, syrup, rum, onion, salt and 2 cups (500 milliliters) of reserved cooking liquid. Pour this mixture over beans. Cover and bake in a 350°F oven for 2 hours, adding more cooking liquid as needed during last 30 minutes of cooking if the beans have no liquid or are not tender. Remove from oven. Combine brown sugar and melted butter. Drizzle over beans. Bake, uncovered, for another 30-45 minutes or until liquid has evaporated. Serves 6.

CAPONATA

From the region of District 2030-2120
Italy

1 lg. eggplant, unpeeled, cut into 1-inch cubes
4 T. olive oil
¼ c. pine nuts
1 c. finely sliced onion
1 c. chopped celery
2 lg. garlic cloves, minced

4 T. red wine vinegar
¾ c. pitted green olives, coarsely chopped
⅓ c. drained, chopped tomatoes
4 T. capers
Pinch of sugar
Salt and pepper to taste

Sauté eggplant in olive oil and set aside. Place pine nuts in skillet over medium heat and toast until golden brown, stirring constantly. Add the onion and continue to sauté. Add the garlic and celery. Reduce heat and add the vinegar, capers, olives, sugar, salt, pepper and tomatoes. Cook briefly over medium heat. Add eggplant and simmer until eggplant is tender, but celery is still crunchy. Allow to cool slightly, then cover and chill well. Serve with pita bread.

CORN CAKES

From the region of District 6000
USA

1 pkg. corn muffin mix
16 oz. thawed corn (recommend roasted corn if you can find it)

Zest of 1 orange
½ med. onion, chopped
2 T. butter

Use a griddle to cook the corn cakes. Heat to medium-low to medium heat. Mix corn mix in a large bowl as per package directions. Add corn, orange zest and onion. Cut butter into small pieces and add to batter. Spray griddle with non-stick cooking spray. Make corn cakes as if pancakes and cook until golden on each side. Serve hot.

COU-COU

From the region of District 7030
Barbados

6 c. boiling water
4 okras, thinly sliced
2 c. cold water

2 c. cornmeal
1 tsp. salt
1 T. butter

Cook the okras in boiling water for 10-12 minutes. In another bowl, mix the cornmeal and cold water to a paste. When the okras are soft, lower the heat, add salt and cornmeal mixture, stirring constantly with a wooden spoon until the mixture becomes fairly stiff. When mixture breaks away cleanly from the side of the saucepan, the cou-cou is ready. Butter a bowl, turn the mixture out neatly onto it. It will set itself fairly well. Turn it out onto a serving dish, make an indentation in the top and place a knob of butter in it. Serve as a side for any main course, especially with fried flying fish.

CHEELA (Rajasthani Crepe)

From the region of District 3050
India

1 c. Moong Dal (split mung bean), soak in water, leaving half an inch of water above the dal 5 hours prior to cooking, then grind in a grinder)
1 sm. onion, finely chopped

1 green chili, finely chopped
¼ c. cilantro, finely chopped
1 tsp. ginger and garlic paste (opt.)
½ tsp. red chili powder
½ tsp. salt
Cooking oil

Mix all the ingredients, except the oil, slowly pouring water in the mixture, bringing it to a consistency like pancake batter. Heat a non-stick pan on medium-high heat, add for each crepe 1 teaspoon of oil on pan, using a small ladle, take ⅕ of the mixture and pour in the pan, place the bottom side of the ladle in the center first, then spreading outwards in a circular motion until batter is thinly spread out. Then use a spatula cooking each side for 2 minutes (each side should be dark brown). Serve with mint chutney. **Option: Paneer Filling:** Crush ½ cup of paneer (dry curd cottage cheese) and add ¼ cup finely chopped cilantro, 1 teaspoon green chilies, red chili powder, 4-5 drops of fresh lemon juice and a pinch of salt. Mix all together, adding 1 tablespoon on each crepe. Roll and serve. Serves 4.

CHEESE BUREK

From the region of District 2481
Kosovo

3 egg yolks
2 egg whites
1 lb. feta cheese, crumbled
8 oz. cream cheese, softened
4 T. chopped fresh parsley
2 T. chopped fresh dill
1-lb. pkg. filo dough, thawed
½ c. melted butter
½ c. good-quality olive oil

Mix together feta cheese, cream cheese, egg yolks and herbs. Beat the egg whites and fold in. Cut filo dough sheets in half. Mix the melted butter and olive oil and set aside. Brush the bottom and sides of a baking pan. Place a half sheet of the dough at the bottom, brush with oil mixture and layer another sheet on top if it. Brush this second sheet with oil and layer the third sheet. Now place a layer of a third of the cheese mixture. Continue the layers of 3 filo sheets and a layer of cheese until all the cheese is used. Ending up with a layer of cheese on top. Bake in a 375°F oven until golden brown.

FRESH TOMATO BASIL PASTA

From the region of District 7190
USA

½ lb. capellini
2 T. olive oil
3 cloves garlic, minced
4 c. cherry tomatoes, halved
1 c. fresh basil, torn
⅓ c. dry white wine
¼ tsp. black pepper
¼ c. Parmesan cheese
½ tsp. salt

Cook capellini in boiling water for 5 minutes, then drain. Sauté garlic 1 minute in heated olive oil. Add tomatoes, wine and salt. Cook 4 minutes. Remove from heat and stir in basil and pepper. Serves 4.

FAROFA

From the region of District 4310, 4390
Brazil

- 3 T. olive oil
- 2 onions, chopped
- 2 garlic cloves, minced
- ½ red bell pepper, chopped
- 1 carrot, grated
- 4 scallions, thinly sliced, just the white section
- ½ c. blanched and sliced almonds
- ½ c. black or green olives, chopped
- ⅓ c. sultana raisins (soak them in ½ c. dry white wine)
- 1 c. manioc flour or flaky corn farofa or farinha de mandioca
- 2 T. parsley, chopped

Sauté the onion and garlic in the olive oil for 5 minutes. Add the red pepper, carrots and scallions and cook for about 5 minutes. Add the grated carrot. Cook another minute. Add the scallions. Cook another minute. Add the olives and almonds. Reduce the heat to low. Drain the sultana raisins from the white wine and add them to the pan. In a separate frying pan, toast the flour over medium heat. Mix constantly to prevent the flour from burning. Add the flour to the vegetables. Mix well. Serve with parsley sprinkled on top. Enjoy!

PLANTAIN AU GRATIN

From the region of District 7030
Martinique

- 4 ripe plantains
- 6 T. vegetable oil
- 3 T. butter
- 3 tsp. flour
- 1 c. milk
- 1 c. whipping cream
- Salt and pepper to taste
- 6 oz. grated Swiss cheese

Peel and slice the plantains lengthways. Fry the plantains in single layer in the oil at low heat until brown. **To prepare the white sauce:** Melt the butter. Mix in the flour, milk, whipping cream, salt and pepper. Mix well until a sauce consistency is reached. Layer the fried plantains and the white sauce in a baking dish. Let the white sauce be the top layer. Sprinkle the grated cheese on top. Bake at 375°F for 30 minutes.

PSKOVSKY

From the region of District 2230
Belarus

4 big potatoes
2 big carrots

1 c. peas

Sauce:

1 c. vegetable broth
Oil
1½ T. flour

1 c. onion, finely chopped
½ c. canned mushrooms
Celery seed and salt to taste

Wash vegetables, peel and cube. Then stew every vegetable (except peas) separately in a small amount of water. Combine all the vegetables and drain off vegetable broth. **Sauce:** Oil the pan, heat a little, add flour, stirring constantly. Then, very carefully, pour in the broth, so that there are no lumps. Add in onion, celery, mushrooms and salt to taste. Cook on low heat for 15 minutes. Pour the sauce into the vegetable mix and serve warm.

PENNE WITH PEPPERS AND CREAM

From the region of District 6950
USA

3 T. butter
1 T. vegetable oil
1 c. chopped onions
1 c. green peppers, diced into
  ½-inch cubes
1 c. yellow peppers, diced into
  ½-inch cubes

1 c. red peppers, diced into ½-inch cubes
⅔ c. heavy cream
2 T. chopped parsley
½ c. grated Parmesan cheese

Sauté chopped onion in butter and oil. Add diced peppers at medium-high heat and stir. Add salt and pepper. Add cream, stir and turn heat to high. Cook until cream is reduced by half. Cook pasta; drain. Mix pasta with sauce. Add parsley and cheese. Serve at once.

PASCUALINA (Spinach Pie)

From the region of District 4940
Uruguay

2 c. frozen chopped spinach
1½ c. ricotta cheese
½ c. mozzarella cheese
½ c. grated Parmesan cheese
4 T. butter
1½ c. chopped onion
3 cloves garlic, minced
1 c. chopped mushrooms

1 tsp. salt
½ tsp. nutmeg
3 eggs
4 hard-boiled eggs
1 pkg. frozen puff pastry sheets, thawed
Egg wash (1 egg mixed with 1 T. water)

Sauté onion and garlic in the butter until slightly golden. Add salt and nutmeg. Add mushrooms and sauté for 5 minutes. Add spinach and cook for two minutes. Let mixture cool. Mix ricotta, mozzarella, Parmesan and 2 eggs in a large bowl. Add cooled spinach mixture to the cheeses. Season with salt and pepper to taste. Preheat oven to 400°F. Roll out one pastry sheet in a circle and drape pastry over a 9-inch tart pan with a removable bottom, pressing pastry into bottom and sides of pan. Fill tart with spinach-cheese mixture. Slice boiled eggs in half and press them into filling. Roll out other piece of puff pastry and place on top of tart. Seal edges together and crimp with a fork. Brush tart with the egg wash. Use a fork to prick a few holes in the top of the tart as vents. Place tart in oven, lower temperature to 350°F and bake for one hour. If tart is browning too quickly, you can cover the tart with foil loosely. Cool in pan for 45 minutes before lifting tart out of the tart pan with the removable bottom. Serve warm or at room temperature.

QUICHE DENT-DE-LION (Swiss Dandelion Quiche)

From the region of District 1980, 1990, 2000
Switzerland

For the Pastry:

½ lb. plain flour
1 tsp. salt

¼ lb. butter, cold and diced
3 T. cold water

For the Filling:

½ c. chopped dandelion leaves
100g Camembert cheese
½ c. single cream
½ c. milk
3 eggs

½ tsp. salt
Freshly ground nutmeg
Freshly ground black pepper and paprika to taste

(continued)

Mix the butter and flour until mixture resembles bread crumbs. Sprinkle in the salt, then add enough of the water to bring the mixture together as a dough. Cover and keep chilled. Beat together filling mixture of the eggs, milk and cream in a bowl. Chop the Camembert cheese very finely and stir this in. Now add the dandelion leaves. Stir in the salt, nutmeg, black pepper and paprika. Take a quiche dish and grease with butter. Roll the pastry very thin and cover the dish. Prick several times with the tines of a fork, then pour in the egg and dandelion filling. Transfer to an oven preheated to 180° Celsius or 350°F and bake for about 30 minutes or until the pastry is golden and the filling is just set. Allow to cool before slicing into wedges and serving.

RAJASTHANI GATTA CURRY

From the region of District 3050
India

2 c. besan (gram flour)
2 T. ghee (clarified butter) or oil
1 T. plain yogurt
½ tsp. red chili powder
¼ tsp. turmeric powder

¼ tsp. garam masala (a blend of ground spices)
¼ tsp. ajwain (carom seeds)
Pinch of hing (asafetida powder)
½ tsp. salt

In a bowl, add besan, ghee, red chili powder, garam masala, carom seeds and hing (asafetida powder) and mix. Add plain yogurt, mix well into a doughy consistency (add water if needed). Roll the dough into 1-inch diameter and 5- to 6-inch long round cylinder shape roll. Add into boiling water and cook for 5-7 minutes. Strain the boiled rolls, then cut them into small pieces about ½ inch thick. Gatta dumpling is now ready. Keep aside.

Curry:

2 c. water
1 c. plain yogurt
½ tsp. red chili powder
¼ tsp. turmeric
½ tsp. coriander powder
¼ tsp. garam masala
1 tsp. cumin seeds
Pinch of hing (asafetida powder)

1 tsp. kasoori methi (fenugreek leaves)
1 tsp. ginger and garlic paste (opt.)
1 T. oil
½ tsp. salt
Handful picked cilantro leaves

Stir in a bowl, water, plain yogurt, red chili powder, turmeric powder, coriander powder and salt, then put aside. Heat a deep pan medium to medium-high heat and add oil. Once oil is heated, add hing and cumin seeds (the seeds should pop in the pan first), then add the curry mixture. Stir at medium heat until it comes to a boil, cooking for 5-10 minutes. Add your gatta dumpling in the curry, then turn the heat to low

(continued)

and cook for another 5-7 minutes. Stir in kasoori methi and garam masala, then top off with cilantro to garnish. Serve hot with chapattis (whole wheat unleavened flatbread). Serves 4.

SWISS ROESTI

From the region of District 2000
Switzerland/Liechtenstein

1 kg raw potatoes
1 sm. T. salt

3-4 T. oil
Thin sliced onion rings

Peel the potatoes and pass them over a grater to get fine sliced potato sticks. Heat the oil, butter or dripping in the pan and add the sliced potatoes together with the sliced onion rings. Turn all regularly, add salt and if you like some pepper or nutmeg to get a mass well mixed with the oil or butter. On a medium heat, fry the mass in a covered pan during 20 minutes. During this time, turn the mass regularly so that the potatoes become a slight golden color. After this time, go on frying without lid and form the mass. Fry it on both sides to get a golden colored cake and serve this delicious meal hot.

SMOKED POTATO

From the region of District 5710
USA

1 lg. potato
1 jalapeño pepper
1 T. fried bacon

2 T. grated cheese
¼ c. olive oil
¼ c. lemon pepper

Slice a large raw potato in half. Scoop out a portion (enough for stuffing other ingredients) of the potato center with ice cream scoop. Slice pepper in half, remove seeds if desired. Pack potato with shredded cheese, pepper halves, fried bacon pieces. Hold potato halves together with toothpicks. Mix olive oil and lemon pepper into a thick paste. Cover potato with heavy coating of paste and then wrap potato in aluminum foil. Grill at 350°F until soft. Place in a smoker if available.

SPINACH AND RICOTTA GNOCCHI

From the region of District 6950
USA

1-2 T. finely chopped onion
2 T. butter
10 oz. frozen spinach, thawed
¾ c. ricotta (put in sieve overnight to drain excess moisture)

⅔ c. flour
2 egg yolks
1 c. grated Parmesan cheese
¼ tsp. nutmeg

Sauté onion. Add spinach and cook about 5 minutes; salt to taste. Transfer spinach to bowl. Add ricotta and flour and mix thoroughly. Add egg yolks, cheese and nutmeg. Correct for salt. Shape spinach into small pellets. Dust hands lightly with flour as needed. Cook gnocchi in boiling water. Remove from pot once gnocchi floats to the top of the pot. Place in dish and pour tomato sauce over the gnocchi.

Tomato and Cream Sauce:

3-4 T. butter
3 T. chopped onion
3 T. chopped carrot
3 T. chopped celery

28 oz. tomatoes, chopped with juice
Salt to taste
½ c. heavy cream

Put all ingredients, except cream, in pot. Simmer for 1 hour. Purée contents through a food mill. Add cream and stir/cook for 1 minute until heated.

MANGO RICE

From the region of District 3131
India

3 lbs. rice
6 med. sized green mangoes
A few green chilies
3 c. grated coconut
1¼ pt. gingelly oil or 1¼ lbs. ghee

1 T. mustard seeds
1 T. black gram dhal
1 T. cumin seeds
A few curry leaves
A little turmeric powder
Salt to taste

Clean the rice and put it in boiling water. When it is about three-quarters cooked, remove it from the heat. Drain the excess water and allow the rice to cool. Add the turmeric powder and half the quantity of gingelly oil (or ghee). Mix well. Cut the mangoes into tiny pieces or grate them. Grind the cumin seeds, half the chilies, salt to taste and the coconut gratings. Mix it with the mango pieces and add it to the cooked rice. Fry the mustard seeds, gram dhal, curry leaves and the remaining chilies in oil. Add to the rice. Mix well. Allow to cool and serve.

SPICY STRING BEANS

From the region of District 3220
Sri Lanka

1 lb. frozen or fresh beans (string beans)
4 T. oil
1 tsp. mustard seeds
1 tsp. fenugreek seeds
2 dry chilies
3-4 curry leaves, roughly broken

1½ tsp. chili powder
2 sprigs curry leaves
1 onion, sliced
1½ tsp. salt
¼ c. water
½ c. milk

If using fresh beans, slice them finely. Heat the oil in a pan and add mustard, fenugreek seeds, curry leaves and dry chilies. Stir and add sliced beans and cook for about 20 minutes on medium heat, stirring occasionally. Add the sliced onion and chili powder and cook for about 10 minutes with an open lid. Add the salt and water and cook for about 15 minutes on low heat with a lid on. When the beans are cooked, add the milk and cook for about 5-10 minutes on low heat until the dish has a dry appearance. Serve with rice.

SALOR KOR-KO SAP (Vegetarian Stew)

From the region of District 3350
Cambodia

1 c. coconut milk
2 c. water
2 slices fresh galanga root or frozen galanga root
1 kaffir lime leaves
1 T. minced lemon grass
1 T. mushroom sauce
1 T. sugar
3 T. roasted rice powder
1 tsp. salt

½ tsp. turmeric powder
½ tsp. paprika
1 Asian eggplant, cut in chunks
1 bitter melon, cut in chunks, no seeds
2 c. cubes fresh pumpkin (already peeled, seeded and cut)
6 oz. frozen chopped spinach or ¾ lb. fresh spinach, chopped

Put coconut milk, water, galanga, kaffir, lemon grass, lime leaves, turmeric, paprika and garlic in a blender and blend it. Place eggplant and bitter melon in a soup pot. Pour the coconut milk mixture over and cover the pot with lid. Simmer for 10 minutes, then add pumpkin and spinach. Cover and cook until the pumpkin is tender. Seasoning with sugar, salt, mushroom sauce and roasted rice powder. Stir well. Serve hot with rice or hot bread.

SOBA NOODLES

From the region of District 2500-2840
Japan

2 T. sesame oil
¼ lb. soba noodles, cooked
2 eggs, beaten
1 red capsicum, julienne strips
1 sm. carrot, julienne strips
1 sm. zucchini, julienne strips
1 sm. cucumber, julienne strips
6 snow peas, cut in strips
2 spring onions, sliced
1 T. black sesame seeds
Pink pickled ginger

Warm Soy Dressing:

2 tsp. fresh ginger, grated
1 T. red capsicum, finely chopped
2 tsp. mirin
1 T. rice vinegar
1 T. Japanese soy sauce
2 T. dashi granules (soup stock)

Prepare soy dressing by combining fresh ginger, red capsicum, mirin, rice vinegar, soy sauce and dashi in a small saucepan. Bring to boil, then set aside and keep warm. Heat wok and add 1 tablespoon sesame oil. Stir fry noodles with beaten eggs over high heat until egg is cooked and coating the noodles and the noodles are warm. Set aside and keep warm. Heat remaining oil and stir fry zucchini, carrots and capsicum over high heat for 3 minutes. Add cucumber, snow peas and spring onion and stir fry for another minute. Return noodles to the wok with black sesame seeds and toss until the noodles are warmed through. Dish out in bowls and pour over soy dressing just before serving.

SPINACH & PEANUT BUTTER STEW

From the region of District 9100
Benin

3 onions, sliced
3 tomatoes, peeled and chopped
4 Scotch bonnet chilies, pounded to a paste
2 lbs. spinach, washed, trimmed and chopped
5 T. peanut butter
Salt and black pepper to taste
Oil for frying

Fry the onions in a large pot until soft. Add tomatoes and chilies to the pot and fry for another 2 minutes, then add the spinach. Cook, covered, on medium heat for 5 minutes, stirring often to prevent sticking. Thin the peanut butter with ¼ cup of hot water to form a smooth paste and add to the stew. Season with salt and pepper and cook for a further 10 minutes (continue stirring). Serve immediately.

SWEET-AND-SOUR TOFU

From the region of District 3330-3360
Thailand

650g firm tofu
¼ c. (60ml) vegetable oil
1 clove garlic, sliced
200g green beans, sliced
1 med. brown onion (150g), sliced coarsely
1 med. carrot (120g), sliced finely
200g broccoli, cut into florets
2 trimmed (75g) celery sticks, sliced
2 green onions, chopped

1 T. tamarind sauce
1 T. fish sauce
2 T. oyster sauce
2 T. soy sauce
2 T. sweet chili sauce
2 T. tomato paste
2 T. sugar
2 T. white vinegar
¼ tsp. ground star anise
1 tsp. corn flour
1 c. (250ml) water

Cut tofu in 1 ½ centimeter cubes. Heat oil in large frying pan; cook garlic, stirring, 30 seconds, remove and discard garlic. Cook tofu in batches, in same pan until browned lightly; remove from pan. Cook beans, brown onion and carrot in same pan, stirring until vegetables are almost tender. Add broccoli, celery, green onions, sauces, paste, sugar, vinegar and star anise; cook for 2 minutes. Stir in tofu with blended corn flour and water; stir gently until sauce boils and thickens.

SQUASH CASSEROLE

From the region of District 6840
USA

1 ½ lbs. yellow squash (or can use frozen)
1 c. oleo or margarine (or real butter)
½ c. chopped white onion
¼ c. chopped green bell pepper
½ c. mayonnaise (use mayonnaise as salad dressing gives it another taste that many may not like)

½ c. grated sharp cheddar cheese
1 c. sliced water chestnuts
1 egg and 1 tsp. sugar
Buttered bread crumbs, about 1-2 c. depending on preference

Cook squash, sliced, in hot lightly salted water for 8 minutes and drain (let drain while the remaining ingredients are assembled). Place back into the pot. Sauté onions and bell pepper in 1 cup of oleo (or margarine or real butter). Add cheese and chestnuts into the onion mixture in pan. Whip 1 egg and 1 teaspoon sugar together and add to squash mixture.

(continued)

Add the mixture of onions, bell pepper, cheese, chestnuts and egg and sugar mixture with the squash. Place into a 1 ½-quart casserole (lightly buttered or sprayed with Pam). Top with bread crumbs (½ cup may be enough, depending on preference). Bake at 350°F for 30 minutes. Serve hot. Serves 6-8 persons.

SWAZILAND SAMP

From the region of District 9400
Swaziland

1.5 L. water
1 lb. samp (hominy)
½ lb. sugar beans
2 onions
2 tomatoes
2 carrots, chopped

½ lb. green beans
3 sm. potatoes, chopped
½ lb. shredded cabbage, shredded
1 butternut squash, chopped

Soak the samp in water overnight. Rinse and drain and boil for 35 minutes in more water. Soak sugar beans in water overnight. Then add the washed beans to the samp. Season with salt and boil until samp and beans are soft, but still firm (about 75 minutes). Add all the vegetables, reduce to a simmer and cook for 40 minutes until the vegetables are done and the water evaporated. Add pepper to taste and serve. Great side dish for any main course.

VEGGIE-STUFFED PORTOBELLO MUSHROOMS

From the region of District 7190
USA

1 sm. yellow sweet pepper, cut in bite-size strips
1 sm. red onion, chopped
1 med. zucchini, coarsely shredded
1 carrot, coarsely shredded
1 stalk celery, thinly sliced
2 cloves garlic, minced
2 T. olive oil
1 T. snipped fresh basil

1 T. lemon juice
1 (5-oz.) pkg. fresh baby spinach
½ c. fine dry bread crumbs
½ c. finely shredded Parmesan cheese
4 (4- to 5-inch) portobello mushroom caps, stems removed
4 slices provolone cheese

Preheat oven to 425°F. Line a 15 x 10 x 1-inch baking pan with foil. In a 12-inch skillet, cook sweet pepper, onion, zucchini, carrot, celery and garlic in hot oil over medium-high heat for 4 minutes or until soft. Stir in basil, lemon juice and ¼ teaspoon each salt and ground black pepper.

(continued)

Top with spinach; cover. Cook for 2 minutes or until spinach is wilted. Remove from heat. Stir bread crumbs and half of the Parmesan cheese into spinach mixture; set aside. Remove gills from mushrooms. Arrange mushrooms, stemmed side up on prepared pan. Top each with slice of provolone cheese. Divide spinach mixture among mushroom caps. Bake 15 minutes (mushrooms will water out slightly). Top with remaining Parmesan. Bake 2 minutes more or until heated through. Yield: 4 servings.

VEGETARIAN STEW

From the region of District 9010
Algeria

2 T. vegetable oil
2 lg. onions, chopped
¾ tsp. turmeric
¼ tsp. cayenne pepper
1 ½ tsp. black pepper
½ tsp. salt
3-4 whole cloves
¼ tsp. cinnamon
½ c. tomato paste
2 c. beef stock
3 green zucchini, cut into 3-inch chunks
3 yellow zucchini, cut into 3-inch chunks
3 lg. carrots, scraped and cut into 3-inch chunks
4 med. potatoes, skins on, quartered
3 red or green bell peppers, cored, seeded and quartered
Water to cover
1 c. cooked chickpeas (garbanzos), drained

In a large, heavy saucepan, heat oil and sauté onion over medium heat until translucent. Add all the spices and tomato paste, stirring constantly for 3 minutes. Stir in the stock and bring to a boil. Add all the vegetables, except the chickpeas. Add water to cover. Bring to a boil. Reduce heat and simmer, covered, for 1 hour. Add chickpeas 5-8 minutes before removing from heat. **To serve:** Place a mound of prepared couscous cereal on individual plates. Spoon stew over the couscous. Serve with chili sauce at the side.

VEGETARIAN LENTILS - MOROCCAN-STYLE

From the region of District 9010
Morocco

2 c. lentils
3 tomatoes, chopped
2 med. onions, chopped
4 cloves garlic, finely chopped
  or pressed
5 T. chopped fresh parsley or
  cilantro

2½ tsp. cumin
2½ tsp. paprika
1½ tsp. ginger
½ tsp. pepper
2 tsp. salt
⅓ c. olive oil

Mix all the ingredients in a large pot. Fill with 2 quarts water. Cover the lentils and cook over medium heat for about 1½ hours or until the lentils are tender and the sauce is not watery. Adjust the seasoning if desired and serve. Eat lentils with crusty bread. May also be eaten with a spoon.

MANGO CURRY

From the region of District 3120
India

4 lg. ripe mangoes
½ coconut
2 oz. raisins
1 oz. sugar
3 cloves

1 sprig curry leaves
2 tsp. turmeric powder
1 heaped tsp. mustard seeds
5 dry red chilies
Salt to taste

Peel and slice mangoes into 1-inch cubes. Heat 1½ teaspoons ghee and fry the mustard seeds and chilies until they begin to crackle. Add grated coconut and turmeric and fry until brown. Add mangoes, 1 pint of water, raisins, cloves, sugar and salt to taste. Simmer for about 10-15 minutes. Serve hot with plain boiled rice and garnish with curry leaves.

VEGETABLE STEW (Yataklete Kilkil)

From the region of District 9200
Ethiopia

8 sm. potatoes, peeled, 1-inch cubes
4 carrots, peeled, cut in ¼-inch discs
½ lb. green beans, cut in 1-inch pieces
3 cloves garlic, crushed
2 T. ginger, chopped
2-3 jalapeño peppers, seeded, chopped
3 T. olive oil
½ c. water
½ tsp. ground cardamom
Salt and pepper to taste

Place potatoes, carrots and green beans and 2 teaspoons salt in a large pot. Cover with water and bring to a boil and simmer until all vegetables are cooked through, about 10-20 minutes. Drain and set aside. Place onions, garlic, ginger and peppers in a food processor or blender and purée. In a large saucepan, heat oil over medium heat. Add onion purée and sauté until moisture evaporates. Do not brown. Add cooked vegetables, water, cardamom, salt and pepper. Stir well and simmer on low heat 15-30 minutes. Serves 6.

ZUCCHINI CASSEROLE

From the region of District 6190
USA

4-5 c. sliced zucchini
2 c. boiling water

Cook zucchini in water until just tender; drain. Do not overcook.

2 eggs
1 c. mayonnaise
1 onion, chopped
1 c. grated Parmesan cheese
¼ c. chopped green pepper
Dash of salt and pepper

In a large bowl, beat eggs. Stir in remainder of ingredients. Add zucchini. Turn into greased 1½-quart baking dish. Dot with 1 tablespoon margarine and 2 tablespoons buttered bread crumbs (optional). Fresh parsley sprinkled over makes a nice addition. Bake at 350°F for 30 minutes until bubbly. Test center to make sure the custard is set. Serves 6.

Main Dishes

Helpful Hints

- Certain meats, like ribs and pot roast, can be parboiled before grilling to reduce the fat content.

- Pound meat lightly with a mallet or rolling pin, pierce with a fork, sprinkle lightly with meat tenderizer, and add marinade. Refrigerate for 20 minutes and cook or grill for a quick and succulent meat.

- Marinating is a cinch if you use a plastic bag. The meat stays in the marinade and it's easy to turn. Cleanup is easy; just toss the bag.

- It's easier to thinly slice meat if it's partially frozen.

- Adding tomatoes to roasts naturally tenderizes the meat as tomatoes contain an acid that works well to break down meats.

- Whenever possible, cut meat across the grain; this will make it easier to eat and also give it a more attractive appearance.

- When frying meat, sprinkle paprika on the meat to turn it golden brown.

- Thaw all meats in the refrigerator for maximum safety.

- Refrigerate poultry promptly after purchasing. Keep it in the coldest part of your refrigerator for up to 2 days. Freeze poultry for longer storage. Never leave poultry at room temperature for over 2 hours.

- When frying chicken, canola oil provides a milder taste, and it contains healthier amounts of saturated and polyunsaturated fats. Do not cover the chicken once it has finished cooking because covering will cause the coating to lose its crispness.

- One pound of boneless chicken equals approximately 3 cups of cubed chicken.

- Generally, red meats should reach 160° and poultry should reach 180° before serving. If preparing fish, the surface of the fish should flake off with a fork.

- Rub lemon juice on fish before cooking to enhance the flavor and help maintain a good color.

- Scaling a fish is easier if vinegar is rubbed on the scales first.

- When grilling fish, the rule of thumb is to cook 5 minutes on each side per inch of thickness. For example, cook a 2-inch thick fillet for 10 minutes per side. Before grilling, rub with oil to seal in moisture.

MAIN DISHES

AFELIA

From the region of District 2450
Cyprus

2½ lbs. lean pork without bone, cubed
2 c. red wine
2 T. coriander seed, lightly crushed
1 stick cinnamon
½ c. olive oil
Salt and lots of freshly ground black pepper

Mix together cinnamon, coriander seed, salt, pepper and wine; pour over your pork. Marinate meat in refrigerator overnight. When you are done marinating, lift out the meat and save the marinade. Heat the oil in a heavy based pan and brown your cubes of meat. When well browned, remove the meat from the pan. Drain all oil from the pan and then return the meat to the pan. Add all the marinade and enough water to cover meat. Bring to a boil, then cover the pan with a lid and reduce the heat to cook the meat gently for about 30 minutes or until tender. Most of the liquid should have evaporated to leave a thick sauce. If not, continue to cook uncovered until the excess liquid is gone. Serve with potatoes.

BEEF AND BEER STEW

From the region of District 1030-1140
England

1 lb. boneless beef chuck or round steak, 1 inch thick
¼ c. olive oil
3 med. onions, sliced
2 cloves garlic, chopped
3 T. all-purpose flour
1 c. water
1 lg. (about 16-oz.) can dark beer
1 bay leaf
2 T. packed brown sugar
2 tsp. salt
½ tsp. dried thyme leaves
¼ tsp. pepper
2 T. vinegar
1 c. cooked chopped bacon
Minced parsley
Hot, cooked noodles

Cut beef into ½-inch slices; cut slices into 2-inch strips. Sauté onions and garlic in olive oil until onion is tender, about 10 minutes. Remove

(continued)

onions. Sauté and stir beef in remaining oil, about 15 minutes. Stir in flour to coat beef; gradually stir in water. Add onions, beer, bay leaf, brown sugar, salt, thyme and pepper. The water should cover the beef. Add more if necessary. Heat to boiling, reduce heat. Cover and simmer until beef is tender, 1 to 1½ hours. Remove bay leaf. Stir in vinegar, sprinkle with bacon and parsley. Serve over hot noodles. Serves 6.

BRUNEI BERIANI RICE

From the region of District 3310
Brunei Darussalam

1 chicken (about 900g)
1 T. poppy seed
2 cloves garlic
2 chilies
2-3 T. salt
1 T. curry powder
1-inch piece ginger
2 c. shallots, sliced

5 T. butter
5cm cinnamon stick
5 whole cloves
10 cashew nuts
10 almonds
2 c. coconut milk
2½ c. fine rice

Cut the chicken in 6-8 equal pieces. Grind the garlic, ginger, chilies, poppy seed, almonds and cashew nuts together. Heat the pan and sauté chicken pieces in butter. Add the ground ingredients followed by curry powder and salt. Stir until all the ingredients have mixed together and coated the chicken. Cook for 10 minutes. Take 2 cups of coconut milk. Add salt. Add the rice and cook until the rice has absorbed all the milk and then add the chicken mixture to rice and cook on a very low flame. When all the flavors are incorporated, in about 20-30 minutes, the dish is ready to serve.

BELGIUM MEATBALLS IN BEER

From the region of District 2170
Belgium

2 lbs. ground beef
1 lb. ground pork
2 ¼ c. bread crumbs
1 ½ c. milk
2 lg. eggs
1 med. shallot, finely chopped
3 T. fresh parsley, finely chopped
Salt and pepper to taste
1 dash of nutmeg
½ c. all-purpose flour
½ c. unsalted butter

2 T. olive oil
2 med. onions, finely chopped
5 med. Belgian endive, cored and chopped
2 tsp. sugar
Salt and pepper to taste
3 T. flour
3 c. beer
1 c. chicken stock
½ c. fresh parsley, finely chopped

Soak bread crumbs in milk for 10 minutes and squeeze dry. In mixing bowl, combine bread crumbs, ground meats, parsley, salt, pepper, nutmeg, eggs and shallots. Mix well. Form into 2-inch diameter meatballs. Dust with ½ cup flour. In deep Dutch oven, heat the butter and oil, add meatballs and sauté until well browned, about 6 minutes. Remove to a platter and set aside. Add onion and endives to pan, cook over low heat, stirring constantly for 10 minutes. Sprinkle with salt, pepper, 3 tablespoons flour and sugar. Cook, stirring for 1 minute. Add beer and broth, bring to a quick boil. Reduce heat to a simmer and return meatballs to the pan. Simmer partially covered, until the meat is cooked through and has absorbed the flavors of the sauce, 35 minutes. Sprinkle with parsley and serve. Serves 8.

BAKED KOTLOTI

From the region of District 5170
USA

4 slices dry bread
1 lb. hamburger
½ lb. sausage or ground pork
1 ½ tsp. salt
½ tsp. pepper
2 T. parsley, chopped

3 eggs, separated
2 T. butter
3 T. flour
1 can beef consommé or chicken stock
¼ c. sour cream

Soak bread in warm water for 30 minutes, then squeeze dry and tear up finely. Combine bread, hamburger, sausage, salt, pepper, parsley and egg yolks with meat. Beat the egg whites until stiff, but not dry and fold into the meat mixture with a fork or with your hands. Form meat

(continued)

mixture into 8 or 10 oval patties. Heat a large frying pan. Add the butter and brown the meat patties on both sides. Transfer the patties into a casserole dish. Make roux from the drippings by adding the flour. Stir well, then add beef consommé or chicken stock to make the gravy. Adjust the seasoning. Stir in the sour cream and pour gravy over the meat patties. Bake at 350°F for 25 minutes. Serve with rice, noodles or potatoes. This tastes like a meatloaf, but the bread and egg whites add an unusual lightness.

BESHBARMAK

From the region of District 2430
Kazakhstan

2 kg lamb with bones   **10 c. water**

Dough for noodles:

500g flour   **250ml water**
2 eggs   **1 tsp. salt**

Vegetables:

4 onions   **1 onion**
1 c. minced chives   **1 carrot**
3 T. minced parsley   **3 T. oil**
1 tsp. ground black pepper

Make a rich broth of the lamb by cooking it on slow heat, covered with water for 3 hours, until the meat is easily separated from the bones. While lamb is cooking, mix the dough ingredients and cut into circles 2 millimeter wide. When lamb is ready, take it out of the broth, remove the bones and cut the meat into bite-sized slices. Boil the circle noodles in the broth and drain them out, reserving the liquid. Chop 2 onions and cook until golden in oil. Chop one carrot and fry in a skillet together with the onions. Add the sliced meat. Add chives, parsley and pepper and keep aside. Cut remaining onions into thin rings. **To serve:** Put lamb in the middle of a big serving plate. Place one layer of noodles around. Sprinkle lamb and noodles with black pepper and onions, cut into thin rings. Broth is served separately. Sprinkle broth with some chopped chives and parsley and pour over the noodles and lamb.

BAHAMIAN RICE

From the region of District 7020
Bahamas

1 T. vegetable oil
1 onion, chopped
½ c. green bell pepper, chopped
¾ c. diced, salted pork
2 T. tomato paste
15-oz. can pigeon peas, cooked and drained
2 slices bacon, cooked and crumbled (opt.)
1 tomato, chopped
½ tsp. dried thyme
Salt and pepper to taste
1 c. coconut water
5 c. water
1 tsp. browning sauce
3 c. uncooked rice

Heat oil in a large pot. Add the onion and fry until translucent. Stir in the green pepper, tomato paste, tomato, bacon, salted pork and pigeon peas. Season with salt, pepper and thyme. Bring to a simmer. Stir in the coconut water, water and browning sauce and bring to a boil. Stir in the rice. Return to a boil, then stir, cover and reduce the heat to low. Simmer for about 45 minutes until rice is tender. Stir occasionally.

BOULANEE

From the region of District 2430
Tajikistan

1 c. mashed potatoes
½ tsp. salt
½ tsp. coriander powder
½ tsp. cayenne pepper powder
½ bunch chopped cilantro
4 green onions, chopped
1 lb. ground beef
½ tsp. freshly ground black pepper
1 pkg. square egg roll wrappers
Corn oil

To the potatoes, add salt, cayenne pepper, cilantro and green onions and mix. Meanwhile, brown ground beef with pepper, salt and coriander. Mix ground beef with mashed potatoes. Let cool. Take an egg roll wrapper and place a spoonful of filling in the middle. Wet the edges of the wrapper and close, making a triangle. Fold the ends of the triangle into the pastry, making a small envelop. Flatten with your hand. Heat oil and fry the boulanee until brown on both sides, about 4-5 minutes. Serve with yogurt or tomato sauce.

CHICKEN STEW (Canja de Gahlinha)

From the region of District 9100
Cape Verde

1 chicken, cut up into bite-size pieces
300g rice (1 ⅓ c.)
4 T. olive oil
2 onions
1 bay leaf

2 T. paprika
2 tomatoes, chopped
2 cloves garlic, minced
1 tsp. chili paste (or more if desired)
Sage leaves for garnishing

Clean and wash the chicken, then cut into serving pieces. Add to a pot along with the salt, garlic, onion, oil and bay leaf. Cover and allow to marinate overnight. Next day, cook until the meat has browned. Add about 2½ cups water and bring to a boil, now add the tomatoes, paprika and chili paste along with the rice. Stir to mix thoroughly, then return to a boil, then reduce to a simmer and cook, covered, for about 30 minutes. By this time the rice should have cooked and absorbed all the water. Spoon the stew onto serving platters and place in the center of the table. Decorate with fresh sage leaves and add more chili paste if desired.

CHICKEN IN ORANGE SAUCE (Pollo con Naranja)

From the region of District 4815-4940
Argentina

4 lbs. chicken, quartered
Freshly ground pepper
Salt
5 T. butter
1 c. chicken stock

1 c. orange juice
Grated rind of 1 orange
1 T. flour
2 eggs
3 T. heavy cream

Season the chicken pieces with salt and pepper. Heat the butter in a heavy casserole and sauté the chicken pieces, one or two at a time, until golden on both sides. Set aside as they are done. Pour off the fat from the casserole into a small bowl and reserve. Return the chicken pieces to the casserole, putting the legs in first with the breasts on top, as the breasts cook more quickly. Add the chicken stock, orange juice and grated orange rind. Cover and simmer for 30-45 minutes or until the chicken is done. Lift out the chicken onto a serving dish and keep warm. Mix the flour with a tablespoon of the reserved fat and stir it into the liquid in the casserole. Bring to a boil and cook, stirring for a minute or two. Reduce the heat to low. Beat the eggs with the cream. Slowly stir 1 cup of the thickened liquid from the casserole into the egg mixture, then pour the mixture into the casserole and cook, stirring with a whisk

(continued)

until the sauce is lightly thickened, a minute or two. Do not let the sauce boil as it will curdle. Pour some of the sauce over the chicken and serve the rest in a sauceboat. Serve with rice or mashed potatoes.

PACENA PATKA (Roast Duck)

From the region of District 1913
Croatia

1 med. duckling
3 T. butter
1 c. bread crumbs
2 eggs, well beaten
1 c. mushrooms, sliced

1 c. sour cream
3 T. chopped green onion
1 tsp. chopped parsley
Salt and pepper to taste

Melt the butter over low heat. Increase the heat and sauté the mushrooms in the butter. Mix together the mushrooms, bread crumbs, parsley, green onion and sour cream. Add the well beaten eggs and season with salt and pepper. Stuff the bird with this mixture. Place dabs of butter on the duckling. Season the outside with salt and pepper. Place the duck in the oven and roast at 350°F until the duck is golden and the skin is nicely crisped.

CHICKEN WATERZOOI

From the region of District 1620, 1630
Belgium

3 stalks celery, julienned
4 med. carrots, julienned
5 boneless, skinless chicken breast halves
2 T. vegetable oil
2 T. unsalted butter
1 T. peppercorn
½ lb. sliced mushrooms

1 lg. leek, white part only, thinly sliced
Fresh thyme (a few sprigs)
3 minced shallots
10 oz. ale
2½ c. half-and-half
Salt and pepper

Steam the celery and carrots for 4 minutes and set aside. Heat the oil and one tablespoon butter in a deep skillet; sauté chicken until golden and juices run clear (about 4 minutes per side). Cut into large strip pieces and set aside. Add remaining butter to pan and lightly sauté the shallots, mushrooms, leek, and thyme for about 5 minutes. Add the ale and peppercorns, increase heat and simmer for about 10-15 minutes until the liquid is reduced by half, stirring to loosen brown bits in the pan. Stir in half & half and simmer for 12 minutes until sauce thickens. Add chicken, celery and carrots; heat through. Add salt and pepper to
(continued)

taste and serve immediately. Serve with steamed new potatoes and more ale. Serves 6.

CEVICHE DE CAMARON (Shrimp)

From the region of District 4400
Ecuador

3 lbs. med. shrimp, shelled and deveined
2 c. bitter orange juice
1 med. onion, finely chopped
1 fresh hot red or green pepper, seeded and finely chopped

2 lg. tomatoes, peeled, seeded and chopped
Ground pepper and salt

Boil the shrimp in a saucepan of salted water for about 2-3 minutes until cooked. Drain the water out and then add orange juice, onion, red/green pepper, tomato and seasoning. Allow it to stand for an hour. Serve along with toasted corn.

CAYMAN CREPES

From the region of District 9150
Cayman Island

4 crepes
4 oz. lobster tail, diced
4 oz. sm. shrimp, diced
4 garlic cloves, chopped

2 onions, chopped
8 oz. fine bread crumbs
¼ c. heavy cream

Sauce:

2 tsp. shallots, chopped
8 oz. shrimp, chopped
¼ c. white wine

2 tsp. fresh basil, chopped
3 oz. béchamel
2 oz. cream

Lightly sauté onions and garlic in olive oil. Add lobster, shrimp and cook slowly, then add 2 teaspoons basil and heavy cream and reduce for 2 minutes. Add remaining ingredients and leave to cool before placing in crepe. **Sauce:** Sauté shallots in butter with white wine and reduce. Add chopped shrimp and 2 teaspoons basil and cook for one more minute. Finish by adding cream, béchamel and seasoning. Fill mixture into 4 crepes. Fold crepes and serve.

CHICKEN IN PEANUT SAUCE

From the region of District 9150
Cameroon

¼ c. peanut oil
1 chicken, cut up into bite-sized pieces
2 onions, cut up
3 cloves garlic, minced
1 c. tomato paste
1 c. peanut butter
1½ c. water
Black pepper
Salt

Heat oil in a deep pot and add the chicken. Fry it on both sides until it is browned. Remove the chicken and set aside. Add onions and garlic to the chicken pot and fry well. Stir in tomato paste and simmer for a few minutes. Return chicken to pot with 1 cup of water and let chicken cook until almost tender. Remove chicken and set aside. Add peanut butter into the pot and mix well with the tomato sauce mixture. Add the ½ cup water if necessary to cook chicken. Add the chicken and simmer until chicken is done. Add black pepper and salt to taste.

CALICO BEANS

From the region of District 6270
USA

½ lb. hamburger
½ lb. Canadian bacon
1 c. chopped onions
1 (15-oz.) can pork & beans, drained
1 can lima beans
1 can kidney beans
½ c. ketchup
1 tsp. salt
¾ c. brown sugar
½ c. molasses
2 tsp. sugar

Brown and slightly cook meat and onions. Add other ingredients. Mix well. Bake for 40 minutes at 350°F.

CARURU

From the region of District 4410-4440
Brazil

3 lbs. fresh shrimp
¼ lb. ground dried shrimp
3 T. butter
Salt
4 T. coriander, fresh
½ c. peanuts, ground, roasted
⅓ c. olive oil or Spanish oil
1¼ c. boiling water
2 c. coconut, fresh grated

2 T. Manioc meal (maize meal)
  or bread crumbs
½ lb. okra, fresh or frozen (10 oz.)
2 tomatoes, chopped and peeled
2 T. green pepper, chopped
¼ c. onion, chopped
Pepper to taste

Sauté the fresh shrimp in butter until opaque and tender about 4 minutes. Remove and set aside. Remove shrimp with slotted spoon to platter; reserve. Reduce heat and in the same skillet sauté onions until soft. Add green pepper, tomatoes, okra and ground shrimp. Stir well. Pour boiling water over coconut. Mix with manioc meal or substitute. Stir into tomato mixture. Simmer, covered, over low heat until okra is tender, about 25 minutes. Add reserved shrimp to vegetable mixture; cook for about 5 more minutes or until shrimp is warm. Stir in oil, peanuts and coriander. Season to taste.

CHICKEN WITH ARTICHOKES

From the region of District 6950
USA

6 chicken breast fillets
  (3 breasts, cut in half)
½ c. flour
2 T. butter
2 T. oil
1 med. onion, sliced
1-2 garlic cloves, chopped

1 can artichoke hearts,
  quartered
3-4 oz. white wine
1 can chopped tomatoes
1-2 sun-dried tomatoes, cut into
  bite-size (opt.)
Salt and pepper

Season the flour with salt and pepper. Dredge the chicken breasts in the flour. Heat the oil and butter in pan. Sauté chicken for 1-2 minutes on each side. Add onion and garlic and cook a little longer. Add wine, tomatoes and artichokes and simmer about 5-8 minutes. Salt and pepper to taste.

CARNE EN JOCON (Beef in Tomato Stew)

From the region of District 4250
Guatemala

1 med. onion, finely chopped
2 red or green bell peppers, seeded and chopped
1 fresh hot green pepper, seeded and chopped
3 cloves garlic, chopped
2½ lbs. lean, boneless beef chuck, cut into 1-inch cubes
10-oz. can Mexican green tomatoes and liquid from the can
3 med. tomatoes, peeled and coarsely chopped
½ tsp. dried oregano
Salt and freshly ground pepper
1 bay leaf
2 cloves
1 c. beef stock, more or less if needed
2 stale tortillas or 3 T. cornmeal

Sauté the onion, peppers and garlic until the onions are soft. Add the meat and all the other ingredients, except the tortillas. Cover and simmer gently until the beef is tender, about 2½ hours. Remove bay leaf. If using tortillas, soak them in cold water, squeeze them out and crumble like bread crumbs. Add to the casserole and simmer, uncovered, until the sauce is thickened. If using masa harina or cornmeal, mix it with a little cold water and stir into the stew, cooking just until the sauce is thickened (cornmeal will take a few minutes longer to thicken). Serve the stew on a bed of Guatemalan rice.

CHICKEN CACCIATORE

From the region of District 2030-2120
Italy

1 broiler chicken, cut up
1 c. flour
¾ c. olive oil
1 c. sliced onion
1 c. diced mushrooms
3 c. canned tomatoes
2 cloves garlic, crushed
1 tsp. salt
¼ tsp. pepper
½ c. white wine
Pinch of oregano

Put flour in a bag with the cut-up chicken. Let the flour coat the chicken. Brown chicken in oil. Remove and set aside. Add onion and sauté until tender, but not brown. Add the mushrooms and sauté about 5 minutes more. Now add the tomatoes, garlic, salt, pepper and oregano. Cover and simmer for 20-25 minutes until chicken is done. Add wine and cook for 5 more minutes. Serve warm over noodles.

CORONATION CHICKEN

From the region of District 1240-1290
England

4 cooked and diced chicken breasts
½ c. apricot preserves
2 c. mayonnaise
½ c. onion, finely chopped
1 T. curry powder
½ c. red wine
½ c. chicken stock

2 tsp. tomato paste
1 bay leaf
Pinch of salt
Pinch of pepper
2 T. lemon juice
3 T. whipping cream, lightly whipped

Mix mayonnaise and apricot preserves and set aside. Heat oil and sauté onion for 4 minutes. Add curry powder and sauté for 2 minutes. Add wine, chicken stock, tomato paste and bay leaf. Bring to a boil. Now add salt, pepper and lemon juice. Simmer, uncovered, 5-10 minutes. Remove bay leaf and cool. Slowly add this to the mayonnaise mixture. Add cream. Fold in the diced chicken. Serve on a bed of lettuce. Serves 8.

CHEESE CROWNED TENDERLOINS

From the region of District 5360
Canada

4 (4-oz.) beef tenderloin or top sirloin grilling steaks
¼ c. herbed Boursin or cream-style cheese

½ c. seedless raspberry jam
¼ c. balsamic vinegar

In medium oiled skillet over medium-high heat, brown steaks 3-4 minutes on each side. Remove to baking pan and top each steak with one-quarter of the cheese. Broil 3 minutes or until cheese is browned. Meanwhile, stir jam and vinegar into skillet and bring just to boil. Serve steaks on a pool of sauce, drizzling a little over top. Preparation time: 2 minutes. Cooking time: 10 minutes.

CHILI CRAB

From the region of District 3310
Malaysia/Singapore

2 kg crabs, shells removed, lungs discarded, cut into serving pieces

3 eggs, lightly beaten
4 T. vegetable oil

Spices, coarsely pounded:
6 lg. chilies
1 med. onion
6 cloves garlic

3 slices ginger
400ml water

Sauce:
8 T. tomato sauce
2 T. chili sauce
1 tsp. salt
4 T. soy sauce

1 T. sugar
3 T. cornstarch, diluted in 6 T. water

6 pieces man tou, steamed buns or sliced French loaf

Place crabs roe into beaten eggs; crack the shell of crab pincers and set aside separately with egg mixture and crab in the refrigerator. Fry pounded spices in 4 tablespoons hot oil until fragrant. Add crabs and stir fry. Add water to cover most of the crabs. Add tomato and chili sauce and allow to boil. Add salt, soy sauce and sugar. Boil for 5 minutes, then add crab roe and egg mixture. Thicken with cornstarch. Bring to a boil. Transfer to plate and serve with man tou, steamed buns or slice French loaf. Serves 4-6.

CHICKEN BIRYANI

From the region of District 3140
India

2 black cardamom
2 T. chopped coriander leaves
2 sticks cinnamon
2 each: cloves and green cardamoms
½ tsp. cumin and coriander powder

2 T. each of chopped ginger and garlic
½ tsp. mace (nutmeg will do)
6 pieces peppercorns
2 green chili
2 T. lime juice
1 tsp. turmeric powder

Grind above ingredients to a paste.

(continued)

800g chicken, med. pieces
2 c. flavored rice (basmati)
3 med. sized onions, sliced
4 T. oil (or ghee)
2 lg. onions, fried

½ tsp. saffron color, mixed with water to make ⅛ c. saffron milk
Salt to taste
2 c. yogurt

Grind the ingredients to be ground to a fine paste. Mix this paste with yogurt and salt. Make cuts on the chicken pieces and rub this marinade into them well. Marinate in the refrigerator for at least four hours. In a large vessel, combine the rice, water, salt and cook until the rice is half done. Drain the excess liquid and spread the rice on a plate to cool. Heat the oil in a heavy-bottomed pan until hot and fry the sliced onions until they are crisp and golden brown. Add the marinated chicken pieces, mix well with all other ingredients and add fried onion. In a large heavy-bottomed pan, add chicken with marinade and top a layer of rice topped with a portion of the saffron milk. In this way arrange alternate layers of melted clarified butter (ghee), butter, chicken, rice and saffron milk until they are all used up. Make sure the top most layer is of rice topped with melted clarified butter (ghee), butter and saffron milk. Cook on high heat for first 10 minutes and next 10 minutes medium heat and next 10 in low heat. Cover it with a tight fitting lid. Cook on very low level. Garnish with slices of boiled eggs, nuts or raisins.

CHICAGO-STYLE DEEP-DISH PIZZA

From the region of District 6440
USA

Crust:

2 pkgs. RapidRise dry yeast (½ oz.)
1¾ c. warm water
½ c. vegetable oil

5 T. olive oil
½ c. cornmeal
5 c. flour

Filling:

⅓ lb. sliced mozzarella cheese
3 c. Italian-style whole peeled tomatoes, drained and squished
1 tsp. basil
1 tsp. oregano
2 cloves garlic, minced
Salt to taste
½ c. Italian sausage, hot or mild

¼ c. yellow onions, peeled and sliced thin
¼ c. thin sliced pepperoni
½ c. mushrooms, sliced
½ c. sweet bell peppers, cored and sliced thin
1 c. grated Parmesan cheese
4 T. olive oil

(continued)

In a mixing bowl, dissolve the yeast in water. Add the oils, cornmeal and half of the flour. Beat for 10 minutes. Now add remaining flour and then knead for 5 minutes. Place the dough in a clear oiled mixing bowl. Cover and let it rise. When risen, punch down and let it rise again. Oil your deep-dish pizza pan. Dust hand with flour if the dough is sticky. Place some dough in the pan and push it out to the edges using your fingers. Put in enough dough so that you can run it up the sides of the pan. Make it about ⅛ inch thick throughout the pan. **For the filling:** Place the cheese in a layer on the bottom of the pie. Next, add the tomatoes and the basil, oregano, garlic, salt and all the other ingredients, reserving the Parmesan cheese for the top. Drizzle olive oil over the top of the pie and you are ready to bake. Bake the pie in a 475°F oven until the top is golden and gooey and the crust a light golden brown, about 35-40 minutes.

CHICKEN CURRY

From the region of District 9220
Seychelles

1 (2- to 3-lb.) whole chicken, cut into pieces
1 T. garam masala
1 T. garlic powder
2 T. olive oil
2 onions, chopped
1 c. chicken broth

1 (10.75-oz.) can condensed cream of chicken soup
4 potatoes, peeled and cubed
4 T. curry powder
Salt and pepper to taste
2 oz. golden raisins

Rub the chicken with garam masala and garlic powder. In a large sauté pan over medium heat, brown chicken in olive oil in a large pot. Remove chicken and sauté onions in the same oil until golden. Return the chicken to the pan and cover with the broth. Simmer until the meat is tender and can be easily picked off of the bone. Remove the chicken to cool. Mix the soup into the broth in the pan, then add the potatoes and the curry. Simmer until tender. As soon as the chicken is cool enough to handle, remove the meat from the skin and bones and if necessary, cut into bite-size pieces. When the potatoes are done, add the meat to the potato mixture and heat through. You may add golden raisins at this point if desired, adjust seasonings and serve!

CAJUN TAILS CRAWFISH ETOUFFEE

From the region of District 6200
USA

½ c. butter
1 c. finely chopped onions
1 clove garlic, chopped fine
2½ c. water
½ c. chopped green onion tops
Salt and pepper to taste (may also add cayenne pepper if you like a little heat)

Hot steamed rice
1 lb. crawfish tails or cleaned shrimp
1 T. Worcestershire sauce
2 tsp. cornstarch
½ c. water
1 T. chopped fresh parsley and onion tops

Melt butter in Dutch oven over low heat. Add onions and garlic. Sauté over medium heat until clear. Add 2½ cups water; bring to a boil, add crawfish or shrimp. Cook over low heat for 5 minutes. Stir occasionally. Add Worcestershire, add seasoning to taste. Dissolve cornstarch in ½ cup water. Pour into stew. Allow to thicken, simmer for one or two minutes, stirring occasionally. Add onion tops and parsley and remove from heat. Serve over hot cooked rice. Serves 4.

CHICKEN YASSA

From the region of District 9100
Gambia

1 big chicken
1 c. white wine
1 tsp. ginger powder
1 lb. onion, sliced fine
¼ c. butter
3 big peppers, diced
2 bay leaves

1 tsp. crushed peppercorns
¼ c. lemon juice
2 lemons, sliced fine for garnish
2 tomatoes, sliced fine for garnish
4 c. chicken stock

Cut chicken into fourths. Let rest in marinade of wine, ginger and salt for 10 hours. Remove chicken from marinade and sauté chicken in the butter. Add all other ingredients plus ½ cup marinade. Cover and cook on a low fire until tender. If there is too much broth, remove chicken and reduce the liquid on a high flame. Put chicken on platter. Pour thickened broth over chicken and garnish with sliced tomatoes and lemon. Serve with rice.

CHICKEN IN WINE

From the region of District 1640-1790
France

3 oz. butter
1 T. oil
3½-lb. oven-ready chicken
1 lg. onion, thickly sliced
¾ lb. carrots, thickly sliced
1 T. fresh thyme leaves
Salt

Black pepper
1 bay leaf
1¼ c. Muscadet (wine)
1¼ c. fresh chicken stock
1 lb. button mushrooms
4 egg yolks
Freshly grated nutmeg

Heat the oil and half the butter in a large casserole or pan. Add the chicken and fry for a few minutes on all sides. Remove from the pan and set aside. Place half the onions and carrots in the casserole, then place the chicken, breast side up, on top. Cover with the remaining onions and carrots. Add the bay leaf, thyme, salt and pepper, then pour over the stock and wine. This should cover half of the bird. Add more stock if necessary. Bring to the boil, cover and simmer for 40 minutes. Add the mushrooms, then turn the chicken over. Continue to simmer, covered, for a further 30 minutes. At the end of the cooking time, remove the chicken to a warmed serving platter. Lift out the vegetables with a slotted spoon, remove the bay leaf and arrange the vegetables around the chicken. Keep warm. Return the casserole to a high heat and boil rapidly for 5-8 minutes to reduce the liquid. Meanwhile, melt the remaining butter in a pan and lightly fry the remaining mushrooms. Sprinkle over the other vegetables surrounding the chicken. Keep warm. In a bowl, beat the egg yolks together with the nutmeg. Add a little of the cooking liquid to the eggs; mix well, then stir into the casserole. Remove from the heat and stir once. **To serve:** Pour a little of the sauce over the chicken and serve the rest separately.

CHEF STEVE MILES' CHICKEN A L'ORANGE

From the region of District 6900
USA

1 orange, peeled, sliced and seeded
1 (8 oz.) frozen orange juice concentrate
3 c. chicken stock
4 chicken breasts, boneless, skinned and sliced into ¼-inch strips

Flour to dust
4 cloves garlic, crushed
6 T. orange liqueur
Salt and pepper to taste
1 stick butter
1 lg. onion, sliced

(continued)

Combine orange juice and chicken broth and simmer for ¼ hour. Melt butter in skillet. Flour chicken and sauté with onions and garlic until chicken is brown; season with salt and pepper. Add liqueur and orange sauce and simmer for 30 minutes. Serve garnished with sliced orange.

CROWDIE AND CHIVE RAVIOLI WITH RED CHARD AND ROAST BEETROOT DRESSING

From the region of District 1010
Scotland

Pasta:

140g pasta flour	30ml olive oil
2 eggs	

Filling:

280g Crowdie	Salt and pepper
Handful fresh chives	

Beetroot Dressing:

1 beetroot	45ml olive oil
10ml red wine vinegar	Pepper

To make pasta: Weigh 140 grams pasta flour into a large bowl. Add 1 egg and 1 egg yolk; mix well. Knead dough until pliable. Cover dough and chill for at least 30 minutes. Place crowdie into bowl for filling. Wash chives, chop in half and cut; place into bowl with crowdie. Add salt and pepper and mix crowdie mixture well. Roll pasta dough out and put through pasta machine. Using a round cutter, cut out pasta circles. Place a teaspoon of crowdie filling into the center of each pasta circle. Using a pastry brush and water, lightly dampen the outside of circle and carefully pinch closed; place on floured surface to dry. Half fill a pan with water and put onto boil. Peel and dice beetroot, toss in olive oil and red wine vinegar. Then add pepper; cover. Place ravioli into pan of boiling water until cooked. Drain pasta, garnish with red chard and serve with beetroot dressing.

ZIGINI

From the region of District 9200
Eritrea

2 lbs. stewing beef, in cubes
¼ c. vegetable oil
2 lg. onions, chopped
4 cloves garlic, crushed
1 lg. tomato, diced

Salt and pepper
¼ c. chopped fresh coriander (cilantro)
3 T. Berbere (less for a milder stew)

Fry the meat on high heat in oil until brown, add the onion and sauté until translucent and eventually add the garlic and 3 tablespoons Berbere seasoning. Add the tomato and boil slowly until the meat is tender and the stew has thickened (about 60 minutes). More water may be added until the meat is tender. Garnish with coriander and serve hot on Injera (Ethiopian flat bread).

Berbere:

½ tsp. ground ginger
¼ tsp. ground coriander
¼ tsp. ground cardamom
¼ tsp. ground fenugreek
Pinch of ground cloves
Pinch of ground allspice

Pinch of ground cinnamon
½ T. salt
2½ T. cayenne pepper
1 T. paprika
½ tsp. fresh ground black pepper

For the Berbere: Combine the spices and roast in a dry skillet on low to moderate heat, stirring constantly, for about 5-10 minutes or until roasted. To store extra spices, place in an airtight jar.

ESCUDELLA

From the region of District 1700
Andorra

2 c. white beans, soaked overnight
1 sm. ham bone
1 beef marrow bone
1 chicken, cut into several pieces
1 lb. raw pork sausage, sliced
3 slices cured ham, cut in chunks

1 lg. potato, cut in eighths
¼ c. rice
1 c. pasta noodles (or pasta shells)
1 c. cooked chickpeas
1 c. chopped cabbage
Salt and pepper according to your taste

Cook the sausage pieces in a deep pot with vegetable oil over medium heat until browned. If you don't have Dutch oven, a pot or flame-proof

(continued)

casserole dish will do just as well. Rinse the dry white beans in cold water and tie the ham bone and marrow bone in cheesecloth. Put the beans, bones in cheesecloth, cooked sausage, chicken and ham in the pot or casserole. Fill it up with 8 cups of cold water and add salt according to taste. Bring to a boil, then reduce the flames and let it cook gently, covered, for about 1 hour. A good test of seeing whether it is ready is to check that the beans are cooked and whether the chicken is very tender. Remove the bones and discard them. Remove the chicken pieces and put them aside. Add more liquid if necessary to cook the other vegetables and rice. Bring it to a rapid boil. When it's boiling, put in the cabbage, potatoes, rice, noodles, cooked chickpeas and add pepper to taste. Turn the flames down to a medium heat. Cook for 20 minutes. You can test to see whether it's ready by checking on the softness of the rice and potatoes. Before serving, put the chicken back inside the pot. Cook for a few more minutes so everything is heated together again. Season to taste. Serve warm.

ENSALADA DE BACALAO

From the region of District 7000
Puerto Rico

1 lb. boneless salted cod fish
6 white potatoes
2 lg. red onions, peeled and sliced into rings
4 sliced hard-boiled eggs
1 ½ c. diced tomatoes

½ c. olive oil
½ c. Spanish olives
3 cloves garlic, finely crushed
3 T. white vinegar
1 sm. jar red pimientos

Soak fish in water for 24 hours to remove the salt. Change water every 8 hours. After 24 hours, boil the fish in fresh water, at low heat, simmer for about 1 hour until the fish is tender and flaky. Remove from heat and water; break the fish into bite-size pieces and let it cool. Boil the potatoes. Let it cool and cut in large cubes. Rub mashed garlic all around a large salad bowl. Place the fish in the salad bowl as the first layer. Add the other ingredients of onions, tomatoes and olives. Make layers until all the fish, onions, tomatoes and olives are used up. Combine vinegar and olive oil and drizzle over the salad. Toss until all ingredients are well coated with the dressing. Add sliced, boiled eggs and pimientos.

EMPANADAS

From the region of District 4340, 4350
Chile

Pastry:

3 c. flour	¼ c. shortening
1 T. baking powder	¾ c. beef or vegetable stock
1 tsp. salt	

Pino Filling:

3 T. oil	1 tsp. oregano
1 c. onions, chopped	1 c. beef or vegetable stock
3 cloves minced garlic	¼ c. black or green olives
1 lb. ground beef	1 T. flour
¾ tsp. paprika	1 beaten egg
1 tsp. cumin seed	

Mix the flour, baking powder and salt together in a large bowl. Rub in the shortening with your fingers, breaking it up into small pieces. If using oil, simply stir it in. Stir in just enough stock to form a mass. Remove it to a floured work surface and knead for about 5-10 minutes or until smooth. Add a little flour if it is too sticky. Cover it with a towel or bowl and let it rest at least 30 minutes. While the dough is resting, heat the oil in a sauté pan over medium flame. Sauté the onions until they are translucent, 3-4 minutes. Add the cumin seed and oregano, garlic and paprika and sauté 1-2 minutes more. Add the ground beef, salt and pepper and sauté until it is cooked through, 5-7 minutes. Stir in the water or stock and olives and bring to a simmer. Sprinkle flour over all and stir in well so that there are no lumps. Simmer for another 5-8 minutes or until lightly thickened. Remove from heat and set aside to cool. Preheat oven to 375°. Cut the rested dough into 12 equal portions. Lightly flour a work surface and roll each portion out into a 6- to 8-inch round. Add about ¼ cup of filling to the center of the pastry round, leaving a ½-inch border. Wet the edges with a finger dipped in water, fold over into a half moon and seal the edges with the tines of a fork or by rolling them up into a scalloped edge. Lay out on a baking sheet. Brush tops with an egg beaten with a little water if you like. Bake for 30-40 minutes until browned on top. Serve warm.

FRESH FISH STEAMED, BENGALI-STYLE

From the region of District 3060
India

1 lb. fresh fish or prawn
Pinch of turmeric powder

Salt to taste

Paste:

2 green chilies
3 tsp. black mustard

1 x 1-inch piece of coconut
1 tsp. mustard oil

Grind mustard, green chilies and coconut to make a fine paste. Mix mustard oil, paste and fish. In a small tight container, steam the fish, no pressure for five minutes. Let it cool down inside the steamer. Serve with hot rice.

FISH IN COCONUT SAUCE (Kokoda)

From the region of District 1380-1430
Finland

3 mahi-mahi or white fish fillets
½ c. lime juice
½ tsp. sea salt
1 c. thick coconut cream (not milk)

2 onions, finely chopped
1 hot pepper, de-seeded and finely chopped
2 tomatoes, de-seeded and finely chopped

Cut the fish into bite-size pieces and place in a glass bowl only. Add the lime juice and salt. Mix well, cover and marinate in refrigerator for 10 hours. Just before serving, add coconut cream, onions and the pepper. Stir thoroughly, then place onto serving platter using slotted spoon. Top with chopped tomatoes and serve on a bed of lettuce.

FRENCHY'S VEAL CUTLETS PARMIGIANA

From the region of District 6840
USA

1 lb. veal cutlets (have butcher cut into one-half inch slices)
3 T. grated Parmesan cheese
6 T. olive oil
½ lb. mozzarella cheese, sliced
1 c. bread crumbs (Italian preferred, but plain will do)

2 lg. eggs
Salt and pepper to taste
2 c. marinara sauce to your liking*

(continued)

Place veal cutlets between two sheets of wax paper and pound thin. Mix 3 tablespoons of grated Parmesan cheese and 1 cup bread crumbs. Beat 2 large eggs into a shallow bowl and salt and pepper lightly. Warm a large frying pan on stove and add six tablespoons of oil (olive oil in preferred, but oil of your preference can be used, no lard). Warm oil until hot. Dip cutlets into eggs and then into bread crumbs (both sides) and place into frying pan with the hot oil. Fry about 5 minutes or until golden brown on each side. Place on a cookie sheet with paper towels to absorb grease and keep warm. Continue cooking until all cutlets are cooked. In a large lasagna-type pan or a baking pan, place browned cutlets on bottom. Pour your marinara or tomato sauce over top and place thin slices of mozzarella over top. Layer veal, sauce and cheese until all used. Bake at 300°F for 15 minutes or until cheese is slightly browned. Serve very hot.

*Do not use sauce with meat. Mushrooms would be okay in the sauce. If you like more sauce, use about one more cup. Too much sauce will make the veal Parmigiana too juicy.

FEIJOADA

From the region of District 4470-4680
Brazil

5 c. dried black beans
½ lb. smoked bacon
1 lb. hard-cured chorizo
    sausage, thinly sliced
1 lb. beef sirloin, cut into 1-inch
    cubes

2 onions, finely diced
2 T. minced garlic
2 bay leaves
1 sm. fresh chile pepper,
    chopped
Salt

Soak the beans in water overnight and then drain. In a large, heavy-bottomed pan, cook bacon in oil over medium-high heat. Add sausage and beef and cook until browned. Add the onions and garlic and cook for about 3 minutes. Add 8 cups of water, drained beans, bay leaves and chile pepper. Simmer the beans for about one hour or until they are soft and the sauce is thick. Add salt to taste. The sauce should be thick. the beans should be very soft. Add more water and cook longer if meat or beans are not cooked. Be sure not to burn the beans at the bottom of the pan. Keep stirring frequently towards the end.

FRENCH POTATOES WITH SMOKED SAUSAGE

From the region of District 1913
Croatia

2 kg potatoes
1 ½ c. sour cream
4 eggs, hard-boiled
¾ c. oil

Salt and pepper to taste
Red paprika
½ lb. smoked sausage, cooked

Cook potatoes in jacket, then peel and slice. Repeat with hard-boiled eggs. Prepare greased oven-proof dish, placing alternative rows of potatoes and eggs and sausage. First and last row should consist of potatoes. Now mix oil with sour cream, salt and pepper. Pour over potatoes. Cook on a high temperature until potatoes are golden brown. When cooked, sprinkle with red paprika. Serve with salad.

FISH CALULU

From the region of District 9150
Sao Tome and Principe

1 kg grouper, cut into lg. steaks
½ kg peeled prawns
3 tomatoes, blanched, peeled and chopped
3 T. palm oil
2 aubergines, peeled and cubed (eggplant)
2 onions, chopped

2 T. flour
4 okra, finely chopped
Sm. bunch marjoram, chopped
¼ kg sweet potato leaves or collard greens
4 whole peppercorns
3 cardamom pods

Add the tomatoes, aubergines, palm oil, okra and onions to a saucepan. Crush the peppercorns, cardamom pods in a pestle and mortar and add these along with the marjoram, fish and prawns and shredded collard greens to the pot. Season with salt and add sufficient water to just cover everything. Bring to a boil, reduce to a simmer and cook for about 20 minutes or until the fish is done. Dissolve the flour in a small volume of water and add to the pan. Allow the dish to thicken and serve with boiled, mashed plantains.

FISH PIE

From the region of District 4250
Belize

2 lbs. boiled fish filet, minced
1 c. bread crumbs
½ c. evaporated milk
2 sm. sweet peppers, chopped
1 lg. onion, chopped
1 tsp. lemon zest

1 tsp. ground pepper
¼ tsp. salt
2 T. melted butter or olive oil
2 cabbage leaves
3 hard-boiled eggs, sliced thick

In a mixing bowl, combine the fish, lemon zest, pepper and salt (or you may substitute the lemon, pepper and salt for 1 tablespoon of lemon pepper seasoning), ½ cup bread crumbs, milk, sweet pepper and mix well to form a soft consistency. Put cabbage leaves on the bottom of a greased loaf pan. Add ½ the mixture. Layer the mixture with a layer of the hard-boiled eggs. Add the remaining mixture of fish. Cover with the remaining bread crumbs and the melted butter. Bake for 40 minutes at 350°F or until golden brown.

TOURTIERE

From the region of District 7010, 7040
Canada

2½ lbs. pork, ground
2 garlic cloves, minced
Pinch of ground nutmeg
Pinch of ground sage
1 hot green pepper to taste

1 c. finely chopped onion
2 c. grated potato
½ c. raisins
2 c. boiling water
1 pastry for double crust pie

Place pork, onion, garlic, mace, sage, grated potato and raisins in large heavy pot. Cover with water and boil for 30 minutes, stirring frequently until meat is no longer pink and water is evaporated. Remove from heat and set aside to cool. Skim off excess fat. Preheat oven to 400°F. Prepare the pastry. Line a pie plate with half of the pastry. Prick with fork and bake 10 minutes. Cool. Pour cooled meat mixture into pie shell. Cover with top crust. Crimp and seal edges and cut vents to allow steam to escape. Bake 15 minutes. Reduce heat to 350°F and bake 20 more minutes or until crust is light brown and filling is bubbly. Serve hot.

PRAWN MASALA

From the region of District 3271
Pakistan

½ kg prawns
4 T. curd
1 heaping tsp. ginger/garlic paste
½ tsp. salt

Baghar: (sauté)
6-8 fresh curry leaves
½ tsp. mustard seeds (rai)

4 T. fried onion
½ tsp. mix spice
1 tsp. chili powder
½ tsp. black pepper powder
¼ c. oil

¼ tsp. fenugreek seeds (methi seeds)

Heat oil, add fenugreek seeds, mustard seeds and curry leaves and prepare baghar. In a bowl, mix ginger/garlic paste, salt, chili powder, pepper and little water. Now mix this in the baghar. Fry the masala. Add curd and fry. Add the prawns and fried onions and fry well. Lastly, add mix spice. Yield: 4 servings.

GREEK SHRIMP

From the region of District 2470
Greece

2 sm. onions, chopped
3 T. olive oil
1½ c. tomato wedges
¼ c. dry white wine
½ tsp. salt
Fresh ground pepper to taste

1 bay leaf
½ tsp. crushed oregano
2 T. chopped fresh parsley
1 lb. frozen shrimp
1½ tsp. cornstarch
4 oz. feta cheese, crumbled

Sauté the onions in oil. Drain tomatoes; reserve juice. Chop tomatoes coarsely and add to skillet along with wine, salt, pepper and bay leaf. Cook over high heat for 6 minutes. Mix cornstarch and reserved tomato juice and stir in. Cook over medium heat until thickened. Add shrimp and cook on low heat until pink and curled. Remove from heat and stir in cheese. Garnish with fresh parsley and oregano. Serve immediately.

ISLAND CHICKEN

From the region of District 7020
Jamaica

2 broiler-fryer chickens, halved
1 tsp. salt

1 tsp. pepper

Caribbean Paste:

¾ c. dark brown sugar
¼ c. dark rum
1 T. lime juice
2 tsp. lemon pepper
1¼ tsp. ginger

½ tsp. cloves, ground
¼ tsp. cinnamon
½ tsp. garlic powder
3 drops hot pepper sauce

4 T. dark rum
1½ c. mango chutney

Lime, sliced
Parsley

Sprinkle salt and pepper over washed and dried chicken. Set aside. In a small bowl, make Caribbean paste by mixing together all 9 ingredients listed above. Place the chicken, skin side up, in a large shallow baking pan. Rub Caribbean paste evenly over the chicken. Bake in a 400°F oven for 50 minutes or until the chicken is fork-tender. In a blender, place chutney and 4 tablespoons of dark rum. Blend well. Spoon chutney mixture over chicken and bake about 3 minutes more or until chutney is warm. Arrange chicken on a serving platter. Garnish with lime and parsley.

JERK CHICKEN

From the region of District 7030
Grenada

For the Marinade:

1½ onions, chopped
⅔ c. finely chopped scallion
½ tsp. cinnamon
¼ c. minced pickled jalapeño pepper or to taste (wear rubber gloves)
2 tsp. black pepper
6 drops pepper sauce or to taste

3 T. soy sauce
¼ c. vegetable oil
3 garlic cloves
1 tsp. dried thyme, crumbled
1½ tsp. salt
1½ tsp. ground allspice
¼ tsp. freshly grated nutmeg
20 chicken wings (about 3¼ lbs.), the wing tips cut off

Mix all the ingredients in a blender and marinate chicken in the marinade overnight. Arrange the wings in one layer on an oiled rack set over a

(continued)

foil-lined roasting pan, spoon the marinade over them and bake the wings in a preheated 450°F oven for 30-35 minutes or until they are cooked through.

JAPRAK

From the region of District 1910
Bosnia & Herzegovina

½ kg mutton, cubed fine
1 kg veal, cubed fine
50g rice
1 c. chopped onion
1 egg
2 cloves garlic
½ c. cooking oil

½ c. double cream
Pepper
Salt
Paprika
Fine chopped parsley
50 grapevine leaves
Beef stock

Boil the grapevine leaves for 20 minutes in salty water. Drain the leaves and leave to cool. Melt the oil in the frying pan. Add the mutton and veal and sauté for 3 minutes. Then add garlic and parsley to the meat. Now add rice, egg, pepper, paprika and salt. Stir thoroughly. Gradually add ¾ cup of cold water which cooks the rice. When rice is done, fill the grapevine leaves with the mixture creating small cylindrical parcels. You may even tie them up. Fill the dish tightly with the parcels and then add enough beef stock until all the parcels are covered with it. Cook slowly for 2 hours. When done, remove parcels onto serving platter. Mix stock with the double cream and pour over parcels. Goes well with boiled potatoes.

KANGKONG BELACAN

From the region of District 3310
Malaysia/Singapore

Spice Paste:

2 T. dried shrimp, soaked, set aside the water
3 cloves garlic

2 tsp. shrimp paste
3 red chilies
6 shallots

Blend the above.

3 T. vegetable oil for frying
300g kangkong, cut into 6cm length (water spinach)

1 ½ tsp. sugar
Salt to taste

(continued)

Fry blended spices in hot oil on high heat for 2 minutes. Reduce heat and fry until fragrant. Add kangkong, sugar and salt. Turn up heat to high and stir fry for 3 minutes. Serve hot with rice. Serves 4.

KOREAN BBQ

From the region of District 3590-3750
Korea

4 lbs. beef ribs
3 garlic cloves, crushed
¼ c. sesame seed, toasted
1 c. green onions
1 tsp. pepper

2 T. sesame oil
2 c. soy sauce
¾ c. sugar
¼ c. oil

Mix garlic, sesame seeds, green onions, pepper, sesame oil, soy sauce, sugar and oil in a bowl. Pour over the short ribs. Cover and let stand at room temperature for 4 hours. Barbecue over coals or run under broiler, turning and basting often with marinade until meat is tender.

KENTUMERE (Fish and Spinach with Tomatoes)

From the region of District 9100
Ghana

½ c. palm oil
1 c. onions, coarsely chopped
½ tsp. cayenne pepper

1 ½ c. chopped tomatoes
1 c. kippered herring
5 c. fresh spinach, chopped

Heat the oil in a large skillet or heavy pot, then sauté onions and pepper together. Stir in the tomatoes, along with the remaining ingredients. Cook at moderate temperature for 15 minutes or until fish is tender and flaky. Serve kentumere with white rice and plantains.

MIDWESTERN CHILI

From the region of District 6490
USA

4 med. onions, chopped
3 garlic cloves, crushed
¼ c. vegetable or olive oil
1 tsp. oregano
2 bay leaves, crumbled
2½ lbs. ground beef
3 T. chili powder
1½ cans chopped tomatoes, do not drain

20 oz. red kidney beans, do not drain
2 tsp. salt
3 T. apple cider vinegar
Crushed red pepper flakes to taste

In a large soup pot, heat the oil over medium heat. Add chopped onions and garlic. Sauté until onions are soft. Add oregano, bay leaves and ground beef and sauté for 5 minutes. Add half of the chili powder, tomatoes and kidney beans. Reduce heat to low and simmer, stirring occasionally, about 1 hour. Add remaining chili powder and salt, vinegar and red pepper flakes. Simmer for an additional 15 minutes. Serve hot. Makes 10-12 servings.

MACAO CHICKEN

From the region of District 3450
Macao

1 whole chicken, cut into 8 pieces
½ tsp. saffron
¼ c. white wine
¼ tsp. salt
¼ tsp. pepper
3 bay leaves, crumbled
Olive oil for frying
4 med. potatoes, cut into chunks
1 med. yellow onion, peeled and chopped

1 clove garlic
1 tsp. red curry paste
1 lg. tomato roughly chopped
2 tsp. salt
½ c. evaporated milk
1 c. thick coconut milk
3 hard-boiled eggs, cut into quarters
Few slices chourico
6 black olives
2 T. desiccated coconut
Pepper to taste

Prepare the marinade by combining saffron, white wine, salt, pepper and bay leaves in a bowl. Marinate chicken in the marinade for 1 hour. (Do not remove skin or bones from chicken.) Heat oil in a large wok and sauté onion and garlic over high heat until soft. Stir in curry paste and add chicken to seal. Add chopped tomato, salt and about 1 cup of water. Cook for 20 minutes over medium heat. Add potatoes and leave

(continued)

on medium heat for a further 10-20 minutes until chicken is cooked through. Stir in coconut milk and evaporated milk and remove from heat. Check for seasonings. Turn into a large serving dish and garnish with egg, chourico, olives, desiccated coconut and freshly ground pepper. Place under the oven grill for 10 minutes until lightly browned on top.

MACKEREL ESCABECHE (Saba Nanban Zuke)

From the region of District 2650
Japan

Sauce:

600ml dashi
120ml dark soy sauce
30ml mirin
30ml vinegar
Juice of 1 lemon
30 oba (shiso leaves)
30g ginger

10 mackerel fillets
Flour as needed
4 miyoga, chopped and soaked in water

30g sesame seeds, roasted
1 daikon
30ml honey
20g sugar
Ichimi togarshi (ground chili powder), according to taste

Vinegar water (1 part vinegar to 2 parts water)

For the sauce: Place all the ingredients in a bowl and mix well. Remove central bone from the mackerel piece, dredge in flour and deep-fry at 170° Celsius. While fish is still hot, immerse it in the sauce. Immerse the soaked miyoga in the vinegar water. When the fish and sauce mixture has cooled, serve it on a plate topped with the miyoga. Serves 10.

MAFFE TIGA (Peanut Chicken)

From the region of District 9100
Guinea

4 c. water
3 soup cubes
2 lg. onions, chopped
4 cloves garlic
3 T. tomato paste
¼ tsp. cayenne pepper
Pinch of oregano
1 T. lemon juice
1 lg. tomato, diced (remove seeds first)
1 lb. sugarless natural peanut butter
2 boneless chicken breasts, cut into sm. pieces
3 whole hot peppers (broken if you want it spicy)
3 bay leaves
Salt and pepper to taste
1 T. oil

Sauté the onion and garlic in the oil until tender. Add all the ingredients, except the peanut butter and chicken. Let it simmer for about 30 minutes. Add the peanut butter and simmer for another 10 minutes. Add the chicken breast. Simmer until the chicken breast is done (about 15 minutes). The sauce should be thick. Serve this dish over rice.

MEXICAN LASAGNE

From the region of District 4100, 4130
Mexico

1 pkt. lasagne noodles
1 lb. lean ground beef
1 c. onion, chopped
3 c. salsa
1 ½ c. Monterey Jack cheese
¼ c. cilantro, chopped
1 tsp. chili powder
2 c. low-fat ricotta cheese

Heat oven to 375°F. Cook and drain noodles. Brown beef, onion, cilantro and chili powder and set aside. In a bottom of ungreased rectangular pan, place 5 noodles. Layer with beef mixture, then top with 1 cup of ricotta cheese and then 1 ¼ cups salsa. Repeat with remaining noodles, beef mixture, ricotta cheese and salsa. Sprinkle with Monterey Jack cheese. Bake, uncovered, for 35 minutes or until hot. Let stand for 15 minutes before cutting.

MALAYSIAN SPICY PRAWNS

From the region of District 3300, 3310
Malaysia

2 lbs. fresh prawns
1 bunch fresh coriander leaves or scallions

Salt and pepper to taste
2 T. oil

Spice Paste:

1 inch galangal or fresh ginger, chopped
3 spring onions, chopped

1 stalk lemon grass, chopped
3 dried chili peppers
2 cloves garlic, chopped

Mix all the ingredients for the paste in a blender. Blend well and set aside. Heat wok and drizzle in the oil. When wok is hot enough, add the spice paste into the wok. Stir fry until fragrant. **Caution:** Do not burn. Add prawns to mixture. Add half the coriander or scallions. Add salt and pepper. Remove prawns when they turn translucent and arrange on platter. Sprinkle remainder of coriander or scallions on prawns. Serve immediately.

LAMB CHUBBAGIN

From the region of District 9010
Mauritania

1 kg lamb meat, cubed (you can substitute camel meat)
1 ½ kg rice
1 ½ c. oil
1 sm. cabbage, cut into wedges
2 med. sweet potatoes, peeled and cut into chunks
1 aubergine (eggplant), cut into chunks
3 carrots, cut into chunks

1 ½ onions, coarsely chopped
6 chilies (or to taste)
½ c. tomato purée
3 garlic cloves
1 smoked and dried fish
Few bissap (hibiscus) leaves, trimmed of stems
3 maggi soup cubes
Salt and black pepper to taste

Sauté the lamb in the oil for about 8 minutes. Meanwhile, mix the tomato purée with 1 cup water to form a thick paste. Add this to the pan along with the onion and a little salt. Combine thoroughly. Now add the vegetables. Wash and flake the dried fish, removing all the bones. Add the flaked, dried fish into the pan, then add the remaining hot chilies. Tie the bissap leaves into a bundle and add to the stew. Add a little water if it is too dry. Cover pot and reduce heat. Meanwhile, wash rice and wrap in a cloth and add this to the pot, allowing the rice to steam inside the main pan when you close the lid on it. Cook for about 30

(continued)

minutes. Now discard the bissap leaves. Next, remove the meat and vegetables and place in a bowl to keep warm. Open the rice and stir into the remaining sauce. Season with 1 maggi cube and some water, enough to cook the rice tender. Stir to combine. Continue cooking until the rice is tender and the mixture is almost dry. Transfer the rice to a serving dish. Place meat and vegetables in the center. Typically this is served with nocose made from 3 garlic cloves, black pepper, 2 maggi cubes, a little slivered onion all pounded together into a paste. If desired, the bissap leaves can also be pounded into this condiment. Let everyone spoon the dish into their plates.

MEAT STEW (Korma)

From the region of District 3272
Afghanistan

1 lb. lean stewing beef or lamb
½ c. oil
1 lg. onion, finely chopped
3 garlic cloves, crushed
1½ c. water
Salt

Freshly ground black pepper
¼ tsp. hot chili pepper (or more)
3 c. spinach, chopped
2 tsp. cumin
6 T. coriander leaves, chopped

Cut meat into ¾-inch cubes. Heat oil in a heavy pan, add onion and fry gently until transparent. Increase heat, add garlic and meat cubes and fry, stirring often, until juices evaporate and meat begins to brown. Add water, salt and pepper to taste, chili pepper and cumin. Bring to a slow simmer and reduce heat. Cover pan and simmer gently for 1 to 1½ hours until meat is tender. Time depends on cut of meat used. Add spinach and coriander and cook for further 10-15 minutes. Spoon over a bed of rice and serve.

MBAWA YA TOMATI (Chicken Wings with Tomatoes)

From the region of District 9220
Mayotte

3 kg chicken wings
4 onions
2 tins tomato paste
5 T. palm oil (or groundnut oil with paprika for color)

1 tsp. ground cumin
Salt and black pepper to taste

Heat the oil in a pot, add the chopped onions and fry for a few minutes before adding the cumin, pepper and salt. Mix well, then add the tomato purée. Add 500 milliliters water to form a sauce and mix well. Then add

(continued)

the chicken wings. Bring to a boil, then allow to boil briskly for 15 minutes. Serve on a bed of rice.

NEW ENGLAND POT ROAST, ALA JANE

From the region of District 7980
USA

5- to 6-lb. beef rump roast
4 med. size onions, chopped
1 c. flour
⅛ c. olive oil

1 bay leaf
Coarse salt to taste
Black pepper to taste
Water

Heat oil in Dutch oven, place onions in hot oil and let them brown. Place roast in brown bag filled with flour, salt and pepper. Shake until roast is coated. Place roast in Dutch oven with onions. Sear roast until browned on all surfaces. Turn heat down to simmer and add water to cover roast. Cook until water has evaporated and onions continue to darken/burn. Add same amount water and repeat for up to 5 hours. Retain some liquid after last boil to use as gravy. Meat should fall apart.

NGEGE (Tilapia with Groundnut Sauce)

From the region of District 9200
Uganda

2 lbs. tilapia fish fillets
Salt and black pepper to taste
½ c. cooking oil
2 onions, finely chopped
2 T. tomato paste

½ tsp. garlic powder or 2 cloves garlic, mashed
½ c. unsweetened peanut butter
1 spoonful curry powder

Rub salt and pepper onto the fillets. Heat oil in deep-frying pan until very hot. Fry fish in hot oil on both sides until fish is browned and crispy. Reduce heat and cover until fish is done. Remove fish from pan. Place fish in covered dish in warm oven. Increase heat under frying pan. Fry the onions and garlic in the same pan, until fully cooked. Remove onions and place them over the fish. Reduce heat. Add peanut butter and curry powder and tomato paste to frying pan. Mix well with remaining oil. Reduce heat to very low. Slowly stir in enough water to make a smooth sauce. Pour sauce over fish and onions. Serve with Ugali or rice.

NASI GORENG

From the region of District 7030
Surinam

8 oz. cooked rice
8 oz. grilled and diced chicken breasts
3 T. butter
½ c. diced onion
½ tsp. shrimp paste
3 bouillon cubes

4 cloves garlic, mashed
Black or white pepper
6 strips (like matchsticks) of ginger
8 T. soy sauce
3 twigs celery, chopped coarsely

In a skillet, heat the butter and sauté onions. Add the grilled chicken, shrimp paste, bouillon cubes, ginger, garlic and a dash of black/white pepper. Stir all the ingredients and sauté until bouillon can be powdered by the back of the spoon. Add the rice, soy sauce, continue stirring until the rice turns light brown. Turn the stove off, add the celery and stir.

OXTAIL

From the region of District 9320
South Africa

1 kg oxtail
15ml oil
1 onion, peeled and chopped
4 cloves garlic, peeled and crushed
2 ribs celery, diced
2 bay leaves

1 sprig thyme
300ml dry white wine
500ml beef stock
2 carrots, peeled and coarsely chopped
150 green beans, top and tailed

Preheat the oven to 200° Celsius. Roast the oxtail pieces in a roasting tray until golden on the edges, turning once. Meanwhile, heat the oil in a large casserole pot on a medium heat. Add the onion, garlic and celery and fry for a minute. Add the bay leaves, thyme, wine, beef stock and the browned oxtail pieces. Reduce the oven temperature to 170° Celsius. Cover the casserole pot and put in the oven for about four hours, stirring occasionally. Add the carrots and beans and season with salt and pepper. Cook for another 30 minutes or until the vegetables are tender. Serves 4.

PAN SEARED LOIN OF VENISON WITH MILLEFEUILLE POTATOES

From the region of District 1010
Scotland

4 lg. potatoes
110g carrots
110g turnips
60g butter
1 clove garlic

Thyme
140g loin of venison
100ml red wine
150ml veal stock
Salt and pepper

Preheat oven to 180° Celsius. Wash, peel and re-wash potatoes. Crush garlic, wash and prepare thyme. Melt butter in a frying pan and add garlic and thyme. When sizzles, remove from the heat. Set mandolin to setting number 2 and thinly slice potatoes. Place grease-proof paper circles into Dariol molds and arrange potatoes into molds. Pour butter sauce into Dariol molds with sliced potatoes. Place frying pan on a high heat and put Dariol molds in pan. When butter reaches bubble stage, cook potatoes in pan for a further 4 minutes. Wash, peel and re-wash turnips and carrots, dice. Boil turnips and carrots in large pan (from cold water) for 20 minutes with a pinch of salt. Remove Dariol molds from frying pan and place onto a baking tray and place into oven for 20 minutes. Test turnips and carrots with skewer and mash thoroughly with 10 grams butter. Lightly season venison with salt and pepper. Put a frying pan on the heat with a dribble of olive oil for venison and lightly seal venison and then place onto baking tray and into the oven for 4 minutes. Add veal stock and red wine to pan venison sealed in and heat (simmer). Remove venison from oven and leave to rest for 3 minutes. Remove potatoes from the oven and serve venison, potatoes, carrot and turnip mash with veal sauce to garnish.

POLYNESIAN PORK STEAK

From the region of District 9920
French Polynesia

6 pork steaks
8 oz. plum sauce
½ c. flaked coconut
4 T. water
2 T. vinegar
4 T. cooking oil

1 T. soy sauce
½ tsp. salt
½ tsp. ground ginger
½ tsp. lemon peel, grated
1 dash of pepper

Trim fat from steaks. Brown steaks in oil. As they are browning, season generously with salt. Combine the rest of the ingredients and pour over steak. Cover and simmer 40 minutes or until meat is tender and done. Remove meat to a warm platter, spoon sauce over them and serve.

QUICK & EASY CHICKEN FETTUCCINE FOR TWO

From the region of District 5110
USA

1 T. butter (or margarine)
1 clove garlic (or ½ to 1 tsp. garlic pepper)
1 T. flour
¾ c. 2% milk
¾ c. grated Parmesan-Reggiano cheese

1 chicken breast, cooked and chopped or pulled apart
½ c. peas (or any frozen colorful veggie)
4 oz. pasta (mini bowties or mini penne)

Prepare pasta as directed, just before it reaches al dente, add the chicken and veggies and continue cooking until pasta is done. Strain water out and place in serving bowl. **Sauce:** Melt the butter in a saucepan over medium heat, add the garlic and sauté. (If using garlic pepper, skip this step.) Add flour and stir until thick and bubbly (add garlic pepper here). Add milk slowly, stirring constantly until combined. Add cheese, stir until smooth, pour onto the pasta, toss lightly and serve.

PASTEL DE CHOCLO

From the region of District 4320, 4340
Chile

3 T. oil
1 lg. onion, finely chopped
3 garlic cloves, minced
1 ¼ lbs. ground beef
¾ tsp. paprika
1 tsp. cumin
1 tsp. oregano
1 beef broth
1 T. flour

1 lb. frozen or fresh corn
¼ c. cornmeal
2 T. cornstarch
Milk as needed
1 tsp. sugar
Salt and pepper to taste
1 T. butter
3 tsp. sugar

Preheat oven to 375°F. Heat the oil in a sauté pan over medium flame. Add the onion and sauté until soft and lightly brown. Stir in the garlic and sauté for another 1-2 minutes. Add the ground beef, paprika, cumin, oregano, salt and pepper and sauté, until everything is mixed and the meat is almost brown. Pour in the water or stock and bring to a simmer. Sprinkle in the flour and stir well so that there are no lumps. Simmer for another 5-8 minutes until lightly thickened. Remove from heat and set aside. Place the corn, cornmeal, cornstarch and 1 teaspoon sugar in a food processor and process until well puréed. With the blade running, add the milk a little at a time until the corn forms a thick batter.

(continued)

Season to taste with salt and pepper. Melt 1 tablespoon butter in a large saucepan. Add the corn purée and cook, stirring constantly, until well thickened, about 5-8 minutes. Set aside. Spread the beef mixture in a greased casserole dish. top with the cooked corn purée and spread out evenly over the dish. Sprinkle the 3 teaspoons sugar over the corn topping. Set the dish in the oven and bake for 30-40 minutes or until bubbling and golden brown on top. Serves 6.

PIROSHKI

From the region of District 2430
Kyrgyzstan

1 lb. ground beef, lean
1 c. shredded cabbage
½ c. onion, chopped fine
½ c. parsley, chopped fine
Salt and pepper
2 T. olive oil

1 chopped hard-boiled eggs
3 pkgs. biscuit dough (30 biscuits) (or make your own bread dough)
1 raw egg, separated

In a deep skillet, sauté the onions in oil until translucent. Add ground beef and brown. Add the cabbage and let it wilt and cook. Add the parsley, salt and pepper and let it mix well. Stir in the cooked eggs. Preheat oven to 400°F. Roll each biscuit dough into thin circles. Put tablespoon of meat mixture in the center of each circle and top with another circle. Roll and dab a little of the egg white around the edges to seal the biscuit dough. Pinch and flute edges. Put fluted side down on greased cookie sheet. Brush piroshki with beaten egg yolk and bake for 10 minutes in oven until golden. Serve with sour cream or chutney.

PAD THAI

From the region of District 3330-3360
Thailand

12 oz. Pad Thai noodles
10 c. cold water
¼ c. olive oil
2 T. garlic, chopped
16 med. shrimp, shelled and deveined
4 oz. firm brown tofu, cut into ¼-inch cubes
3 eggs, beaten

¼ c. crushed unsalted peanuts
3 T. fish sauce
3 T. rice vinegar
2 T. sugar
2 tsp. paprika
1 tsp. crushed red pepper or cayenne pepper
4 oz. fresh bean sprouts
¼ c. leeks, cut into long shreds

(continued)

In a large bowl, soak noodles in cold water 45 minutes. Drain in a colander and set aside. Sauté garlic in olive oil until slightly brown. Add shrimp and tofu and sauté 1 minute. Add eggs and stir. Add noodles, fish sauce, peanuts, vinegar, paprika, sugar and red pepper and stir for 3 minutes. Remove from heat and transfer to a platter. Sprinkle with bean sprouts and leeks and serve. Serves 8.

PORK COLOMBO

From the region of District 7030
Guadeloupe

900g or 2 lbs. pork meat, cut in pieces
3 T. oil
3 chives, minced
4 parsley sticks
2 red chiles, minced
1 thyme stick
1 onion, minced
1 zucchini, cubed
1 aubergine (eggplant), cubed

4 potatoes, peeled and cubed
1 green mango, chopped in cubes
6 cloves garlic, mashed
¼ tsp. ground coriander
2 T. Colombo powder
1 pinch clove powder
Juice of 1 lemon
2 T. white vinegar
Salt and pepper to taste

Put the meat in a bowl with salt, pepper, 3 mashed garlic cloves, 1 chopped chili, the clove powder and vinegar. Let it soak for about 1 hour. Sauté in oil, the chives, onion and the rest of garlic. Then add the coriander, thyme, meat, chopped mango and chili and let the meat brown. Add the aubergine, the zucchini and the potatoes. Next, add the Colombo powder mixed with a little water. Cover the meat with water, put the lid on the saucepan and let simmer about one hour. Stir occasionally. Add additional salt and pepper if desired. Add lemon juice before serving.

RISOTTO

From the region of District 1730
Monaco

2 L. pale vegetable stock
1½ lbs. Arborio (or other risotto) rice
20 asparagus spears
1 c. white wine
8 T. black truffle coulis

¼ c. onion, finely chopped
5 garlic cloves, chopped
½ c. olive oil
Salt and freshly ground black pepper to taste
1 batch Parmesan Tuiles

(continued)

Take 14 of the asparagus spears and slice diagonally into 1-inch pieces. Bring the stock to a boil and add the asparagus. Heat olive oil in a pan and sauté the onions and garlic for about 3 minutes. Add the rice and sauté for another 3 minutes. Stir in the white wine and cook, uncovered, until all the liquid has been absorbed, stirring constantly. Add the stock with asparagus to the rice a cup at a time, each time cooking until the liquid has been absorbed before adding more. Continue cooking in this way until the rice is tender and the mixture has a creamy consistency (this will take about 25 minutes). Season with salt and black pepper. Slice the remaining asparagus spears in half lengthways. Divide the risotto between five plates and drizzle with 2 tablespoons of the black truffle coulis for each place before garnishing with the Parmesan Tuiles and cut asparagus.

RAPPIE PIE

From the region of District 7820
Canada

10 lbs. potatoes, peeled (put them into cold water as you peel them)
1 (8-lb.) whole chicken
1 lb. pork chops
2 coarsely chopped onions
1 lb. salt pork
3 qt. water
2 cans chicken gravy
Salt and pepper

Combine gravy, water, chicken, pork chops, onion, salt and pepper. Bring to a boil and simmer. When meat is cooked, remove from the stock and let it cool. Remove meat from bones. Return all bones and skin back to pot. Continue simmering for another 2 hours. Peel the potatoes. Place them in cold water to prevent browning. Run the potatoes through a juice extractor. Reserve the potato liquid to determine the exact quantity. Place the potato pulp in a big bowl or pot. Any starch settled at the bottom of the potato liquid should be added to the potato pulp. Cut salt pork into strips and fry to extract fat. Now stir into the potatoes enough liquid that measures equal to the potato liquid. When you have about half of the stock added to the potatoes, stir in the extracted salt pork fat and continue stirring in hot stock if needed, but be sure it is very well mixed and there are no potato pulp lumps and it is not runny. Mixture will be thick enough to hold a standing spoon. Butter and flour and baking casserole dish. Pour half potato mixture into pan and sprinkle entire surface of potatoes with salt and pepper. Cover evenly with chicken and pork. Top with remaining potato mixture. Preheat oven to 400°F. Bake 2¼ hours or until top has a crispy golden crust.

RIKKITA BEEF

From the region of District 7030
Saint Kitts and Nevis

2 lbs. beef or steak
2 tsp. hot pepper
6 cloves garlic
4 hot peppers, finely cut

2 tsp. curry powder
2 c. white wine or 2 c. champagne
2 c. Italian dressing

Poke holes in the beef and marinate with garlic, champagne and 4 hot peppers in plastic bag. Put in a large pan with curry powder and 2 teaspoons hot pepper and beef marinade. Cook meat until fully cooked. Place meat in bowl and pour Italian dressing on meat and serve.

SKOUDEKHARIS

From the region of District 9220
Djibouti

1 kg chicken, diced or cubed (substitute lamb if desired)
6 T. oil
4 lg. onions, chopped
Salt and black pepper to taste
1 tsp. ground cumin
1 tsp. ground cloves

2 tsp. minced garlic
1 kg fresh tomatoes, blanched, peeled and chopped
1 tsp. ground cardamom seeds
2 tsp. chopped red hot chilies
1 kg rice
2 c. water

In a large pot, sauté the onions in oil until translucent. Add the meat and cook until browned, then add the tomatoes and allow to cook for a few minutes. Add all the spices, cover with water and allow to simmer gently for one hour (may need less time for chicken and more time for lamb). When the meat is tender, add the rice and 2 cups water; bring to a boil. Reduce to a simmer and cook for 20 minutes or until the rice is done. Cook for a few more minutes if there is liquid in the pot. The dish should be dry. Serve immediately.

SNAPPER A LA SICILIANA

From the region of District 6840
USA

- 6 T. butter
- 3 T. capers, thoroughly washed and drained
- 2 T. slivered black olives
- 4 red snappers or ocean perch, ½ to ¾ lb. each, cleaned with heads and tails on
- Salt
- ½ c. olive oil
- Freshly ground black pepper
- 2 T. lemon juice
- 2 T. finely chopped fresh parsley, preferable the flat leaf Italian-type

Preheat oven to 425°F. In a 6- to 8-inch skillet, melt 4 tablespoons of butter over low heat until it becomes a light brown, but do not burn it. Stir in the capers and olives and remove pan from the heat. Wash the fish quickly inside and out, under cold running water and dry with paper towels. Salt the inside of each fish lightly. In a shallow flameproof 12-inch baking dish, heat the oil and the remaining 2 tablespoons of butter over moderate heat until it begins to sizzle. Stir in the oregano and a few grindings of black pepper into the oil mixture in baking dish. Roll the fish in the herbed fat in the baking dish. Leave the fish in the baking dish and place on the middle shelf and bake, basting the fish with the hot oil (in baking dish) every five minutes for 20-30 minutes or until the fish are firm to the touch. With a slotted spatula, carefully transfer them to a heated platter. Warm the butter and caper sauce, stir in the 2 tablespoons of lemon juice and parsley and pour it all over the fish. Serve with pasta, rice or potatoes.

STEAMED FISH

From the region of District 3310
Singapore

- 4 firm white fish filets (snapper, bass, etc.)
- 2 T. fresh ginger, grated
- 3 red chilies, seeded and chopped finely
- 3 cloves garlic, chopped finely
- 1 bunch coriander leaves, chopped
- 3 spring onions, chopped
- 2 tsp. lemon juice
- A couple lemon wedges to serve as garnish

Use a bamboo steaming basket. You may layer it with banana leaves or baking paper. Arrange the filets and top with ginger, garlic, red chilies and coriander. Cover the lid and steam over wok for 6 minutes. Remove the lid, sprinkle spring onion and lemon juice on fish. Cover and steam for another 20 seconds or until fish is cooked through. **Do not overcook!** Serve with lemon wedges with rice.

SETTLER'S BEANS, THE LENEXA WAY

From the region of District 5710
USA

- 5 brats or 5 mild Italian sausage
- 1-lb. pkg. premium smoked bacon
- 1 sweet yellow onion
- 2 (16-oz.) cans Van Camp's pork and beans
- 2 (16-oz.) cans butter beans, drained
- 2 (16-oz.) cans dark red kidney beans, drained and rinsed
- ½ c. catsup
- ½ c. spicy barbecue sauce (Gates Original)
- ½ c. brown sugar
- ½ c. sugar
- 6 T. white vinegar
- ½ tsp. salt
- 2 dashes black pepper
- 1 tsp. chili powder or ground chili to taste
- 4 T. hot and spicy mustard
- 4 T. molasses
- 1 Fresno pepper (red, med. hot pepper)
- 1 green bell pepper
- 1 T. minced garlic
- Add 2 T. liquid smoke (if cannot smoke sausage)

Hickory smoke or grill the sausage, then quarter each long ways and cut into pieces. Cook the bacon in a skillet, then remove it and cut or tear it into ½-inch pieces. Chop the onion, then sauté it in the bacon grease until soft (drain off the grease when done). Mix all ingredients in a large bowl, then transfer to the 9 x 13-inch baking dish. Cook for 1 hour at 350°F, covered. Serve warm. Recommend not eating near an open flame.

SHREDDED BEEF

From the region of District 4060
Dominican Republic

For Broth:

- 2 lbs. beef brisket
- 1 sprig parsley
- 1 bay leaf
- 3 lg. onions, peeled and quartered
- 1 garlic clove, peeled
- 1 carrot, peeled and cut into chunks
- 1 tsp. salt
- 1 tsp. peppercorns

(continued)

For Sauce:

1 lg. green bell pepper, skin removed	1 lg. onion, peeled and chopped
3 garlic cloves, peeled and minced	1 bay leaf
1 tsp. salt	1 c. tomato sauce
½ tsp. freshly ground pepper	1 c. reserved beef broth
¼ tsp. dry leaf oregano	½ c. dry white wine
⅓ c. vegetable oil	1 tsp. white wine vinegar
	1 (6-oz.) jar pimientos, drained and sliced

Place the meat in a large heavy pot and cover it with water. Add all the ingredients for the broth and bring to boil over high heat. Reduce to a simmer and cook for 2 hours. Remove the meat from the pot and set aside to cool. Reserve 1 cup of broth. **Sauce:** Cut the green pepper in half, cut the pepper into thin strips and set it aside. Mash the garlic, salt, pepper and oregano into a paste. Set aside. Heat the oil in a large skillet over medium heat. Sauté the chopped onion until it is translucent, about 4 minutes. Reduce the heat to a medium-low and stir in the garlic mixture and bay leaf and cook for two minutes. Stir in the tomato sauce, broth, wine and vinegar and simmer for 6 more minutes. While the sauce is cooking, shred the meat with your fingers into 4-inch strands. Stir the meat and the green pepper strips into the sauce, cover and simmer for about 20 minutes to blend the flavors. Remove the bay leaf, transfer the shredded beef and sauce to a serving dish and garnish with pimientos.

SALT FISH AND GREEN FIG PIE

From the region of District 7030
Saint Lucia

2½ lbs. green figs	3 sweet peppers, cut into strips
1 lb. salt fish	2 tomatoes, thinly sliced
¾ lb. cheese	1 onion, sliced
½ c. milk	½ tsp. black pepper
1 T. lime juice	1 tsp. bread crumbs

Boil the green figs until tender. Peel and mash the figs and sprinkle with lime juice. Remove the salt from the fish by soaking it in water for several hours. Remove the skin and bones and shred fish. **To prepare the dish:** Press half of the crushed fig in a greased baking pie dish. Sprinkle half of the shredded fish on fig. Spread layer of sweet peppers, then a layer of half the onion, then half the tomatoes, half the cheese and half black pepper. Repeat layers, beginning with green fig and ending with grated cheese and black pepper. Top with milk and sprinkle with bread crumbs. Bake in an oven at 180° Celsius or 250° Fahrenheit for 30 minutes or until the cheese has melted and is golden brown. If

(continued)

the cheese is getting too brown, place a loose piece of foil over the dish for a few minutes before the end of the cooking time.

STUFFED GRAPE LEAVES

From the region of District 2450
Armenia

1 c. uncooked rice, thoroughly washed
½ c. pine nuts
2 c. chopped onions
1 tsp. salt
½ c. olive oil
1 ½ c. boiling water
3 T. lemon juice

½ c. raisins
¼ tsp. cinnamon
¼ tsp. allspice
¼ tsp. black pepper
¼ tsp. paprika
½ c. chopped parsley
About 50 grape leaves

Sauté onions in olive oil. Add rice, pine nuts and salt and simmer for 30 minutes or until all the water is absorbed. Mix in the remaining ingredients, except grape leaves, and let stand for 15 minutes. Roll enough mixture into each grape leaf carefully folding the leaf so that mixture is secure inside. Arrange on platter and serve.

SAUERBRATEN AND POTATO DUMPLINGS

From the region of District 6270
USA

Sauerbraten:

2- to 3-lb. boneless chuck roast
½ c. flour
Salt and pepper to taste
2-3 T. cooking oil (or enough just to cover bottom of pot)

2 to 2 ½ c. water
¼ c. vinegar
2 T. pickling spices (preferably bundled in a square of cheesecloth to make a sachet)

Cut meat into serving-size pieces, about 2 x 2 inch. Combine flour, salt and pepper and coat pieces of meat with the mixture. Heat cooking oil in a Nesco or Dutch oven, then brown meat on all sides in hot oil. Add water, vinegar and pickling spices. Liquid should just cover the meat. Bring to a boil, then reduce heat to 250°F and simmer until meat is tender, about 2 ½ to 3 hours. Remove pickling spices before serving. A gravy should have formed in the pot, but if the liquid needs to be thickened, add flour as needed.

(continued)

Potato Dumplings:

4-5 med. potatoes (or instant potatoes, prepared serving for 4)
1 egg
1 to 1½ c. flour
Salt, pepper and herbs to taste

Prepare potatoes by cooking and mashing. Refrigerate mashed potatoes for several hours (potatoes must be cold or dumplings will fall apart). When ready to cook the dumplings, add egg, 1 cup flour and herbs and seasonings to the mashed potatoes and mix gently until a stiff dough forms. Add more flour as needed. Bring a large pot of water to a boil, then form dough into balls and gently lower them into the boiling water. (I usually make balls larger than a golf ball, but smaller than a tennis ball.) Boil gently for 5-6 minutes until cooked through.

SAUERBRATEN

From the region of District 1930-1950
Germany

1½ c. cider vinegar
3 c. water
2 med. onions, coarsely chopped
2 tsp. salt
3 bay leaves
1 lemon, cut into 8 wedges
1 tsp. whole black peppercorns
½ tsp. whole cloves
5-lb. top round roast
½ c. vegetable oil
¼ c. all-purpose flour
1 c. beef broth
⅔ c. packed dark brown sugar
¾ c. gingersnap cookie crumbs

Combine vinegar, water, onions, salt, bay leaves, lemons, peppercorns, cloves and bring to a boil. Cool. Place beef in bowl. Pour marinade over. Cover and chill 2 days, turning beef every eight hours. Preheat oven to 350°F. Remove beef from marinade and reserve the marinade. Place beef in roasting pan and roast beef until tender, about 2½ hours. Transfer beef to carving board; cool. Pour any accumulated juices from roasting pan into marinade. Strain marinade and reserve 2 cups; discard the rest. Fry the flour in oil in a heavy large skillet. Stir over medium heat until dark brown, about 10 minutes. Gradually mix in 2 cups marinade. Boil until thick, stirring often, about 8 minutes. Mix in sugar and cookie crumbs. Bring mixture to a boiling point. Season to taste with salt and pepper. Turn off heat. Slice beef and arrange in large baking dish. Pour sauce over meat and serve. If preparing a day in advance, preheat oven to 400°F. Bake beef until heated through, about 15 minutes and then pour warmed sauce over it.

SHRIMP JAMBALAYA

From the region of District 6840
USA

2 lbs. peeled and deveined shrimp
4 c. cooked rice
2 T. tomato paste
1 tsp. sugar
4 cloves garlic, minced
1 c. onion, chopped
2 c. water

½ c. celery and bell pepper, chopped
¼ lb. oleo
½ tsp. flour
½ c. shallots and parsley, chopped fine
Tony Chachere's seasoning to taste

Cook rice separately. Chop shrimp and set aside. Melt oleo and add chopped onions, celery, bell pepper and garlic in a heavy pot. Cook, uncovered, over medium heat until onions are wilted. Add tomato paste and cook, stirring for about 15 minutes. Lower heat if necessary to avoid sticking. Add 1½ cups water. Season to taste. Add sugar and cook, uncovered, over medium heat for about 40 minutes, stirring occasionally or until oil floats to the top. Add shrimp and stir for another 20 minutes. Dissolve flour in ½ cup water and add. Cook another 5 minutes. Mix ingredients with cooked rice, add shallots and parsley. Mix again. This recipe can be doubled easily to feed a hungry bunch. Serves 6-8.

SPICY RICE WITH BEEF

From the region of District 1470
Denmark

2dl rice equals 170g
4dl water
2-3 tsp. curry
¼ tsp. pepper
A twig of thyme
4 tsp. dry stock
½ tsp. salt
500g beef, minced
200g maize

2 onions, chopped
2 garlic cloves
2 leeks in rings
1 red or green paprika, roughly chopped
250g peas
Parsley, chopped
2 tsp. salt
Pepper

Fry curry and pepper in oil; add boiling water with stock, then add the rinsed rice, salt and a twig of thyme. Bring to boil and cook at the lowest heat for 20 minutes. Fry onions, garlic and meat in oil. Add the leek rings and maybe a little water. Add maize when the meat mix is boiling. Finally add the peas, chopped paprika and parsley. Taste before serving. Meat mixture and rice may be mixed. Serve with a green salad. Serves 4 pairs.

TUNA PILAF

From the region of District 6420
USA

1 sm. onion, thinly sliced
½ c. diagonally sliced celery
1 T. vegetable oil
1 (10-oz.) pkg. frozen mixed vegetables

½ c. water
1 (5-oz.) can tuna, drained well
1 (8-oz.) can sliced water chestnuts, drained
⅓ c. soy sauce

In a large heavy skillet (electric skillet works well). Cook and stir onion and celery in hot oil until onion is tender. Add mixed vegetables and water. Heat just to boiling; cover tightly and simmer for 10 minutes or until vegetables are tender. Add remaining ingredients; stir/toss gently until well mixed. Heat through and serve.

PASTELLES

From the region of District 7030
Trinidad & Tobago

3 c. pre-cooked cornmeal
3 lg. chicken breasts, cooked with a dash of ginger and thyme
1 lb. beef briskets
3 lg. white potatoes, diced
2 lg. carrots, diced
2 med. onions, diced
4 cloves garlic, minced
2 T. green seasoning (thyme and basil)

1 seeded Scotch bonnet
2 tsp. chicken bouillon powder
½ c. raisins
1 c. sliced green olives
1-inch cube fresh ginger
1 T. olive oil
1 tsp. salt
¼ c. vegetable oil
Banana leaves or aluminum foil

Dice the beef into ¼-inch cubes and keep aside. Dice onions, potatoes and carrots into ¼ cubes. Place olive oil in a large pot with a lid and add the Scotch bonnet, onions, minced garlic and green seasoning. Cook on medium until onions and garlic are soft and add beef and cook on high heat until no longer pink. Stir in chicken, potatoes and carrots and bouillon powder. Cover and simmer on medium-low heat for 10-15 minutes until the potatoes are cooked. Stir the olives and raisins. Taste and add salt if needed. Set this filling aside to cool. Mix cornmeal with 4 cups warm water and 1 teaspoon salt. Make a soft but manageable dough. Form dough into balls the size of an egg. Warm vegetable oil and lightly coat banana leaf or foil squares with oil. Press out each ball of dough on prepared leaf or foil. Place ⅔ cup of filling on flattened dough and fold dough around the meat filling. Fold up the

(continued)

leaf or foil to secure the pastelles. Tie leaf packages with string, not needed for foil packages if folded tightly. If pastelles will not be eaten immediately, freeze the uncooked in freezer bags. Otherwise, steam packages for 30 minutes in a covered pot.

WIENER SCHNITZEL

From the region of District 1910, 1920
Austria

2½ lbs. veal or pork
1¼ c. all-purpose flour
4 eggs
2 T. vegetable oil

Salt and pepper to taste
4½ c. bread crumbs
¼ c. oil for frying

Cut the veal into ½-inch strips. Roll strips in flour and keep aside. Beat eggs, 2 tablespoons oil, salt and pepper in a shallow bowl. Coat the veal strips in this mixture and then roll in bread crumbs and fry in the hot ¼ cup oil until golden brown.

CHICKEN SATAY WITH PEANUT SAUCE

From the region of District 3310
Malaysia/Singapore

½ chicken, deboned and cut into 2 x 3cm

15 bamboo skewers/satay sticks

Blended Ingredients:

2cm galangal
2cm ginger
5 cloves garlic
2 T. coriander powder
1 T. fennel powder

2 T. turmeric powder
Salt
Sugar
3 T. cooking oil

Marinate the chicken with the pounded galangal, ginger, garlic, coriander powder, fennel powder, turmeric powder, sugar and salt and mix together. Thread as kebabs 5 pieces of the chicken in each skewer. Keep aside for 30 minutes. Grill the chicken over burning coals, constantly sprinkling cooking oil over the meat. Turn over and continue grilling until the chicken is cooked.

Peanut Sauce:

500g dry fry peanuts and ground

(continued)

Blended:

1cm galangal	2 cardamoms
1cm ginger	3 cloves
4 cloves garlic	1 star anise
10 shallots	1 inch cinnamon sticks
2 T. chili powder	2 T. cooking oil
1 stalk lemon grass, smashed	Salt
1 T. coriander powder	Sugar
½ T. fennel powder	½ L. water

Fry in oil the blended ingredients, galangal, ginger, garlic and shallots until fragrant and add the chili powder, lemon grass, coriander powder, fennel powder, cardamoms, cloves, star anise, cinnamon sticks, salt, sugar and water and peanuts. Simmer until the sauce thickens. **To serve:** Arrange a few sticks of chicken satay on a plate and serve with a bowl of peanut sauce, cucumber and sliced onion. Satay also goes very well with compressed rice.

KHICHERI (Spiced Rice)

From the region of District 3030
India

1 lb. rice	1 tsp. garam masala
4 T. green dhal	6 cloves garlic
2 lg. onions	1 piece ginger
2 sm. potatoes	5-6 green chilies
1 (2-inch) piece coconut	½ bunch coriander leaves
1 tsp. turmeric powder	Oil
1 tsp. red chili powder	Ghee
1 tsp. cumin seeds	Salt to taste

Chop onions and green chilies finely. Mince the coriander leaves, ginger and garlic. Peel the potatoes and cut into small cubes. Grind the coconut piece to a fine paste. Fry onions in a combination of 1 tablespoon ghee-1 tablespoon oil. When the onions are light brown, add the minced garlic, ginger and green chilies. Then add the garam masala together with the turmeric, red chili powder, cumin seeds and ground coconut. Fry for a while, put in the rice and dhal and fry both until crisp. Pour in warm water until it is about 2 inches above the level of the rice. If the water dries up, more warm water may be added. Add potato cubes and salt. When the water starts bubbling, lower the heat and simmer until rice is done. Sprinkle coriander leaves on top before serving.

MOUSSAKA

From the region of District 2470-2484
Greece

2 lg. eggplants
1 ¼ lbs. ground beef or lamb
Vegetable oil
2 med. onions, chopped
2 cloves garlic, minced
1 tsp. salt
1 c. canned tomatoes
2 T. tomato paste

¼ tsp. thyme
½ tsp. oregano
½ tsp. nutmeg
3 T. chopped parsley
¾ c. red wine
2 unbeaten eggs
½ c. bread crumbs
1 c. grated Parmesan cheese

White Sauce:

¾ c. butter
¾ c. flour
3 c. milk

5 egg yolks
½ tsp. salt
¼ tsp. pepper

Skin the eggplant and cut into ½-inch slices. Sprinkle with salt and set aside for about 40 minutes. Rinse and pat dry. Brown the eggplant in a little oil as possible and set aside. Brown meat in vegetable oil with onions and garlic. Add salt, tomatoes, tomato paste, thyme, oregano, nutmeg, parsley and wine. Cover and simmer for 30 minutes. Cool. Mix in unbeaten eggs and half of the crumbs and stir until well mixed. **To assemble:** Sprinkle bottom of a 13 x 9-inch baking dish with remaining crumbs. Cover with the eggplant. Spoon meat mixture over the eggplant. Pour white sauce over this mixture. Top with cheese. Put another layer of eggplant, meat and white sauce and cover with cheese and bake at 350°F for 45 minutes. **For the white sauce:** Melt butter. Add flour slowly, stirring constantly. Remove from heat. Slowly stir in the milk. Return to heat and stir until the sauce thickens. Beat egg yolks well. Gradually stir yolks, salt and pepper into the sauce. Blend well.

Desserts

Helpful Hints

- Keep eggs at room temperature to create greater volume when whipping egg whites for meringue.

- Pie dough can be frozen. Roll dough out between sheets of plastic wrap, stack in a pizza box, and keep the box in the freezer. Defrost in the fridge and use as needed. Use within 2 months.

- Place your pie plate on a cake stand when ready to flute the edges of the pie. The cake stand will make it easier to turn the pie plate, and you won't have to stoop over.

- When making decorative pie edges, use a spoon for a scalloped edge. Use a fork to make crosshatched and herringbone patterns.

- When cutting butter into flour for pastry dough, the process is easier if you cut the butter into small pieces before adding it to the flour.

- Pumpkin and other custard-style pies are done when they jiggle slightly in the middle. Fruit pies are done when the pastry is golden, juices bubble, and fruit is tender.

- Keep the cake plate clean while frosting by sliding 6-inch strips of waxed paper under each side of the cake. Once the cake is frosted and the frosting is set, pull the strips away, leaving a clean plate.

- Create a quick decorating tube to ice your cake with chocolate. Put chocolate in a heat-safe, zipper-lock plastic bag. Immerse it in simmering water until the chocolate is melted. Snip off the tip of one corner, and squeeze the chocolate out of the bag.

- Achieve professionally decorated cakes with a silky, molten look by blow-drying the frosting with a hair dryer until the frosting melts slightly.

- To ensure that you have equal amounts of batter in each pan when making a layered cake, use a kitchen scale to measure the weight.

- Prevent cracking in your cheesecake by placing a shallow pan of hot water on the bottom oven rack and keeping the oven door shut during baking.

- A cheesecake needs several hours to chill and set.

- For a perfectly cut cheesecake, dip the knife into hot water and clean it after each cut. You can also hold a length of dental floss taut and pull it down through the cheesecake to make a clean cut across the diameter of the cake.

DESSERTS

PEPPARKAKOR (Ginger Cookies)

From the region of District 2350-2360
Sweden

¾ c. butter
⅔ c. brown sugar
⅔ c. molasses
1 lg. egg
1 tsp. baking soda

1 tsp. cinnamon
1 tsp. ginger
½ tsp. cloves
3¼ c. flour, sifted

Preheat oven to 350°F. Mix together the butter, sugar and molasses until smooth and creamy. Add the egg and beat well. Stir in the baking soda, cinnamon, ginger and cloves. Slowly add the flour to make a stiff dough. Add enough flour to make dough easy to handle without sticking to fingers or cookie press. Using a cookie press, press out several long strips of dough on ungreased cookie sheets. Bake for 7 minutes until cookies are medium brown. Remove them from the oven and let rest for 1 minute before cutting them into 2-inch pieces. Remove cookies from cookie sheets when cool. Store in an airtight container. Makes 7-8 dozen.

PAPAYA PIE

From the region of District 7030
Antigua and Barbuda

6 c. diced ripe papayas, no seeds
3 tsp. lime juice
½ tsp. lime zest
Pinch of cinnamon

1 dash of orange extract
½ c. flour
½ c. sugar
4 egg whites
1 lg. pre-baked pie shell (sweet)

Coarsely mash the papayas. Add lime juice, zest, cinnamon and orange extract. Fold in flour and sugar. Beat egg whites until stiff and fold into mixture. Pour into pie shell. Bake 25 minutes until top is just brown. Serve chilled.

QUICK CHEESECAKE

From the region of District 6670
USA

1½ c. graham cracker crumbs
2 T. butter
2 tsp. sugar
2 (8-oz.) pkgs. cream cheese
1 c. sugar

5 egg yolks
1 pt. sour cream
1 tsp. vanilla extract
1 tsp. lemon juice
5 egg whites, beaten stiff

Mix crumbs, butter and sugar and line a cake pan. Mix cream cheese, sugar, yolks, sour cream, vanilla extract and lemon juice. Carefully mix in egg whites. Pour into crumb pan. Bake at 300°F for 1 hour. Cool. Chill and serve.

PUMPKIN PATCH SQUARES

From the region of District 6510
USA

Bottom Crust:

1 c. flour
½ c. each: oatmeal, soft butter and brown sugar

Topping:

½ c. each: chopped pecans and brown sugar

2 T. butter

Pumpkin Filling:

2 c. pumpkin
1 can evaporated milk
2 eggs
¾ c. sugar

½ tsp. salt
1 tsp. cinnamon
½ tsp. ginger
¼ tsp. cloves

Combine bottom crust ingredients until crumbly. Press into 13 x 9-inch pan. Bake at 350°F for 15 minutes. Blend pumpkin ingredients and pour over baked crust. Bake at 350°F for 20 minutes. Combine topping ingredients and sprinkle over pumpkin filling. Bake at 350°F for 15 minutes. Cool and cut into squares.

POTATO CHIP PECAN COOKIES

From the region of District 6900-6920
USA

1 pkg. Duncan Hines golden sugar cookie mix
1 egg
1 T. water
1½ c. crushed potato chips, divided
½ c. chopped pecans

Preheat oven to 375°F. Grease cookie sheets lightly. Combine cookie mix, contents of buttery flavor packet from mix, egg, water, ½ cup potato chips and pecans in large bowl. Stir until thoroughly blended. Form dough into 36 (1-inch) balls. Roll in remaining 1 cup crushed potato chips. Place 2 inches apart on cookie sheets. Flatten dough with fork. Bake at 375°F for 8-10 minutes or until golden brown. Cool 1 minute on cookie sheets. Remove to cooling racks. Cool completely. Store in airtight container.

PAWPAW PIE

From the region of District 9150
Congo

1 unbaked pie crust
½ c. lemon juice
1 med. pawpaw, skin and seeds removed
2 lg. eggs
Sugar to taste
1 c. milk
1 tsp. grated lemon peel

Thinly slice the pawpaw (papaya) and marinate in lemon juice for at least 2 hours. Drain well and place the slices onto the pie shell. Beat the egg with milk and sugar. Add grated lemon peel. Pour over fruit and bake in a hot oven for about 35 minutes. You may also make the pie by mashing the pawpaw and mixing with other ingredients, including 1 teaspoon cornflour. Bake as above and serve with whipped cream.

RIBEI (Semolina Dessert)

From the region of District 2000
Liechtenstein

1 lb. semolina
1¼ c. milk
1 c. water
1 level T. sea salt
Grapeseed oil
40g butter
Sugar, to garnish

(continued)

Combine the milk, water and salt in a pan. Bring to a boil, then add the semolina. Take off the heat, cover and allow to soak for at least 3 hours. Heat grapeseed oil in a pan, add the soaked semolina mixture and cook over medium heat, stirring frequently for 5 minutes. Gradually add the butter and continue to cook in this manner for about 20 minutes more, or until golden brown crumbs begin to form in the mixture. Turn into a bowl, garnish with plenty of sugar, then serve accompanied by a coffee and fruit compote.

RAISIN CARROT CAKE

From the region of District 6440
USA

½ c. butter or margarine
1 c. sugar
½ tsp. grated orange peel
2 eggs
⅓ c. water
½ c. applesauce
2 c. sifted flour

1½ tsp. baking powder
1½ tsp. baking soda
¼ tsp. nutmeg
½ tsp. cloves
1½ c. raisins (may be chopped)
2 c. finely grated carrots

Blend together butter, sugar and orange peel. Beat in eggs, one at a time, and add water and applesauce. Sift together dry ingredients and beat into creamed mixture. Stir in raisins and grated carrots. Pour into 2 (8-inch) round pans or one (8 x 12-inch) oblong greased pan. Bake at 350°F for 35-45 minutes until toothpick in center comes out clean. Cool completely before frosting. Frost with favorite cream cheese or butter cream frosting. Sprinkle chopped nut topping (optional).

RICE PUDDING

From the region of District 4240
Costa Rica

3 c. rice
5 c. milk
4 c. sugar
2 T. vanilla
½ tsp. ground cinnamon

½ tsp. ground cloves or 6 whole cloves
½ tsp. grated fresh nutmeg
½ c. butter
1 c. raisins

Cook rice, uncovered, in 9 cups of water for 45 minutes until rice is quite soft. Stir in other ingredients and simmer for ½ hour. Serve warm, or refrigerate at least four hours to serve cold.

RUM CAKE

From the region of District 7230
Bermuda

1 ½ c. chopped pecans
1 pkg. yellow cake mix
1 (3.4-oz.) pkg. instant vanilla pudding mix

4 eggs
½ c. water
½ c. vegetable oil
½ c. rum

Glaze:

½ c. butter
¼ c. water

1 c. white sugar
¾ c. dark rum

Heat oven to 325°F (165° Celsius). Grease and flour a 10- to 12-cup bundt pan. Sprinkle the nuts on the bottom of the pan. In a large bowl, mix together the cake mix, pudding mix, eggs, water and oil and rum. Pour over the nuts. Bake in the preheated oven for 50 minutes or until a toothpick inserted into the cake comes out clean. Let rest for 15 minutes and then invert onto a serving platter. In a saucepan, melt butter, sugar and water until it comes to a boil. Continue boiling for 4 minutes. Get it off the heat and stir in the rum. Brush glaze over top and sides of cake.

RUSSIAN ALMOND COOKIE

From the region of District 2230
Belarus

2 c. sifted cake flour
½ tsp. almond extract
½ tsp. salt
¼ tsp. vanilla

1 c. butter
½ c. almonds, split in half
½ c. powdered sugar

Sift flour and salt twice. Cream butter; gradually add sugar, beating well. Add flavoring. Gradually stir in flour, mixing well. Chill and roll into balls the size of a walnut. Flatten and place on a greased baking sheet. Press half an almond on top of each cookie. Bake in a slow oven (300°F) until brown, 18-20 minutes. Yield: about 48 cookies.

SHREWSBURY CAKES

From the region of District 1030-1140
England

2½ c. all-purpose flour
1 tsp. ground cinnamon
1 tsp. ground nutmeg
1 tsp. baking soda
1 tsp. cream of tartar

1 c. butter, softened
½ c. granulated sugar
2 eggs
Ground nutmeg (opt.)

Mix together flour, cinnamon, nutmeg, baking soda and cream of tartar and set aside. Beat butter with an electric mixer on high speed for 30 seconds. Add sugar; beat until fluffy. Add eggs, one at a time, beating well. Add flour mixture, a quarter at a time, beating well until incorporated. Chill the dough for about an hour. Roll dough about ¼ inch thick on a lightly floured surface. Cut into 2½-inch rounds with a cookie cutter. Place on ungreased cookie sheet. Sprinkle with nutmeg if desired. Bake in a 375°F oven for 7-9 minutes or until very light brown. Enjoy Shrewsbury cakes!

SOUR CREAM POUND CAKE

From the region of District 7570
USA

½ lb. butter
3 c. sugar
6 eggs
1 c. dairy sour cream
3 c. pre-sifted all-purpose flour

¼ tsp. baking soda
Pinch of salt
½ tsp. almond extract
1 tsp. vanilla

All ingredients should be at room temperature. Preheat oven to 325°F. Cream butter in a large mixing bowl. Gradually add 3 cups sugar, beating constantly. Add 2 eggs, one at a time. Then add 1 cup sour cream. Add 4 eggs, one at a time, scraping bottom and sides of bowl and beating well. Sift together 3 cups pre-sifted all-purpose flour, ¼ teaspoon soda and pinch of salt and add to sour cream mixture. Beat and beat, scraping bowl often. Add ½ teaspoon almond extract and 1 teaspoon vanilla. Turn into greased and floured tube pan and place in preheated oven for 1½ hours. This is a very moist cake, keeps well and may be frozen.

SAN KA YA (Thai Coconut Custard)

From the region of District 3330-3360
Thailand

5 eggs
¼ c. brown sugar
¼ c. white sugar
1 c. thick coconut milk

1 c. winter squash, seeded and rind removed, thinly sliced or shredded

Beat eggs well in a mixing bowl. Add coconut milk and stir. Add brown and white sugars and stir until dissolved. Add squash and stir well. Pour mixture into a 9 x 9-inch baking pan. Place ½ cup water into a steamer or Dutch oven large enough to hold the custard pan. Bring water to a boil over high heat and place pan with custard inside. Be sure that the water does not get into the custard. Cover and steam over high heat for 30 minutes. Serve at room temperature.

TRUFFLE LAYER CAKE

From the region of District 1470
Denmark

Cake Bottoms:

1 ¼ dl milk
65g chocolate
65g butter
2 eggs

170g sugar
170g wheat flour
½ tsp. sodium bicarbonate
   (alternative baking soda)

Filling:

75g orange marmalade
2 sm. oranges
17 sm. macaroons
7 ½ dl double creme

400g bitter chocolate with no less than 50% cacao
Orange liqueur

Bottoms: Melt the chocolate with 2 tablespoons of water. Stir in milk and butter and bring it to boil. Cool it. Beat the egg yolks with the sugar and stir in the chocolate milk. Mix the flour and the sodium bicarbonate and mix with the egg chocolate milk. Whip the egg whites stiff and turn them gently into the mixture. Pour the dough into a round buttered form, with a loose bottom, diameter 24 centimeters, and place it in a well warm oven (200° Celsius) approximately 30 minutes. Control with a knitting pin or similar, if it's done. **Filling:** Stir the orange marmalade with juice of one orange. Cut the chocolate bottom into 3 chocolate bottoms, and smear orange marmalade/juice mix on top of the 2 bottoms. Chop and melt carefully the chocolate over water bath, cool

(continued)

it a little and turn it into the light whipped cream, then orange liqueur. Soak the macaroons with the rest of the orange juice. Place one bottom on a dish, cover with half of the macaroon mix, then 1/5 of the truffle creme, next layer like this, and on top the last bottom, then cover with the rest of the truffle creme. Place in refrigerator for at least 4 hours before serving. Decorate with scratched chocolate or fresh fruit. Can be served with some fresh fruit and/or raspberry sauce (not too sweet). Can easily be frozen, then thaw for one hour or more. Makes 8-10 pieces.

TAMBI ZA NAZI NA ZABIBU

(Vermicelli Cooked in Coconut Milk with Raisins)

From the region of District 9200
Tanzania

½ lb. vermicelli
2½ c. hot coconut milk
¼ lb. sugar
500-750ml hot water (2-3 c.)
¼ lb. raisins, washed and soaked in warm water for 60 minutes

A few drops vanilla extract
2 T. ground cardamom
Slivered, blanched almonds (opt.)

Cook the coconut milk, vermicelli, sugar, cardamom and vanilla extract on high for about 2 minutes. Reduce the heat to a low simmer, then cook, uncovered, for about 30 minutes or until the liquid has evaporated and the vermicelli is tender (if the vermicelli is still too hard add a little more coconut milk and continue cooking). Add the raisins and almonds, then stir to combine. Continue to cook for about 3 minutes to heat through, then take off the heat. Spread on a large platter and serve.

GUYANA BLACK CAKE

From the region of District 7030
Guyana

¼ lb. cherries
¼ lb. prunes
¼ lb. dried cherries
¼ lb. currants
¼ lb. candied citrus
3 c. rum
1 lb. brown sugar for browning
½ lb. butter

½ lb. brown sugar
½ tsp. baking powder
1 tsp. cinnamon
½ lb. flour
12 eggs
4 oz. lemon peel
½ lb. butter

(continued)

Soak the dried fruit in 2 cups of rum. Store in airtight container for two weeks. Heat 1 pound of the sugar until it turns dark brown. It will smoke and smell burnt. When it turns brown black pour in ¼ cup water and turn off the heat. Be careful not to burn yourself with the splatter. This is the caramel to brown the cake. Let it cool. Grind the soaked fruit in a processor. Cream the butter and sugar. Add the eggs, beat well. Add the soaked fruits and rum. When it is well blended, pour the caramel. Add the flour with the baking powder, cinnamon and lemon peel. Pour mixture in a baking pan and bake in a slow oven (about 300°F) for two hours. Brush cake with the remaining cup of rum. Remove cake from pan after 24 hours. Store airtight in the refrigerator.

GIBANICA (Cheese Strudel Pie)

From the region of District 2483
Serbia

1 pkt. prepared filo (phyllo) pastry
1 kg cottage cheese
6 eggs
1 ¼ tsp. salt

½ c. oil
1 c. milk
½ c. buttermilk
4 T. butter
1 T. milk

Mix cottage cheese and eggs. Beat thoroughly after you add each egg. Season with the salt, then beat in the oil, milk and buttermilk. Mix until thoroughly combined. Place one sheet of filo dough in the base of a deep pan. Dip almost all the remaining pastry sheets in the cottage cheese batter and place them in the pan any which way, broken sheets and all, so that you have many overlapping layers (but reserve 2, undipped pieces for the top along with ½ cup batter). Place the last 2 filo dough pieces to cover the top of the dish, then spoon the remaining batter and the 1 tablespoon milk over the top. Finely dice the butter and use to dot the top of the dish. Transfer to an oven preheated to 300°F and bake gently for about 40 minutes or until nicely browned on top. Remove from the oven and gently invert onto a plate. Serve warm, sliced into squares and accompany with a glass of beer.

GRAHAM CRACKER BROWNIES

From the region of District 7090
USA

2 (14-oz.) cans sweetened condensed milk
12-oz. bag chocolate chips (can substitute butterscotch chips)

13-oz. box graham cracker crumbs

(continued)

Preheat oven to 350°F. Grease and flour a 9 x 13-inch pan. Stir together all ingredients. Spoon into the 9 x 13-inch pan. Bake for 30-35 minutes until middle is set. Cool before cutting.

JENNY'S MUFFINS

From the region of District 5100
USA

2 c. almond meal
1 tsp. apple cider vinegar
1 tsp. baking soda
3 bananas
Handful chopped walnuts
3 eggs

2 T. maple syrup
⅛ c. oil (grapeseed/canola)
Pinch of salt
1½ c. shredded carrots (about 3 lg. carrots)
1 tsp. vanilla

Butter 2 muffin tins. Mash bananas with a fork. Add eggs, vanilla, maple syrup, oil and vinegar. Mix well. Add 2 cups almond flour, baking soda, salt and mix well. Gradually add to the egg mixture. Add the nuts and the carrots and mix well. Pour into the muffin tins and bake at 350°F (or 180° Celsius) until done.

KAYMAKLI KURU KAYISI (Cream-Stuffed Apricots)

From the region of District 2420-2440
Turkey

1½ lb. dried apricots
3 c. sugar
3 c. water
1 tsp. lemon juice

1 lb. mascarpone (sweet cheese)
1 c. pistachio nuts, chopped

Soak the apricots in cold water for 24 hours and drain. Heat the sugar and water together over medium heat for 10 minutes, then add apricots. Cook the apricots until they are tender and syrup is formed. Add the lemon juice and remove from heat. With a slotted spoon, transfer apricots to a plate to cool. When cool, open the apricots and fill with sweet cheese. Arrange the apricots (slit side up) on a platter, pouring over them as much syrup as they can absorb. Garnish with grated nuts. Usually serves 20.

KOLACHE

From the region of District 2240
Czech Republic

½ c. warm water
2 (.25-oz.) pkgs. active dry yeast
1 c. warm milk (110°F/45° Celsius)
½ c. white sugar

1 tsp. salt
½ c. melted shortening
2 c. sifted all-purpose flour
2 eggs
3 c. all-purpose flour

Filling:

Cooked apricot halves, chopped
1 c. brown sugar

⅓ c. chopped almonds
⅓ tsp. cinnamon

Prepare yeast by mixing it with ½ cup of lukewarm water. Set aside to rise for 15 minutes. In a big mixing bowl, mix together 1 cup milk, ½ cup sugar and 1 teaspoon salt. Add milk slightly warm. Add ½ cup melted shortening and 2 cups sifted flour. Mix well. Add in 2 beaten eggs and yeast mixture and mix well. Set aside to rest until bubbly. Add 3 cups of flour and blend well. Knead well and set aside to rise for 45 minutes. Punch down and let rise again for 1 hour. Mix all the ingredients of the filling together. Roll dough out on a floured board and cut 3-inch squares. Make an indentation in the middle and fill with one teaspoon of the filling. Bake at 425°F for 15 minutes. Remove and cool. Serve warm or cool.

KAHLUA COFFEE BROWNIES

From the region of District 6840
USA

1 c. unsalted butter
1 T. instant coffee
4 oz. unsweetened chocolate
4 whole eggs
2 c. sugar

1½ c. all-purpose flour
⅛ tsp. salt
1 c. bittersweet chocolate chips
1 c. white chocolate chips

Icing:

1 (8-oz.) pkg. cream cheese, room temp.
¼ c. unsalted butter

2 T. Kahlua
2½ c. powdered sugar

Melt the butter in a medium saucepan over low heat. Add the coffee and stir until dissolved. Remove the saucepan from the heat, add the unsweetened chocolate and stir until smooth. Add the eggs, one at a time, and continue mixing. Add the sugar and mix well. Add the flour

(continued)

and salt and gently combine. Using a spatula, fold the chips into the batter. Spread the batter evenly into the prepared baking dish. Bake at 350°F for 20 minutes or until a toothpick comes out clean. Remove and let cool before icing. In a large bowl, beat the cheese and butter for 3 minutes until creamy. Add the Kahlua and powdered sugar and mix until completely blended. Using a spatula, spread the icing on the brownies. Serves 12.

KNAFEH

From the region of District 2450
Palestine

½ lb. phyllo pastry
8 oz. melted butter
4 c. fresh milk
2½ c. sugar
1 c. water

6 T. semolina
2½ c. ricotta cheese
1 T. freshly squeezed lemon juice
2 c. diced pistachios

Put phyllo pastry in a large bowl and pour melted butter over it and shred it. Divide it into 2 parts. Spread ½ of the phyllo lightly in a 12 x 12-inch baking tray. Bake at 350° until pastry gets brownish, then remove it and let it cool. Boil milk in a pot and add semolina and ½ cup sugar, mixing constantly. When the mixture gets thick, remove it from fire and add the ricotta cheese and stir well. Spread the mixture on the baked pastry. Cover the mixture lightly with the second part of the phyllo pastry. Bake at 350°F until it gets brownish. Timing varies according to oven. **For the syrup:** Mix 2 cups sugar, water and lemon juice. Bring it to a boil and let the sugar melt. Cut the knafeh into square pieces, pour some of the syrup on each square and add pistachios on top.

KUGLICE OF SMOKAVA (Fig Balls)

From the region of District 1913
Croatia

400g figs
300g sugar
50g walnuts, ground

Lemon peel and juice
Orange peel and juice
Little rum

Cut the figs, add ground walnuts, chopped lemon and orange peel and juice, rum and sugar. Mix well together. Roll them into little balls and roll them in sugar.

BISKUTTINI TAR-RAHAL (Village Biscuits)

From the region of District 2110
Malta

1 lb. flour	Grated rind of 1 lemon
1 lb. sugar	Pinch of clove powder
4 eggs	Pinch of cinnamon powder
1¼ tsp. baking powder	Royal Icing

Beat the eggs, add the sugar and beat again. Add flour, baking powder, lemon rind and spice powder. With the aid of a spoon, form the mixture into round biscuits. Place on pre-greased and floured baking trays. Bake in a moderate oven for some 15-20 minutes or until the biscuits are golden. When cool, drizzle with Royal Icing.

BERRY COFFEE CAKE

From the region of District 7780
USA

Cake:

1½ c. flour	2 eggs
2 tsp. baking powder	¼ c. milk
½ tsp. baking soda	6 T. melted butter
½ tsp. salt	1 tsp. vanilla extract
½ c. honey	

Topping:

2 c. blueberries, fresh or frozen	½ c. honey
1 T. flour	2 T. lemon juice

Place blueberries in bottom of a greased 9-inch cake pan, distribute evenly. Sprinkle with flour and drizzle with honey and lemon juice (topping). Set aside. In a small bowl, combine flour, baking powder, baking soda and salt. Set aside. In a medium bowl, combine honey, eggs, milk and vanilla; beat with a fork until well mixed. Add flour mixture and mix well. Stir in melted butter and mix well. Pour batter over blueberries in pan. Bake at 350°F for 30-35 minutes or until toothpick inserted in center comes out clean. Cool in pan on wire rack for 15 minutes. Invert pan on plate and serve. Top with whipped cream if desired.

BLACK BUTTER (Apple Butter)

From the region of District 1110
Jersey/Channel Island

5 lbs. apples
2 pt. sweet apple cider
1¼ lbs. sugar

1 tsp. clove powder
2 tsp. cinnamon powder
Clarified butter

Core and peel the apples and chop into small pieces. Next, boil the apple cider until it is reduced in half. Add the apples and cook until they are tender. Remove the apples and purée them. Return them to the pot and add the sugar and spices and cook for another one hour until the mixture thickens and turns brown. Pour into clean jelly jars and top with clarified butter. Seal and keep for at least 3 months. The butter should turn dark brown, almost black. Serve as a side to any dish.

BOLO POLANA (Cashew Nut and Potato Cake)

From the region of District 9210
Mozambique

3 med. sized boiling potatoes, peeled and quartered
¾ lb. unsalted butter, softened
2½ c. sugar
3 T. flour
3 c. roasted, unsalted cashews, finely chopped in blender or nut grinder

3 tsp. fresh lemon peel, finely grated
3 tsp. fresh orange peel, finely grated
9 egg yolks
5 egg whites

Preheat oven to 350°F. Boil and mash the potatoes and let it cool. Grease a 9-inch springform pan. In a large bowl, mix softened butter and sugar together using a wooden spoon or electric mixer until light and fluffy. Add the potatoes, cashews and lemon and orange peels; mix well. Add the egg yolks, one at a time, and continue to stir until well blended. Beat the egg whites until stiff. Slowly fold egg whites into the potato batter. Pour the batter into the pan, smoothing the top with a spatula. Bake for about 1¼ hours or until top is brown. Let cool for 10 minutes, then remove the cake onto a wire rack. Serve cake warm or at room temperature.

COCONUT CAKE

From the region of District 9910
Vanuatu

4 ½ c. coconut, fresh and grated
250g unsalted butter
8 eggs

2 ½ c. fine sugar
2 c. self-rising flour

Preheat the oven to 350°F (150° Celsius). In a bowl using an electric mixer, whisk sugar and butter until light and creamy. Then add the eggs, one by one, into the butter and sugar thoroughly. Fold in the flour and grated coconut into the above mixture. Butter and flour a round or square 20 centimeter baking tin and pour mixture into it. Bake for 1 ½ hours.

CUSTARD PUDDING

From the region of District 4370, 4380
Venezuela

8 T. sugar

1 c. water

For the Custard Pudding:

8 eggs
2 c. sweetened condensed milk
2 c. evaporated milk

1 tsp. vanilla extract
3 T. raisins

Preheat the oven to 150° Celsius, 300° Fahrenheit, gas mark 2. Make the caramel with sugar and water. Allow the sugar to dissolve over a low heat, then bring to the boil. Continue to boil rapidly until it is medium golden brown color, then remove from the heat immediately. Pour the caramel into the base of an ovenproof dish, swirling around the bottom and slightly up the sides. Place the remaining ingredients in a large mixing bowl and mix very well. Pour the batter into the caramel lined dish, cover with aluminum foil, then bake for about 1 ½ hours. Cool and chill before serving.

CREMA CATALANA

From the region of District 2201
Spain

6 egg yolks
½ lb. sugar
3 c. milk (¾ L.)

2 cinnamon sticks
2 pieces lemon peel
3 T. corn flour

(continued)

Beat the egg yolks until light. Then whisk in ¾ of the sugar. Place the milk in a saucepan together with the cinnamon and lemon peel; bring to the boil and then remove from the heat and strain. When cool, whisk the milk with the egg mixture. Dissolve the corn flour with a little milk and whisk into the mixture. Place the mixture over a low heat and cook, stirring constantly, until it begins to boil. Put the custard into a pudding bowl or smaller individual bowls and allow to cool before placing in the refrigerator. Before serving, sprinkle a little sugar on top and caramelize it by placing under a hot grill briefly until the sugar melts and turns brown.

CRESCENT BAKE

From the region of District 7500
USA

2 pkgs. crescent rolls
1 egg yolk
½ c. sugar

2 (8-oz.) pkgs. cream cheese
1 tsp. lemon juice

Blend yolk, sugar and cream cheese. Press 1 crescent roll package into 9 x 13-inch pan. Spread with cheese mixture. Place other tube of dough over top. Cover lightly. Bake for 30 minutes at 350°F. While warm, top with mixture of ¾ cup confectioners' sugar, 1-2 tablespoons milk and a dash of vanilla.

BUTTER TART PIE

From the region of District 5550
Canada

4 eggs
¾ c. brown sugar, packed
4 T. butter, melted
4 tsp. flour, all-purpose
¾ c. corn syrup

1½ tsp. vanilla
Pinch of salt
2¼ c. currants or raisins
1 pie shell, unbaked

Beat the eggs lightly. Stir in brown sugar, corn syrup, butter, flour, vanilla and salt until blended. Stir in currants or raisins. Pour in pie shell. Bake at 400°F for 5 minutes. Change heat to 250°F. Bake for about 30 minutes longer or until center is just firm to the touch, covering edges of pastry with foil if browning too much. Let cool completely before cutting.

BUTTERLESS SWEDISH NUT CAKE

From the region of District 5950
USA

2 c. sugar
2 c. flour
2 eggs
2 tsp. soda
1 tsp. vanilla

1 (20-oz.) can crushed pineapple
(do not drain)
1½ c. chopped nuts (use
English walnuts)

Mix by hand and put in a greased 9 x 13-inch pan. Bake at 350°F for 45-50 minutes. Let cool before frosting.

Frosting:

1 (8-oz.) pkg. cream cheese   ½ stick margarine

Cream above ingredients and add 1¾ cups powdered sugar and 1 teaspoon vanilla. Spread on cake and sprinkle ½ cup chopped nuts over top. (Cover and store in the refrigerator.) There is no shortening in this recipe.

BOMBONI OD KAVE S LJESNJACIMA

(Coffee and Hazelnut Lollies)

From the region of District 1913
Croatia

200g hazelnuts
120g sugar

6 T. coffee, boiled
10g cocoa

Grind the hazelnuts, then mix with the sugar. Add boiled coffee and cocoa. Mix well. Roll into small balls in the palm of your hand, then roll in crushed hazelnuts and grated chocolate.

BANITZA SARALIA (Sweet Walnut Pastries)

From the region of District 2482
Bulgaria

8 sheets phyllo pastry
Plenty of melted butter

250g chopped walnuts

For the syrup:

225g (8 oz.) granulated sugar
240ml (8 oz.) water

1 tsp. vanilla extract

(continued)

Preheat the oven to 180° Celsius, 350° Fahrenheit, gas mark 4 and lightly grease 2 baking trays. Brush two sheets of pastry liberally with butter and place one on top of the other. Sprinkle a quarter of the walnuts over the top of the two sheets of phyllo. Repeat with the remaining sheets of phyllo and walnuts, then roll lengthways to form a cylinder. Transfer to the greased baking tray and bake for about 30 minutes. Remove from oven and set aside. Meanwhile, make the syrup in a saucepan, bring to the boil the sugar, water and vanilla extract. Stir and then continue to cook for about 10 minutes or until the mixture is thick and syrupy. Pour the hot syrup over the top of the pastry. Set aside for 30 minutes. Cut into slices while warm or at room temperature.

BUSTRENGO (Apple & Polenta Cake)

From the region of District 2070
San Marino

¾ c. polenta
4 eggs
¼ c. bread crumbs
½ c. flour
½ c. sugar
¼ c. marmalade
¼ c. preserved ginger, chopped
¼ c. sugared citrus peel

¼ c. raisins
1 c. milk
2 chopped apples, peeled
½ c. almond paste, crumbled
½ c. cream
½ c. packed brown sugar
½ tsp. cinnamon

Mix the polenta and flour and bread crumbs together. In another bowl, mix the eggs and sugar well. Put all the other ingredients into the egg and sugar mixture; mix well. Now fold in the flour mixture. Mix all ingredients well together. Pour the batter in a greased round cake tin. Bake 45 minutes at 180° Celsius or 350° Fahrenheit. Serve hot with any custard sauce.

ALMOND BARS

From the region of District 1912
Slovenia

1 c. flour
1 c. almonds, ground
¾ c. powdered sugar
¾ c. butter, room temp.

4 egg whites
5 squares chocolate bar, grated
1 egg, lightly beaten

Preheat oven to 350°F. Separate eggs and discard the yolks. Keep the whites. In a large mixing bowl, combine flour, sugar, almonds, butter

(continued)

and egg whites. Mix well. Spread the mixture evenly into a buttered 8-inch square baking pan. Brush the top with the beaten egg. Bake for about 40 minutes. Cool to room temperature and cut into squares. Makes about 30 pieces.

ALFAJORES (Cookies)

From the region of District 4340
Chile

1½ c. butter (3 sticks)
1½ c. sugar
4 egg yolks
2 tsp. vanilla extract
2 c. cornstarch

2 c. flour
4 tsp. baking powder
1 c. dulce de leche or thick jam
Grated coconut or grated nuts (opt.)

In a mixer bowl, beat the butter and sugar together until light and fluffy. Add the egg yolks, beating until they are well mixed. Mix in vanilla extract. Mix the flour, cornstarch and baking powder together. Reduce the mixer speed to low and add the flour mixture in 3 batches, allowing each batch to become incorporated before adding the next. Form the dough into a disc without handling it too much. Wrap with plastic wrap and refrigerate for at least 1 hour. Preheat oven to 350°F. Remove the dough to a lightly floured work surface and roll out to about ⅛ inch thick. Cut out 80 (2-inch) rounds and carefully place the rounds on lightly greased cookie sheets. Bake for 9-10 minutes. They must not brown. Remove from the oven and cool for 5 minutes. Then remove the cookies to wire racks and cool completely. Spread about 2 teaspoons of dulce de leche on the flat half of a cookie and cover it with the flat half of another cookie to form a sandwich. Repeat with the remaining cookies. If desired, sprinkle the finished cookies with powdered sugar. Use more dulce de leche on each cookie so that some squeezes out the sides. Then roll the edges in grated coconut or ground nuts if desired. Makes 40 cookies.

ASABIA EL AROOS (Maiden Fingers)

From the region of District 3272
Afghanistan

½ pkg. (16 oz.) frozen filo dough, completely defrosted

½ c. unsalted butter, melted (opt.)

(continued)

Filling:

¾ c. almonds or pistachios, pulverized in food processor with

⅓ c. sugar

Glaze:

1 egg, beaten

Sugar

Prepare the syrup in advance and chill in the refrigerator. Combine the filling ingredients. Preheat the oven to 375°F. Grease 1 or 2 baking sheets. Cut the filo in half crosswise and again in half, stacking the covering with a slightly dampened towel to prevent drying. Lay 2 rectangles on your work surface with the shorter sides facing you and brush lightly with melted butter. Place a rounded tablespoon of the filling in a line across the shorter side of filo that faces you. Fold the longer edges of the pastry inward, sealing in the sides of the filling and roll the pastry up from the short side, forming a fat cigar shape. Place on the baking sheet with the cut edge down. Repeat with remaining dough. Brush the tops of the pastries lightly with a bit of beaten egg and sprinkle with sugar. Bake for 15-20 minutes until golden brown. Dip the warm fingers into cool sweet syrup (recipe below) and arrange on a serving tray. Serve at room temperature.

Syrup:

3 c. sugar
1 ½ c. water
1 lemon

1 T. orange blossom water or rosewater

Boil the sugar with the water until dissolved and viscous, about 10 minutes. Stir in the remaining ingredients and remove from the heat.

APPLE COFFEE CAKE

From the region of District 6360
USA

2 c. flour
¾ c. granulated sugar
1 c. firmly packed brown sugar, divided
1 tsp. baking powder
1 tsp. baking soda
½ tsp. salt
⅔ c. margarine or butter, melted

2 eggs, beaten
1 c. buttermilk
1 c. chopped Granny Smith apple
½ c. chopped pecans
1 tsp. ground cinnamon
¼ tsp. ground nutmeg
Glaze (recipe below)

Grease 8 x 12-inch glass baking dish. In large bowl, combine flour, granulated sugar, ½ cup brown sugar, baking powder, baking soda and

(continued)

salt. In small bowl, combine margarine, eggs and buttermilk; stir into dry ingredients just until combined. Fold in apples. Spoon batter into greased dish. Combine remaining ½ cup brown sugar, pecans, cinnamon and nutmeg; sprinkle over batter. Refrigerate, covered, several hours or overnight. **To bake:** Heat oven to 350°F. Bake until wooden pick inserted in center comes out clean, 35-40 minutes. Cool slightly; drizzle with glaze. Makes 12 servings. **Glaze:** In small bowl, combine ½ cup powdered sugar, 1 ½ teaspoons soft margarine or butter, ¼ teaspoon vanilla and 1-2 tablespoons milk or cream until smooth and of drizzling consistency. This coffee cake can be assembled and refrigerated several hours or overnight before being baked.

GULAB JAMUN

From the region of District 3271
Pakistan

½ c. milk powder
¼ c. flour
1 tsp. baking powder

½ c. fresh cream
Oil for frying

Syrup:

1 c. sugar

1 ¼ c. water

Sieve flour and milk powder together. Add baking powder and fresh cream and mix well. Make small balls and fry. Cook syrup. Add the balls in syrup. Serve. Yield: 6-8 servings.

BROWN COOKIES (Brune Kager)

From the region of District 1440
Denmark

¾ lb. syrup
9 oz. butter
10 oz. brown sugar
1 T. cinnamon
1 T. ground cloves
½ tsp. cardamom

2 oz. orange peel
1 tsp. baking powder
3 T. rosewater
2 lbs. flour
Almonds

Warm the syrup in a saucepan. Add the butter, orange peel, spices and sugar. Mix in the rosewater. Add the baking powder to the flour and then add the flour to the syrup mixture, kneading thoroughly after each addition. Turn into a bowl, cover and keep cool. Before baking, roll out thinly and cut into rounds. Place well apart on a greased baking sheet, brush with water and decorate with sliced almonds. Bake for 8-10

(continued)

minutes at 400°F (200° Celsius). Make the dough a few days before you want to make the cookies.

BANANA POI

From the region of District 9920
Samoa

2 tsp. vanilla
2 c. half-and-half cream
1½ lbs. ripe bananas
1 grated lemon peel

½ c. sugar, more or less according to taste
Ice

Mash bananas until smooth. Mix in vanilla and cream. Add sugar to taste. Add grated lemon peel to the mixture and stir. The lemon peel will add a faint lemon flavor. Pour over ice and serve. Serves 4.

GÂCHE MÈLEE

From the region of District 1110
Guernsey Channel Islands

1 lb. cooking apples, peeled and sliced
8 oz. self-rising flour
8 oz. brown sugar
3 eggs
3 T. milk

6 oz. butter
Rind of 1 lemon
½ tsp. nutmeg powder
½ tsp. cinnamon powder
Pinch of salt

Chop or thin slice the apples. Cream the butter and sugar and add the eggs. Place all the ingredients into a large mixing bowl and mix thoroughly together. Let sit for an hour. Grease a nine-inch baking tin (do not use Pyrex or ceramic dishes). Cook the Gâche Mèlee at 150° Celsius (gas mark 2) for 2 hours or until the top is golden and the apples are cooked when tested with a sharp knife. Serve warm with cream, ice cream or custard.

GRAHAM CRACKER OR VANILLA WAFER FLUFF

From the region of District 6000
USA

1 pkg. (1 T.) plain gelatin
½ c. cold water
2 egg yolks
½ c. sugar
⅔ c. milk
2 egg whites

2 c. Cool Whip
1 tsp. vanilla
3 T. butter, melted
3 T. sugar
12 graham crackers or vanilla wafers, crushed

Soak gelatin in cold water. While the gelatin is softening, in another bowl beat egg yolks. Add sugar and milk. Cook eggs, sugar and milk over low heat until slightly thickened. Pour hot mixture over softened gelatin and stir until smooth. Chill until slightly thickened. Add stiffly beaten egg whites, vanilla and Cool Whip to chilled mixture. Combine melted butter, crushed graham cracker crumbs and sugar to make delicious sweetened buttered crumbs. Sprinkle half of crumbs in the bottom of a serving dish. Press to the bottom and sides. Add chilled fluff mixture and top with remaining crumbs. Chill until set. Makes 4-6 servings.

TIRAMISU

From the region of District 2030
Italy

6 egg yolks
½ c. sugar
1 lb. mascarpone cheese
1 c. heavy cream
½ c. freshly made espresso coffee

4 T. rum
24 ladyfingers
¼ c. cocoa powder

In a large bowl, mix the egg yolks and sugar until light yellow and smooth. Mix in the mascarpone cheese until thoroughly mixed. In a large bowl, whip the heavy cream until stiff peaks form and fold into the cheese mixture. Mix the coffee and rum. Dip the ladyfingers in espresso rum and line a 9 x 13-inch pan. Pour in half the cheese mixture and smooth. Add another layer of the ladyfingers dipped in espresso rum. Pour the remaining cheese mixture on top and smooth. Chill for 2 hours and dust with cocoa powder before serving.

TOFU CAKE

From the region of District 2500-2840
Japan

1 hard tofu cake (wrapped in paper towel, drained)
3 egg yolks
3 egg whites
7 T. sugar
Dash of salt
6 T. cornstarch

1½ T. lemon juice
½ tsp. grated lemon rind
2 T. cointreau
1 tsp. vanilla essence
3 T. fresh cream
4 sprigs fresh mint leaves (garnish)

Preheat oven to 350°F. Line 8-inch cake tin with baking paper. Blend the tofu in the blender until creamy. Add in 5 tablespoons sugar, egg yolks, lemon juice, lemon rind, salt, cornstarch, vanilla essence and cream. Blend everything together until evenly blended. Stir in the cornstarch. In another mixing bowl, beat up the egg white until you get stiff peaks. Add in the remaining sugar and continue beating until silky. Fold the egg whites into the tofu mixture. Pour the batter into the prepared tin. Bake in oven for about 25-30 minutes, turn off heat and leave in oven to cool. Garnish with mint leaves.

BANANA NA BINJA

From the region of District 4370
Aruba

2 very ripe plantains
3 T. butter
3 T. dark brown sugar

2 T. water
4 T. port wine
Dash of cinnamon

Cut the ripe plantains lengthwise. In a heavy skillet, melt 3 tablespoons butter. Gently sauté the plantain halves until golden on one side. Turn them oven. Now mix brown sugar, water and port wine. Add a dash of cinnamon. Pour mixture over the plantain halves. Simmer gently until the liquid becomes a thick syrup. Serve at once.

CHOCOLATE PIE

From the region of District 7020
Anguilla

4 oz. sugar
4 oz. butter
2 egg yolks
2 loaves white bread crumbs

4 oz. melted dark chocolate
2 beaten egg whites
4 oz. mixed nuts

Whip butter, sugar and egg yolks until nice and creamy; add the white bread crumbs and the melted chocolate. Mix very well, then add the whipped egg whites and then the nuts. Pour in pan and bake in 350°F oven until baked and center is dry. Suggested to be served with warm vanilla sauce and berries.

CORNMEAL COOKIES

From the region of District 9100
Côte d'Ivoire

¾ c. + 2 T. margarine
¾ c. + 2 T. sugar
1 egg
1 ½ c. flour

½ c. cornmeal
1 ¼ tsp. baking powder
¼ tsp. salt
1 tsp. vanilla

Preheat oven to 350°F. In a mixing bowl, beat margarine and sugar together until light and fluffy. Add the egg and vanilla and beat well. In a separate bowl, combine the flour, cornmeal, salt and baking powder. Slowly add the dry ingredients to the margarine mixture and mix well. Drop dough in spoonfuls onto a greased cookie sheet and bake for 15 minutes. Makes 3 dozen.

COCADA

From the region of District 4690
Bolivia

3 c. shredded coconut
¾ c. condensed milk

1 egg
¼ tsp. almond essence

Mix all the ingredients in a bowl and let it sit for 5 minutes. Grease a cookie sheet and drop a tablespoonful for each cookie. Remember to grease the cookie sheet after every batch. Bake at 325°F for 25 minutes until they are golden brown. They burn easily.

ENGLISH PLUM PUDDING

From the region of District 1030-1140
England

1 c. bread crumbs
½ c. all-purpose flour
½ tsp. ground cinnamon
⅛ tsp. ground nutmeg
⅛ tsp. ground cloves
½ tsp. baking soda
½ tsp. salt
1 c. raisins
¼ c. currants
¼ c. cut-up candied fruit peel

¼ c. cut-up candied cherries
¼ c. chopped walnuts
¾ c. ground kidney suet or vegetable shortening
½ c. packed brown sugar
3 eggs, beaten
3 T. brandy
¼ c. brandy (opt.)
Hard sauce

Mix flour, bread crumbs, spices, baking soda and salt. Stir in fruit and walnuts. Mix suet, brown sugar, eggs and 3 tablespoons brandy. Stir this into the flour mixture. Pour into a well greased 4-cup mold; cover with aluminum foil. Steam mold in a Dutch oven until wooden pick inserted in center comes out clean, about 3 hours. You may add more water to the Dutch oven if needed until the pudding is done. Remove mold from Dutch oven and unmold onto a serving plate. Heat ¼ cup brandy until warm; ignite and pour over pudding. Serve with hard sauce.

Hard Sauce:

½ c. butter or margarine, softened

1 c. confectioners' sugar
2 T. brandy

Beat butter, confectioners' sugar and brandy until smooth.

FROZEN LEMON PIE

From the region of District 5360
Canada

1⅓ c. graham wafers crumbs or Oreo cookie crumbs
¼ c. melted butter
2 eggs, separated
¾ c. sugar, separated

Grated rind of a whole lemon
⅓ c. lemon juice (basically the juice of 1 whole lemon)
1 c. whipping cream

Preheat oven to 375°F. In a 9-inch pie plate, mix crumbs and butter; press into sides and bottom of pan. Bake 8-10 minutes. Cool. In medium saucepan over low heat, cook egg yolks, ½ cup sugar, lemon peel and juice, stirring constantly until slightly thickened. Let it come to a good rolling boil for about 1 minute. Mixture thickens considerably upon

(continued)

cooling. Cool. In a small bowl, beat egg whites on high until soft peaks form, beating remaining ¼ cup sugar until stiff peaks form. Set aside. In small bowl, beat whipping cream until soft peaks form. Fold whipping cream and egg whites into lemon mixture. Pile into crust. Freeze. Then wrap completely in foil and plastic. Return to freezer. When you are ready to eat pie, remove 20 minutes before serving. Thaw, unwrapped. Serve and enjoy.

FIGGY DUFF

From the region of District 7820
Canada

2 ½ c. dried bread crumbs
⅓ c. all-purpose flour
¼ tsp. ground allspice
½ tsp. ground cinnamon
¼ tsp. nutmeg
1 c. raisins, soaked in rum until plump

½ tsp. baking powder
¾ c. dark molasses
¾ c. melted butter
¼ c. dark rum
1 c. maple syrup to taste
1 c. whipped cream
Strawberries, sliced

In a large mixing bowl, combine the bread crumbs, flour, soaked raisins, spices, baking powder, molasses, butter and rum. Place the mixture in a pudding bag (close lightly to enable the pudding to expand or use a plastic bag). Don't close the plastic bag, but wrap it in a double layer of cheesecloth, tied tightly above. In a large pot, bring 4 quarts of water to a boil and add the wrapped pudding. Cover and simmer over low heat for 1 ¾ hours. Remove the pudding from the water. When cool enough to handle, unwrap the pudding and transfer to a cutting board. Cut into wedges. Spoon maple syrup on a serving plate. Place pudding wedge over it. Garnish pudding with whipped cream and strawberries.

FLODEKAGER (Danish Cream Cakes)

From the region of District 1440-1480
Denmark

1 ½ c. heavy cream
5 eggs
7 T. sugar

¾ c. flour, sifted
½ tsp. cardamom
½ tsp. baking powder

Preheat oven to 350°F. Butter and flour the muffin tins. In a mixing bowl, beat eggs and sugar. Add baking powder to flour. Add the flour and cardamom powder to the egg mixture. Whip the cream until stiff peaks form. Fold the whipped cream into the flour mixture. Fill the muffin cups ¾ full with the mixture. Bake at 350°F for 10-12 minutes. Frost with desired frosting or top with jam.

FIJIAN PUDDING

From the region of District 9920
Fiji

3 c. freshly grated cassava
1 c. freshly grated coconut
¼ inch freshly grated ginger
1 c. sugar

6 cloves (opt.)
Banana leaves or foil paper (for wrapping)
Steamer

Mix all 5 ingredients together. Divide into 4 equal parts. Wrap in leaves or foil and steam for 40 minutes. Unwrap and serve. Serves 4. Cassava is a shrubby, tropical, perennial plant that is not well known in the temperate zone. The edible parts are the tuberous root and leaves. The tuber (root) is somewhat dark brown in color and grows up to 2 feet long. It is comparable to the potato but has more fiber.

FRESH PEACH PIE

From the region of District 5170
USA

1 lg. single pie shell, baked
4 c. sliced fresh peaches, ripe, but firm
½ c. water

1 c. sugar
3 T. cornstarch
1 T. butter

Crush enough peach slices to make one cup. Arrange rest of the slices in the pie shell. Combine crushed peaches, water, sugar and cornstarch. Bring to a boil, then cook over low heat until clear, about 2-3 minutes. Stir in butter, then pour the cooked mixture over the sliced peaches, making sure all the peach slices are covered. Chill until set. Serve with whipped cream or ice cream.

FRITTERS

From the region of District 4370
Netherland Antilles

1 (¼-oz.) env. dry yeast
½ c. warm water
3 T. sugar
4 c. flour
3 eggs, beaten
½ c. warm water

2 c. seedless raisins
3 apples, peeled and diced
½ tsp. vanilla
1 tsp. salt
1 c. confectioners' sugar

(continued)

Mix the yeast and 3 tablespoons sugar in the slightly warm water and let it rise for 10 minutes. Mix together risen yeast mixture, eggs, water, vanilla and salt and slowly add to the flour. Add raisins and apples; let rise 1 ½ hours. Drop spoonfuls in hot frying oil, dust with confectioners' sugar.

FIG COOKIES

From the region of District 9830
Australia

4 eggs
1 c. butter
1 ½ c. sugar
½ tsp. lemon zest
1 c. honey

4 c. flour, sifted
1 ½ tsp. baking powder
6 T. milk
2 c. dried fig, finely chopped
1 c. desiccated coconut

Cream butter and sugar together. Add eggs, one at a time, ground lemon zest and honey; mix well. Stir in flour and baking powder together, then add milk. Mix in figs and coconut. Drop spoonfuls into the tray. Bake for 10 minutes at 350°F (medium oven temperature). Cool on tray.

FRESH STRAWBERRY PIE

From the region of District 6270
USA

1 baked Never-Fail Pie crust
   (recipe below)
1 qt. lg. firm strawberries
3 T. cornstarch

½ c. water
1 T. lemon juice
¼ tsp. salt
1 c. sugar

Prepare pie crust; cool. Meanwhile, wash and hull berries. In large bowl, combine cornstarch and water, stirring until smooth. Stir in half of berries. Crush berries with fork or potato masher. Stir in lemon juice, salt and sugar. Microwave on high 5-8 minutes, stirring every minute, until mixture thickens. Cool. Cut remaining berries in half. Place in cooled pie crust. Pour cooled strawberry mixture over berries and refrigerate until firm, about one hour. If desired, top with whipped cream or ice cream.

Never-Fail Pie Crust:

1 ½ c. flour
1 T. sugar
¼ tsp. salt

½ c. cooking oil
2 T. milk

(continued)

In bowl, combine flour, sugar and salt. In another bowl, combine oil and milk. Add liquid to flour mixture and mix until well blended. Pat into 9-inch pie plate and prick with fork around sides, bottom and bend of plate. Microwave 4-7 minutes on high or until lightly browned and obviously not doughy, turning dish ¼ turn after 2 minutes, after additional 2 minutes and every 1 minute thereafter (do not overbake).

KEY LIME SQUARES

From the region of District 6960
USA

¼ c. butter, softened
¼ c. granulated sugar
1 tsp. grated lime rind
⅛ tsp. salt
⅛ tsp. lemon extract
1 c. all-purpose flour
Cooking spray

⅔ c. granulated sugar
3 T. all-purpose flour
¾ tsp. baking powder
⅛ tsp. salt
½ c. fresh Key lime juice
3 lg. eggs
1 T. powdered sugar

Preheat oven to 350°F. Place first five ingredients in a medium bowl; beat with a mixer at medium speed until creamy (about 2 minutes). Lightly spoon 1 cup flour into a dry measuring cup; level with a knife. Gradually add 1 cup flour to butter mixture, beating at low speed until mixture resembles coarse meal. Gently press two-thirds of mixture (about 1⅓ cups) into bottom of an 8-inch square baking pan coated with cooking spray; set remaining ⅔ cup flour mixture aside. Bake at 350°F for 12 minutes or until just beginning to brown. Combine ⅔ cup sugar, 3 tablespoons flour, baking powder and ⅛ teaspoon salt in a medium bowl, stirring with a whisk. Add lime juice and eggs, stirring with a whisk until smooth. Pour mixture over crust. Bake at 350°F for 12 minutes. Remove pan from oven (do not turn oven off); sprinkle remaining ⅔ cup flour mixture evenly over egg mixture. Bake an additional 8-10 minutes or until set. Remove from oven; cool in pan on a wire rack. Sprinkle evenly with powdered sugar. Yield: 16 (1 square) servings.

LIBERIAN KANYAH

From the region of District 9100
Liberia

1 c. peanuts, shells and skins removed, roasted
1 c. rice flour
½ c. sugar

(continued)

Use a rolling pin to break and grind the peanuts into small pieces, taking care not to crush them into a powder or paste. Parch the rice flour in a dry skillet, stirring continuously, until it becomes slightly browned. Combine the crushed peanuts and rice (or rice flour). Crush and grind them together until they form a powder. Add the sugar and mix well. Using your hands, press the mixture into a pan and then cut into squares. May be served immediately or stored in airtight container.

LUBKUCHEN

From the region of District 1930
Germany

½ c. packed brown sugar
½ c. honey
1 T. lemon juice
3¼ c. all-purpose flour
¾ tsp. baking powder
1 tsp. baking soda
½ tsp. salt
¼ tsp. powdered ginger
1 tsp. cinnamon

½ tsp. ground cardamom
½ tsp. ground cloves
½ tsp. ground nutmeg
9 T. unsalted butter, softened
1 lg. egg, room temp., lightly beaten
⅓ c. finely chopped citron
Confectioners' sugar

Heat the honey, brown sugar and lemon juice in a small saucepan over low heat until it is just warm and blended and slightly thinned. Beat together butter and egg until blended; add the honey mixture and mix well. In a separate bowl, mix the flour, baking powder and soda, salt, ginger, cinnamon, cardamom, cloves and nutmeg until mixed. Incorporate this into the honey and butter mixture. Lastly add the citron. Knead until mixture is well combined. Butter a baking sheet. Roll dough out ¼ inch thick onto a floured board and cut into small rectangles and put them 1 inch apart on the baking sheet. Bake for 10 minutes in a 350°F oven. When done, cool the cookies; sprinkle with confectioners' sugar. Store in an airtight container. Makes 3 dozen cookies.

LATIYA (Custard Sponge Cake)

From the region of District 2750
Guam

10-inch sponge cake
1 lg. can condensed milk (or 1 qt. whipping cream)
¼ c. cornstarch
2 eggs
1½ c. water

6 T. sugar (1 c. sugar if using whipping cream)
2 tsp. vanilla extract
½ c. butter
1 tsp. cinnamon

(continued)

Slice the sponge cake and spread the pieces in a flat bowl to form a slab. Set aside. Place butter, sugar, water and milk in a saucepan. Bring to a boil. Lower heat and stir in well beaten eggs, vanilla and cinnamon very swiftly so that the mixture does not separate. Bring to a boil, stirring constantly. Mix ⅓ cup of water with cornstarch, stirring until it reaches a smooth consistency. Add the mixture to the milk mixture, stirring until it thickens. Remove from heat and spread over the sponge cake pieces. Sprinkle cinnamon over latiya. May also be served like a custard.

MENI MENIYOUNG (Sesame-Honey Sweet)

From the region of District 9100
Mali

½ lb. sesame seeds
1 c. honey

4 T. unsalted butter

Toast the sesame seeds in preheated oven at 220° Celsius for about 10 minutes. Mix the honey and butter to a small saucepan and heat over a medium-low flame until the mixture begins to bubble and starts to darken (about 5 minutes). Stir the sesame seeds into the honey mixture and spread out some ½ inch thick onto a buttered baking tray. Allow to cool until just warm and cut into sticks. Allow these to cool completely, then serve.

MISHRI MAWA

From the region of District 3050
India

4 T. milk powder
⅓ c. grated paneer (dry curd cottage cheese
4 T. heavy cream
4 T. sugar

5-6 strands saffron
½ tsp. cardamom powder
1 T. chopped pistachio and almonds

Mix milk powder, paneer, cream and sugar. Cook in a pot for 4-5 minutes on medium heat. Stir in cardamom powder and saffron. Turn off heat. Pour mixture in a rectangular tray to cool, sprinkle pistachio and almonds on top. Serve at room temperature.

MAPOPO (Papaya Candy)

From the region of District 9210
Zimbabwe

1 lb. papaya
2½ c. sugar
1 lemon peel, grated
½ tsp. mint, dried or fresh

Peel the papaya and slice into little strips. Place the papaya, mint, grated lemon and sugar over low heat until the sugar dissolves. Cook for 10 minutes, then set aside for half an hour. Reheat over medium heat until the mixture crystallizes. Remove from heat. Mixture will be very hot. Using a spoon and fork, mold into ball or stick shapes.

VERSUNKENER APFELKUCHEN
(Sunken Apple Cake)

From the region of District 1800-1900
Germany

2 c. plain flour
1 c. sugar
1 c. soft butter
3 eggs
Pinch of salt
1½ tsp. baking powder
2 T. milk
3 apples, sliced

Cream the butter and sugar together. Next add the eggs and beat well. Mix the flour with the baking powder and salt and add this to the sugar mixture; mix well. Add milk and incorporate well. Preheat oven to 350°F. Prepare and grease cake tin. Pour half the batter into the cake tin and smooth the top until flat. Layer half the apples on top. Pour in the remaining batter. Push the remaining apples at random into the top batter. Bake in the oven for 25 minutes or longer until the cake is dry when pierced with a toothpick in the center. Turn off the oven and let it rest in the oven for 10 minutes. Let the cake cool. Serve warm.

WHISKEY CREAM PIE

From the region of District 1290
England

¾ lb. graham crackers, finely crushed
5 T. butter
2 T. maple syrup
8 oz. heavy cream
1 lg. egg, room temp.
⅓ c. runny honey
2 T. Scotch whiskey
3 T. toasted, sliced almonds

(continued)

Mix the butter and maple syrup in a pan. Warm it up to blend together. Add this mixture to the graham cracker crumbs. Mix well with a wooden spoon. Press mixture into a 10-inch glass flan dish or pie pan. Freeze for about 5 minutes. In a mixing bowl, whisk the heavy cream until stiff peaks form. Separate the white from the yolk of the egg. Now whisk the white until a soft peak forms. Set aside. Discard the yolk. Stir whiskey and honey into the cream with a metal spoon. Fold in the egg white and pour the mixture over the chilled graham cracker crust. Sprinkle almonds and chill for an hour.

WALNUT TOFFEE

From the region of District 5330
USA

2¼ c. walnuts
2 c. granulated sugar
½ c. water
½ c. light corn syrup

1 c. butter
1 (6-oz.) pkg. semisweet or milk chocolate pieces

Coarsely chop 1½ cups walnuts for toffee. Finely chop ¾ cup walnuts for topping. Combine sugar, water, corn syrup and butter. Heat to boiling, stirring until sugar is dissolved. Cover and cook 5 minutes. Uncover and boil to hard crack stage (300°F). Remove from heat; stir in coarsely chopped walnuts and quickly spread in a buttered 10 x 15 x 1-inch pan. Let candy stand 5-10 minutes. Sprinkle chocolate pieces over candy and let stand a few minutes until melted. Spread evenly with a spatula. Sprinkle with finely chopped walnuts. Let stand until chocolate is set.

NANAIMO BARS

From the region of District 5040
Canada

First Layer:

¾ c. unsalted butter, melted
6 T. cocoa powder
2 beaten eggs
½ c. sugar

1½ c. graham cracker crumbs
1½ c. shredded sweet coconut
1 c. chopped nuts

Second Layer:

2 c. powdered sugar
½ c. unsalted butter
2 T. heavy cream

3 T. vanilla instant pudding powder

(continued)

Top Layer:

5 oz. semi-sweet chocolate squares
3 T. butter

First Layer: Mix the butter, cocoa powder and sugar into a saucepan and over low flame. Let butter melt to mix the ingredients. Next mix in the egg, stirring constantly for 2 minutes until the mixture starts to thicken. Remove from heat and stir in the coconut and graham crackers and nuts. Pour the mixture into the bottom of a greased 9 x 9-inch baking pan and press down firmly to form an even layer. **Second Layer:** Beat together all the ingredients until fluffy. Spread this butter cream mixture over the first layer. Smooth this mixture to look even. **Top Layer:** Melt the chocolate in the butter over a very low flame. When melted and smooth, pour over the butter cream mixture. To cut into bars, first bring to room temperature, then cut with a sharp knife.

OAT-CHOCOLATE CANDY (Havregrynskonfekt)

From the region of District 1470
Denmark

250g oats or 125g oats and 125g desiccated coconut
100g melted butter
200g sugar

50g cacao
7 ssp. strong coffee equals 1dl
Approx. 2 ssp. almond essence, try to taste

Mix the ingredients well together and place it in the refrigerator until it is cold. Roll to small balls between your hands and with the help of a teaspoon let them roll in desiccated coconut, cacao and/or almond flour. Store the ball in the refrigerator. In Denmark this candy is enjoyed during Christmas time.

OLD FASHION BREAD PUDDING

From the region of District 6420
USA

2 c. scalded milk
4 c. coarse bread crumbs
¼ c. melted butter
½ c. sugar

2 eggs, slightly beaten
¼ tsp. salt
½ c. raisins (opt.)
1 tsp. cinnamon or nutmeg

Warm Sauce:

1 c. sugar
2 T. cornstarch
2 c. boiling water

4 T. butter
2 tsp. vanilla, lemon or rum extract

(continued)

If using raisins, plump in hot water for 10 minutes and drain. Pour scalded milk over bread crumbs; cool and add melted butter, sugar, beaten eggs, salt, raisins (optional), cinnamon or nutmeg; pour into buttered 1½-quart casserole. Bake at 350°F for 40-50 minutes. **For warm sauce:** Mix sugar and cornstarch in small saucepan. Gradually add 2 cups boiling water. Bring to a boil and boil for 1 minute, stirring constantly. Then add 4 teaspoons butter and 2 teaspoons vanilla, lemon or rum extract. Keep hot until served.

PEAR TART TATIN WITH MASCARPONE CREAM AND ORANGE GRANITA

From the region of District 1010
Scotland

1 pear
2 oranges
45ml sugar
100ml white wine
150g puff pastry

100g mascarpone
15ml icing sugar
10ml cream
2 drops vanilla essence

Preheat oven to 180° Celsius. Cut orange in half and juice. Pour juice into plastic container and place in freezer. Wash and peel pear. Cut pear in half and remove seeds. Place sugar and white wine in non-stick frying pan on medium-high heat. Place pears into frying pan (flat side down). Roll out puff pastry. Remove pears from pan, dribbling of any excess liquid and place pear onto a chopping board. Cover pears with puff pastry and cut around using knife. Brush pastry with egg wash and sprinkle with a little sugar. Place a small amount of oil on baking tray and place pears on it and into the oven for 25 minutes. Mix 110 grams mascarpone, 15 milliliters icing sugar, 2 drops vanilla essence and 10 milliliters cream together and chill. (Use spoon dipped in hot water to curl cream.) Remove pears from the oven and curl cream into egg shapes and place on pear. Fork frozen orange granita and serve in glass on plate with pear and cream. Garnish granita with mint. Serve.

PEAR FLAN

From the region of District 1520
France

3 lg. pears
3 T. softened butter
8 oz. whipping cream
8 oz. milk

3 eggs
4 oz. sugar
½ tsp. ground cinnamon

(continued)

Preheat the oven to 150° Celsius, 300° Fahrenheit, gas mark 2 and lightly grease an 8-inch flan dish. Peel the pears, cut them in half, remove seeds and cut them into ¼-inch slices. Place the sliced pears in a saucepan with the butter and sauté over a low heat for 6 minutes, turning once. Meanwhile, in a mixing bowl, mix together the eggs, milk, sugar, whipping cream and cinnamon. Drain the pears and arrange in the greased flan case, then pour the egg mixture over the top of the pears and bake for about 40 minutes or until set. Serve warm.

PUMPKIN CHEESE CAKE OR BARS

From the region of District 6270
USA

Crust:

1 pkg. cake mix (I used a spice cake mix, yellow or carrot cake mix would work)

½ c. melted butter

This can be done in a springform pan or a 9 x 13-inch pan. Mix together and press firmly in bottom of pan.

Filling:

1½ lbs. cream cheese, softened, 3 (8-oz.) pkgs. (I used low fat or mix the 2 types)
1 (14-oz.) can sweetened condensed milk
1 (14-oz.) can pumpkin (not pie filling)
4 eggs
1 T. pumpkin pie spice

In large mixer bowl, beat cream cheese and sweetened condensed milk on high speed 2 minutes, scraping bowl as needed. Add pumpkin, spice and eggs. Beat 1 minute longer or until smooth. Pour over prepared crust. Bake 55-60 minutes in cheesecake springform pan or 30-35 minutes in 9 x 13-inch pan. Run knife around edge of pan to loosen. Cool completely on wire rack, then chill for 2 hours or overnight.

PLUM-BERRY TARTS

From the region of District 7190
USA

⅓ c. canola oil
¼ c. butter, melted
2 c. whole wheat or unbleached white flour
1 T. powdered sugar
½ tsp. salt
5-6 T. cold water
¼ c. apricot, cherry or raspberry spreadable fruit

3 plums, halved, pitted and cut in thin wedges
1 c. fresh blackberries and/or raspberries
1 T. fat-free milk
1 oz. semi-soft goat cheese, crumbled (opt.)
2 T. honey

In a small bowl, stir together oil and melted butter until well combined. Cover and freeze for 1 hour or until nearly firm, stirring occasionally. **Dough:** In medium bowl, combine flour, powdered sugar and salt. With pastry blender or fork, cut or stir in butter mixture until pieces are about pea-size. Sprinkle 1 tablespoon water over part of the flour mixture; gently toss with fork. Push moistened pastry to side of bowl. Repeat, using 1 tablespoon of water at a time, until all is moistened. Form pastry in a ball (dough may be wrapped and chilled up to 24 hours). Let stand at room temperature about 30 minutes or until easy to roll. Divide pastry into 6 equal portions. On lightly floured surface, roll each portion to a 6-inch circle. Place on parchment or foil lined baking sheet, leaving 1 inch between pastry rounds. Spoon spreadable fruit on pastry; spread to make 2-inch circle. Top with plums and berries, leaving 2 inches of pastry edge. Fold the edge around the fruit crimping and pleating as you go. Pastry does not have to cover fruit completely. Brush crust with milk. Preheat oven to 400°F. Bake 30-35 minutes or until filling is bubbly and fruit is tender, covering tarts with foil the last minutes of baking. Cool slightly on baking sheet on rack. Sprinkle cheese and drizzle with honey. Serve warm.

PANCAKES

From the region of District 1410
Aland Islands

2 c. milk
45g semolina
4 eggs
80g sugar
2 c. milk

100g plain flour
2 tsp. vanilla
1 tsp. cardamom
Pinch of salt

(continued)

First make the semolina porridge by warming the milk in a pot and gradually adding the semolina while whisking continuously. Let simmer for about 15 minutes, stirring continuously. Leave to cool completely. Whisk eggs and sugar. Add all other ingredients, including the cooled down porridge and stir well to combine. Pour the pancake mixture into a greased ovenproof dish and bake at 200° Celsius for 20-25 minutes until firm. Serve with a dollop of cloudberry jam.

QUINDAO (Brazilian Coconut Torte)

From the region of District 4700-4780
Brazil

10 egg yolks
2 eggs
2½ c. sugar
2 c. unsweetened coconut

Pinch of ground cloves
½ T. unsalted butter, room temp.

Preheat your oven to 325°F. Mix the eggs, egg yolks and sugar until the mixture is creamy. Add the coconut, butter and a pinch of cloves. Mix for another minute or so. Use butter to grease a 9-inch pie pan. Pour the mixture from your food processor into your greased pie pan. Cook the pie in a water bath for around 40 minutes. The top should look dry and a toothpick should come out clean. Let the coconut torte cool for 20 minutes and then unmold it onto a serving plate. Serve right away or refrigerate until you are ready to eat it.

ZUCCHINI BREAD

From the region of District 6270
USA

1 c. oil
3 eggs
2 c. sugar
2 c. zucchini, shredded
1 tsp. salt
1 c. nuts, chopped

3 c. flour
1 tsp. vanilla
3 tsp. cinnamon
1 tsp. baking soda
¼ tsp. baking powder

Mix well. Grease and flour 2 loaf pans. Pour mixture into pans. Bake for 90 minutes at 350°F.

YOGURT MUFFINS

From the region of District 7500
USA

⅓ c. brown sugar
⅓ c. margarine, melted
1 c. low-fat orange yogurt
1 egg, lightly beaten
¼ c. orange juice
½ tsp. orange rind

1 c. all-purpose flour
1 c. whole wheat flour
½ tsp. baking soda
1 dash of nutmeg
Vegetable cooking spray

Preheat oven to 375°F. Mix melted margarine and sugar. Beat together egg, yogurt, orange juice and orange rind. Add margarine and sugar mixture. Add dry ingredients. Mix only enough to moisten. Pour into muffin tins sprayed with cooking spray or lined with muffin cups. Bake 25 minutes.

YORKSHIRE PUDDING

From the region of District 1240-1290
England

1½ c. all-purpose flour, sifted
2 lg. eggs, room temp.
¾ c. milk

2 T. roast beef drippings
3 T. butter, melted

Preheat oven to 425°F. Place the flour in a large bowl. Make a well in the center and break the eggs into it, then slowly add the milk and drippings. Place about ½ teaspoon of shortening in each hole of a 12-hole popover tin and put the tin in the oven for 5 minutes so the shortening melts and is real hot. Remove the tin from the oven. Distribute the batter in each popover hole. As you pour in the batter, it will sizzle. Put popover tin back in the hot oven and bake about 15-20 minutes. The popovers will rise dramatically and be crisp and brown on the top. Serve immediately.

MARMALADE CAKE

From the region of District 1230
Scotland

1 c. butter
⅔ c. sugar
3 lg. eggs

8 T. orange marmalade
2¼ c. self-rising flour
½ c. white raisins (sultanas)

(continued)

Cream the butter and sugar until light and fluffy. Add the eggs, one at a time, beating well between each addition. Mix in marmalade, sultanas and flour. Turn into greased cake pan and bake at 350°F for 45 minutes or until a skewer from the center comes out clean. Cool for 15 minutes and turn out onto rack to cool completely.

MELOMAKARONA

From the region of District 2470
Greece

½ c. sugar
¼ tsp. baking soda
2 egg yolks
¼ c. orange juice
2 T. whiskey
1¼ c. butter, melted and almost cool

3½ c. flour
⅛ tsp. salt
2 tsp. baking powder
½ tsp. ground cloves
1 tsp. cinnamon
½ tsp. orange zest

For the syrup:

1 c. water
2 c. honey

1 c. coarsely ground almonds

Preheat oven to 350°F. Place sugar, orange juice, whiskey, egg yolks and baking soda in a blender; mix until combined. With the motor still running, slowly drizzle in the melted butter through the hole in the top of the blender cover. Mix at high speed until mixture has thickened about 2 minutes. In a large mixing bowl, sift together flour, cloves, cinnamon, orange zest, salt and baking powder. Mix in the egg yolk-butter mixture and knead dough until smooth, about 5 minutes. (Dough will be stiff.) Shape a tablespoon of dough in the palm of your hand to form an oval shape. Place cookies on a cookie sheet, and press the tops lightly with a fork, making a crisscross pattern. Bake about 20 minutes or until golden brown. **To prepare syrup:** Boil a cup of water. Stir in honey, reduce heat to medium and simmer for 6 minutes. Remove from heat. Dip cookies in warm syrup for a few seconds. Place on cookie sheets until syrup soaks into cookies. Sprinkle with nuts and let cool. Tastes good the next day.

MTEDZA CAKE (Peanut Cake)

From the region of District 9210
Malawi

8 eggs, separated
¼ lb. bread crumbs
2 whole eggs

2 tsp. plain flour
¼ lb. finely chopped peanuts
¾ c. sugar

For the Icing (Frosting):

¼ lb. sugar
½ lb. margarine
6 T. water

2 tsp. instant coffee
3 egg yolks
Chopped nuts to decorate

Beat the egg yolks and whole egg in a bowl until thick. Gradually beat in half sugar, bread crumbs and nuts. Continue beating until the mixture is thick. Beat the egg whites until the mixture forms soft peaks. Slowly add the remaining sugar and beat the mixture until it stands in stiff peaks. Gently fold the beaten egg whites into the batter mixture. Fold in the flour. Turn the mixture into a 9-inch cake tin that's been greased and lined and bake in the oven preheated to 140° Celsius. Bake for about 1½ hours or until lightly browned in color and a skewer inserted into the center of the cake emerges cleanly. Remove from the oven, cool for 5 minutes in the tin before transferring to a wire rack to cool completely. **For the icing:** Combine the sugar and water in a pan, heat gently until the sugar dissolves, then simmer for 5 minutes. Meanwhile, cream the egg yolks in a bowl. Pour the syrup over the top and whisk until thick. Add the softened margarine to the egg mixture, then gradually whip in the coffee. Ice the top and sides of the cake. Use chopped nuts to decorate.

MIXED FRUIT SAUTÉ

From the region of District 9350
Angola

4 bananas, peeled and sliced
4 mangoes, peeled and cubed (opt.)
1 pineapple, peeled, cored and cubed

3 oranges, peeled and cubed
3 T. coconut oil
½ c. white grape juice
¾ ground coriander

In a wok or large skillet, sauté all ingredients until thick texture occurs. Serve over vanilla ice cream. Garnish with fresh raspberries and orange zest.

Ten Minute Meals

Helpful Hints

- Never overcook foods that are to be frozen. Foods will finish cooking when reheated. Don't refreeze cooked, thawed foods.

- When freezing foods, label each container with its contents and the date it was put into the freezer. Always use frozen, cooked foods within 1–2 months.

- To avoid teary eyes when cutting onions, cut them under cold running water or briefly place them in the freezer before cutting.

- Fresh lemon juice will remove onion scent from hands.

- To get the most juice out of fresh lemons, bring them to room temperature and roll them under your palm against the kitchen counter before cutting and squeezing.

- Add raw rice to the salt shaker to keep the salt free flowing.

- Transfer jelly and salad dressings to small plastic squeeze bottles – no more messy, sticky jars!

- Ice cubes will help sharpen garbage disposal blades.

- Separate stuck-together glasses by filling the inside glass with cold water and setting both in hot water.

- Clean CorningWare® by filling it with water and dropping in two denture cleaning tablets. Let stand for 30–45 minutes.

- Always spray your grill with nonstick cooking spray before grilling to avoid sticking.

- To make a simple polish for copper bottom cookware, mix equal parts of flour and salt with vinegar to create a paste.

- Purchase a new coffee grinder and mark it "spices." It can be used to grind most spices; however, cinnamon bark, nutmeg, and others must be broken up a little first. Clean the grinder after each use.

- In a large shaker, combine 6 parts salt and 1 part pepper for quick and easy seasoning.

- Save your store-bought bread bags and ties–they make perfect storage bags for homemade bread.

- Next time you need a quick ice pack, grab a bag of frozen peas or other vegetables out of the freezer.

TEN MINUTE MEALS

ASIAN CHICKEN

2 lg. cooked chicken breasts, sliced thin
1 lg. carrot, cut into matchstick pieces
1 T. olive oil
1 sm. can sliced water chestnuts
2 green spring onions, chopped into 1-inch pieces
1 red bell pepper, cut in strips
1 green bell pepper, cut in strips
1 tsp. grated ginger
4 T. Asian sesame salad dressing
1 c. crisp chow mein noodles

Using a wok or a deep sauté pan, sauté the carrots and the chicken in hot olive oil for 4 minutes. Add the rest of the ingredients and sauté until the vegetables are still crisp, but tender, about 4 minutes. Serve hot, topped with crisp chow mein noodles. Serves 2.

BROCCOLI CHICKEN

2 c. Minute Rice, cooked according to pkg.
1 c. frozen chopped broccoli
2 c. shredded, cooked rotisserie chicken
1 c. nacho cheese sauce

Layer a small casserole dish with the prepared rice. In a mixing bowl, combine the broccoli, chicken and nacho cheese sauce. Layer this over the rice and bake in a preheated 400°F oven for 10 minutes. Serve hot. Serves 4.

MANGO SHRIMP

2 mangoes, diced
2 c. cooked whole shrimp
½ c. chopped onion
½ c. chopped celery
½ c. capers, drained
2 T. chopped ginger
2 T. Thousand Island dressing
¼ c. Italian dressing
2 lg. green bell peppers

(continued)

Mix all the ingredients and chill. Cut each pepper in half and scoop out the insides to form 4 cups. Fill each cup with the mango shrimp, letting it overflow onto the plate. Serves 4.

TEMPTING DUCK

1 cooked duck (available at any Oriental eatery)
2 T. ginger, julienned
1 T. mint leaves, chopped

1 T. cilantro, chopped
1 c. red onion, thinly sliced
1 c. salted cashew nuts

Dressing:

2 T. brown sugar
½ tsp. hot sauce
2 T. soy sauce

1 T. lime juice
½ tsp. sesame oil

Remove the meat from the cooked duck and cut into bite-size pieces. In a bowl, combine the duck, ginger, mint, cilantro, cashew nuts and red onion. Prepare the dressing by mixing well all the ingredients for the dressing. Pour over the duck mixture. Serve on a bed of lettuce. Serves 2.

SPICY SALSA TILAPIA

4 tilapia fillets
¼ tsp. salt
2 T. olive oil
¼ tsp. pepper
½ c. black beans
½ c. corn

½ c. finely chopped red bell pepper
¼ c. Italian salad dressing
2 tsp. French dressing
2 hot green peppers

In a mixing bowl, combine the black beans, corn, red bell pepper, salad dressings and hot green pepper. Let this marinate for about 10 minutes. While this is marinating, rub the tilapia fillets with salt and pepper. Fry in the olive oil until cooked, but still firm. Remove onto a plate and top with the marinated salsa. Serves 2-4, according to the size of the fillets.

SALMON BURGERS WITH FRUITY SALSA

1 lb. salmon (skim removed and chopped)
½ c. finely chopped onion
½ tsp. chopped garlic
¼ tsp. cumin powder
¼ tsp. turmeric

1 T. pesto
½ c. dry bread crumbs
2 sm. eggs
1 T. lime juice
Oil for frying

Salsa:

1 chopped mango
1 chopped avocado
¼ c. lime juice

¼ tsp. salt
½ c. chopped cilantro
½ c. chopped onion

In a food processor, combine salmon, onion, garlic, cumin, turmeric, pesto, bread crumbs, eggs and lime juice. Pulse for a few minutes until the mixture forms a mass. Remove into a bowl and form into small patties. Pan fry until the patty is crisp on both sides. Remove onto a paper towel to absorb any oils. Mix all the ingredients for the salsa and spoon over the patties. Makes 2-4 servings, depending on the size of your patties.

TUNA PITA POCKETS

2 lg. pita breads
1 c. chopped tomato
1 c. canned tuna, drained
1 c. chopped cilantro

1 c. chopped mushrooms
1 c. grated cheddar cheese
1 T. olive oil
¼ tsp. salt

Cut the pita bread in halves so that you have 4 nice pockets. In a saucepan, combine tomato, tuna, cilantro, mushrooms, salt and olive oil until heated through. Remove from heat and mix in the cheddar cheese. Fill each pita pocket with the mixture. Wrap each filled pita pocket in a paper towel and microwave for one minute on high. Remove pita pocket from the paper towel and serve. Makes 4 servings.

STUFFED POTATO

4 lg. baked potatoes
1 c. chopped, cooked asparagus
1 c. chopped spinach
1 c. sour cream

¼ c. blue cheese, crumbled
¼ c. cream cheese
Pepper and salt to taste
½ c. crumbled bacon

(continued)

Cut the baked potatoes in half. Scoop out the potatoes, leaving the skin nice and intact for the stuffing. In a mixing bowl, combine the scooped potato, asparagus, spinach, sour cream, blue cheese, cream cheese, salt and pepper. Stuff this mixture into the potato skins and microwave for 2 minutes on high. Garnish with crumbled bacon and serve. Serves 4.

SWEET POTATO FRITTERS

2 c. finely grated sweet potato
¼ c. chives
½ c. crumbled feta cheese
4 beaten eggs
2 green onions, chopped fine
½ tsp. black pepper
½ tsp. salt (more if desired according to taste)
½ c. oil for frying

Combine all the ingredients, except oil, and mix well. Drop by spoonfuls into hot oil until crisp on both sides. Serve with cocktail sauce.

PEANUT BUTTER CHICKEN

2 c. raw chicken breast, diced
2 hot green chilies
2 T. pesto
1 T. lemon juice
1 tsp. hot sauce
1 c. coconut milk
1 T. cooking oil
2 T. crunchy peanut butter

Mix all the ingredients and cook until the mixture comes to a boil and chicken is no longer pink, about 6 minutes. Serve hot over rice or warm bread. Serves 2.

BEAN BONANZA

1 c. cooked chickpeas
1 c. cooked black beans
1 c. cooked kidney beans
1 c. chopped tomato
1 c. chopped red onion
1 c. chopped cilantro
1 c. lemon juice
½ tsp. salt

Mix all the ingredients and let stand for 10 minutes. Serves 6.

SPICY CABBAGE

5 c. thinly sliced cabbage
3 green onions, chopped
½ c. chopped tomatoes
2 chopped hot green chilies
½ tsp. turmeric
½ tsp. garlic powder
¼ tsp. salt, or more if needed
4 T. olive oil
1 c. thick coconut milk
½ c. chopped coriander leaves

Heat the olive oil and sauté the cabbage, onions, tomatoes, chilies, turmeric, garlic powder and salt. When cabbage has softened, add the coconut milk and cook until cabbage is cooked. Garnish with coriander leaves. Serve hot with crisp warm bread. Serves 4.

COCONUT CRUNCH VEGETABLES

1 c. chopped eggplant
1 c. chopped mushrooms
1 c. chopped squash
½ tsp. turmeric
½ tsp. garlic powder
1 chopped green chili
¼ c. chopped cilantro
2 T. desiccated dry coconut
1 c. coconut milk
¼ tsp. salt, or more if needed

Mix all the ingredients and cook until the eggplant is done, but not mushy. Serve with pita bread. Makes 2 servings.

NUTTY VEGETABLES

½ c. cauliflower florets
½ c. broccoli florets
1 c. chopped tomatoes
½ c. chopped eggplant
½ tsp. chopped garlic
¼ tsp. cumin powder
¼ tsp. pepper
¼ c. Ranch dressing
¼ c. vegetable stock
¼ tsp. salt
1 c. slivered almonds

Mix all together and cook until vegetables are crisp, but cooked. Serve hot, topped with almonds. Serves 2.

ROYAL PORK CHOPS

4 thinly sliced pork chops
4 T. olive oil
1 green bell pepper, chopped
1 red bell pepper, chopped
½ c. chopped pineapple
½ c. sliced mushrooms
¼ c. Italian salad dressing
¼ c. Ranch salad dressing

(continued)

Sauté the pork chops in olive oil until no longer pink. Set aside. In the same pan, combine the peppers, pineapple, mushrooms, Italian and Ranch dressing. Cook until vegetables are tender. Spread the vegetables over the pork chops and serve. Serves 4.

CURRY CHICKEN

2 semi-frozen, uncooked chicken breasts
1 c. chopped red onion
1 c. chopped tomatoes
1½ T. curry powder
1 tsp. chopped garlic
1 tsp. chopped ginger
2 T. cooking oil
¼ c. water
Salt to taste

Thinly slice the semi-frozen chicken breast. Set aside. Sauté the onions in oil until tender. Add curry powder, ginger and garlic. Continue to sauté for another minute. Now add the tomatoes, chicken, salt and water. Cook until chicken is no longer pink, about 5 minutes. Serve hot with Naan bread or hot rice. Serves 4.

FRUITY SALAD

2 c. cooked, diced chicken
1 c. seedless grapes
1 c. pineapple chunks
1 c. walnut pieces
1½ c. sour cream

Mix all together and serve on a bed of lettuce.

SPINACH SHRIMP

2 c. raw, peeled shrimp
½ c. Italian salad dressing
4 c. baby spinach
1 c. crisp chopped bacon

In a large sauté pan, sauté the shrimp in the salad dressing until no longer pink. Mix in the baby spinach and cook until the spinach is almost wilted. Mix in the crisp bacon and turn off the heat. Serve immediately with crisp Italian bread. Serves 2.

HAM AND EGG SALAD

2 c. cooked ham, sm. cubed
8 hard-boiled eggs, coarsely chopped
1 c. mayonnaise
1 T. prepared mustard
½ tsp. chopped garlic
2 tsp. chopped dill
½ c. sour cream
4 c. shredded lettuce

Mix all the ingredients and serve on a bed of finely shredded lettuce. Serves 4.

CORNY CHICKEN

2 c. diced, cooked rotisserie chicken
1 c. cooked corn kernels
½ c. onions, sliced fine
½ c. diced tomato
1 pkt. taco seasoning
¼ c. water
1 T. oil
¼ c. chopped cilantro

Over medium heat, sauté the onions in hot oil for 3 minutes. Now add the tomato and continue cooking for 2 minutes. Add the chicken, corn, taco seasoning and water. Cook for 3 more minutes. Turn off heat. Mix in the cilantro. Serve warm. Serves 2.

Recipe Favorites

INDEX OF RECIPES

APPETIZERS & BEVERAGES

AMERICAN-MEXICAN TACO DIP	14
APPLE CIDER DRINK	8
ARTICHOKE SPINACH BAKE	15
AVOCADO SALSA	14
BABA GHANOUSH	16
BAKED MUSHROOMS WITH CHEESE	24
BA-THEETH	12
BUUZ	22
CALENTITA	19
CELEBRATION PUNCH	17
CEVICHE DE OSTRAS	18
CHEESE PUFFS	26
CHIPOTLE CHILE PEPPER GUACAMOLE	20
CONCH FRITTERS	16
COURGETTES IN YOGHURT	6
CRAB CAKES WITH SHRIMP SAUCE	20
CRAB PANCAKES	5
CRAB WON TONS	19
CREMA DE CABRALES	17
CRUNCHY SHRIMP DIP	26
DERAILER	10
DRUNKIN BOURBON	6
FISH HOUSE PUNCH	3
FLAPJACKS	7
FRUIT CHEESE SPREAD	7
FRUIT DIP	7
GROMPEREKICHELCHER	8
HOT ARTICHOKE & SPINACH DIP	8
HOT DEVIL DAIQUIRI	5
HUMMUS	9
KAPPUNATA	27
LAMB KEBABS WITH FETA SAUCE	10
MINI FRATAS	11
MOCHA CREAM	11
MUSHROOM CROSTINI	18
MUSTARD VEGETABLE DIP	11
NEGRONI	15
ONION CRESCENTS	12
OYSTER PÂTÉ	13
PHYLLO SHELLS WITH SAUSAGE STUFFING	13
PICTIONARY PUNCH	24
POTATO PANCAKES/TORTILLAS WITH TUNA	20
PUNCH SLUSH	24
REUBEN DIP	21
ROCKET PUNCH	16
SCOTCH EGGS	21
SEASONED PRETZELS	22
SEVEN LAYER DIP FOR TORTILLA CHIPS	2
SHRIMP ON TOSTONES	23
SIMIT	23
SKEWERED CANADIAN BACON	2
SKEWERS WITH CASHEW NUT SATAY	1
SMOKED FISH PÂTÉ	25
SPICY STRAWBERRY SALSA	25
SPINACH BALLS	25
STUFFED PRUNES WITH BACON	1
TADAM MIMLI	3
TOLTOTT PAPRIKA	4
TONGAN OTAI	3
TONKATSU	4
TUNA TARTAR	9

SOUPS & SALADS

AVOCADO SOUP	29
AZTEC SOUP OR TORTILLA SOUP	29
BELGIAN SOUP	31
BLACK BREAD SOUP WITH FRUIT	30
BROCCOLI RAISIN SALAD	31
BUTTERNUT SOUP	30
BUTTERNUT SQUASH SOUP	32
CABBAGE SALAD	34, 36
CALLALOO SOUP	33
CAPRESE SALAD	33
CAULIFLOWER SALAD	36
CAULIFLOWER SOUP	38
CHICKEN AND MANGO SALAD	38
CHICKEN SALAD	34
CHICKPEA AND NOODLE SALAD	37
COCONUT BEAN SOUP	32
CRAB SOUP	37
CRANBERRY APPLE SALAD	35
CREAM OF CARROT SOUP	34
CRUNCHY MIXED SALAD	36
CUCUMBER SALAD	35
CUCUMBER SOUP-COLD	38

DOVGA	39
EGG LEMON SOUP	40
FASOLADA	41
FIDDLEHEAD SOUP	40
FROZEN YOGURT SALAD	40
FRUITY SLAW	41
GADO GADO	42
GERMAN POTATO SALAD	42
HONDURAN CONCH SOUP	43
HUBOVA POLIEVKA	43
ICEBERG SALAD	44
IRISH CREAM OF TURNIP SOUP	44
KRAUTSALAT	44
LASOPY	45
LEMON PINEAPPLE SALAD	45
LENTIL AND SWEET POTATO SOUP	46
MANGO JICAMA SLAW	47
MARIE'S WEST SIDE SEAFOOD SALAD	48
MARINATED GREEN PAPAYA	46
MOE'S FAVORITE POTATO SALAD	47
MONTSERRAT SALAD	49
MUSHROOM SOUP	48
NEW ENGLAND CLAM CHOWDER	49
NUTTY ORZO SALAD	50
OKRA SOUP	50
PLOUGHMAN'S SOUP	50
POLYNESIAN DRESSING	51
POTATO SALAD	51
RADISH SALAD	52
RAGU JUHA	53
RAUGINTU KOPŪSTAI SRIUBA	52
REJESALAT	52
SALADE COTE CAP VERTE	59
SALADE DE ZAALOUK	62
SEAWEED AND EGG SOUP	58
SHOURABIT SILQ BI LABAN	60
SOPA DE PALMITO	59
SOPPA TA 'L-ARMLA	61
SOUTHWEST SALAD	60
STILTON SOUP	56
SUAASAT	58
SWEDISH CHICKEN SALAD	62
SWEET CORN SOUP	61
TACO SOUP FROM DALLAS VANHEYINGENS RESTAURANT	53
TAMARIND BEEF SOUP	54
TOMATO AND WATERMELON SALAD	47
TOMATOES SALAD	54
TRINI CORN SOUP	55
TUNA AND CHOW MEIN NOODLE SALAD	55
VEGETABLE BACON CHOWDER	56
XORIATIKI	57
ZAMA DE PASOLE VERDE	57
ZESTY BEAN SALAD	57

VEGETABLES & SIDE DISHES

AKKARA	76
ALOO DAM BENGALI	75
ARTICHOKES IN WINE	76
BAKED BANANAS	77
BASIL PESTO	78
CANADIAN BAKED BEANS	78
CAPONATA	79
CHAKALAKA	65
CHEELA	80
CHEESE BUREK	81
CORN CAKES	79
CORNHUSKER'S CASSEROLE	78
COU-COU	80
DAHI VADAS	70
DONGO-DONGO	65
EGGPLANT PIZZA	66
FAROFA	82
FETTAT ADIS	67
FRESH TOMATO BASIL PASTA	81
GRANDMA'S PULUT HITAM	77
GRAVCHE TAVCHE	63
HERBED KIDNEY BEANS	63
ICELAND VEGETABLES	64
ITALIAN SKILLET FRITTATA	64
KAK MAZ MAGGI SQUARE	64
KARTOFLIANKI	65
KOREAN POTATOES	67
LAYERED LENTIL RICE	68
MALAYSIAN VEGETABLE PICKLE	71
MANGO CURRY	93
MANGO RICE	87
MANGO SALSA FOR VEGETABLES & FISH	69
MATOKE	72
MATOKI (GREEN BANANA) BURGERS	70
MONTENEGRIN AUBERGINES	68
MUSHROOM CASSEROLE	69
NSHIMA	72
ONION TART	73

PAN DE MAIZ	75
PAPA'S CHORREADAS	74
PASCUALINA	84
PENNE WITH PEPPERS AND CREAM	83
PLANTAIN AU GRATIN	82
POTATO SALAD-COLD	73
POTATO VARENYKY	74
PSKOVSKY	83
QUICHE DENT-DE-LION	84
RAJASTHANI GATTA CURRY	85
SALOR KOR-KO SAP	88
SMOKED POTATO	86
SOBA NOODLES	89
SPICY STRING BEANS	88
SPINACH AND RICOTTA GNOCCHI	87
SPINACH & PEANUT BUTTER STEW	89
SQUASH CASSEROLE	90
SWAZILAND SAMP	91
SWEET-AND-SOUR TOFU	90
SWISS ROESTI	86
VEGETABLE STEW	94
VEGETARIAN DELIGHT	66
VEGETARIAN LENTILS - MOROCCAN-STYLE	93
VEGETARIAN STEW	92
VEGGIE-STUFFED PORTOBELLO MUSHROOMS	91
ZUCCHINI CASSEROLE	94

MAIN DISHES

AFELIA	95
BAHAMIAN RICE	99
BAKED KOTLOTI	97
BEEF AND BEER STEW	95
BELGIUM MEATBALLS IN BEER	97
BESHBARMAK	98
BOULANEE	99
BRUNEI BERIANI RICE	96
CAJUN TAILS CRAWFISH ETOUFFEE	110
CALICO BEANS	103
CARNE EN JOCON	105
CARURU	104
CAYMAN CREPES	102
CEVICHE DE CAMARON	102
CHEESE CROWNED TENDERLOINS	106
CHEF STEVE MILES' CHICKEN A L'ORANGE	111
CHICAGO-STYLE DEEP-DISH PIZZA	108
CHICKEN BIRYANI	107
CHICKEN CACCIATORE	105
CHICKEN CURRY	109
CHICKEN IN ORANGE SAUCE	100
CHICKEN IN PEANUT SAUCE	103
CHICKEN IN WINE	111
CHICKEN SATAY WITH PEANUT SAUCE	144
CHICKEN STEW	100
CHICKEN WATERZOOI	101
CHICKEN WITH ARTICHOKES	104
CHICKEN YASSA	110
CHILI CRAB	107
CORONATION CHICKEN	106
CROWDIE AND CHIVE RAVIOLI WITH RED CHARD AND ROAST BEETROOT DRESSING	112
EMPANADAS	115
ENSALADA DE BACALAO	114
ESCUDELLA	113
FEIJOADA	117
FISH CALULU	118
FISH IN COCONUT SAUCE	116
FISH PIE	119
FRENCH POTATOES WITH SMOKED SAUSAGE	118
FRENCHY'S VEAL CUTLETS PARMIGIANA	116
FRESH FISH STEAMED, BENGALI-STYLE	116
GREEK SHRIMP	120
ISLAND CHICKEN	121
JAPRAK	122
JERK CHICKEN	121
KANGKONG BELACAN	122
KENTUMERE	123
KHICHERI	145
KOREAN BBQ	123
LAMB CHUBBAGIN	127
MACAO CHICKEN	124
MACKEREL ESCABECHE	125
MAFFE TIGA	126
MALAYSIAN SPICY PRAWNS	127
MBAWA YA TOMATI	128
MEAT STEW	128
MEXICAN LASAGNE	126
MIDWESTERN CHILI	124
MOUSSAKA	146
NASI GORENG	130

NEW ENGLAND POT ROAST, ALA JANE	129
NGEGE	129
OXTAIL	130
PACENA PATKA	101
PAD THAI	133
PAN SEARED LOIN OF VENISON WITH MILLEFEUILLE POTATOES	131
PASTEL DE CHOCLO	132
PASTELLES	143
PIROSHKI	133
POLYNESIAN PORK STEAK	131
PORK COLOMBO	134
PRAWN MASALA	120
QUICK & EASY CHICKEN FETTUCCINE FOR TWO	132
RAPPIE PIE	135
RIKKITA BEEF	136
RISOTTO	134
SALT FISH AND GREEN FIG PIE	139
SAUERBRATEN	141
SAUERBRATEN AND POTATO DUMPLINGS	140
SETTLER'S BEANS, THE LENEXA WAY	138
SHREDDED BEEF	138
SHRIMP JAMBALAYA	142
SKOUDEKHARIS	136
SNAPPER A LA SICILIANA	137
SPICY RICE WITH BEEF	142
STEAMED FISH	137
STUFFED GRAPE LEAVES	140
TOURTIERE	119
TUNA PILAF	143
WIENER SCHNITZEL	144
ZIGINI	113

DESSERTS

ALFAJORES	165
ALMOND BARS	164
APPLE COFFEE CAKE	166
ASABIA EL AROOS	165
BANANA NA BINJA	170
BANANA POI	168
BANITZA SARALIA	163
BERRY COFFEE CAKE	159
BISKUTTINI TAR-RAHAL	159
BLACK BUTTER	160
BOLO POLANA	160
BOMBONI OD KAVE S LJESNJACIMA	163
BROWN COOKIES	167
BUSTRENGO	164
BUTTER TART PIE	162
BUTTERLESS SWEDISH NUT CAKE	163
CHOCOLATE PIE	171
COCADA	171
COCONUT CAKE	161
CORNMEAL COOKIES	171
CREMA CATALANA	161
CRESCENT BAKE	162
CUSTARD PUDDING	161
ENGLISH PLUM PUDDING	172
FIG COOKIES	175
FIGGY DUFF	173
FIJIAN PUDDING	174
FLODEKAGER	173
FRESH PEACH PIE	174
FRESH STRAWBERRY PIE	175
FRITTERS	174
FROZEN LEMON PIE	172
GÂCHE MÈLEE	168
GIBANICA	155
GRAHAM CRACKER BROWNIES	155
GRAHAM CRACKER OR VANILLA WAFER FLUFF	169
GULAB JAMUN	167
GUYANA BLACK CAKE	154
JENNY'S MUFFINS	156
KAHLUA COFFEE BROWNIES	157
KAYMAKLI KURU KAYISI	156
KEY LIME SQUARES	176
KNAFEH	158
KOLACHE	157
KUGLICE OF SMOKAVA	158
LATIYA	177
LIBERIAN KANYAH	176
LUBKUCHEN	177
MAPOPO	179
MARMALADE CAKE	186
MELOMAKARONA	187
MENI MENIYOUNG	178
MISHRI MAWA	178
MIXED FRUIT SAUTÉ	188
MTEDZA CAKE	188
NANAIMO BARS	180
OAT-CHOCOLATE CANDY	181
OLD FASHION BREAD PUDDING	181
PANCAKES	184
PAPAYA PIE	147
PAWPAW PIE	149
PEAR FLAN	182

PEAR TART TATIN WITH MASCARPONE CREAM AND ORANGE GRANITA	182
PEPPARKAKOR	147
PLUM-BERRY TARTS	184
POTATO CHIP PECAN COOKIES	149
PUMPKIN CHEESE CAKE OR BARS	183
PUMPKIN PATCH SQUARES	148
QUICK CHEESECAKE	148
QUINDAO	185
RAISIN CARROT CAKE	150
RIBEI	149
RICE PUDDING	150
RUM CAKE	151
RUSSIAN ALMOND COOKIE	151
SAN KA YA	153
SHREWSBURY CAKES	152
SOUR CREAM POUND CAKE	152
TAMBI ZA NAZI NA ZABIBU	154
TIRAMISU	169
TOFU CAKE	170
TRUFFLE LAYER CAKE	153
VERSUNKENER APFELKUCHEN	179
WALNUT TOFFEE	180
WHISKEY CREAM PIE	179
YOGURT MUFFINS	186
YORKSHIRE PUDDING	186
ZUCCHINI BREAD	185

TEN MINUTE MEALS

ASIAN CHICKEN	189
BEAN BONANZA	192
BROCCOLI CHICKEN	189
COCONUT CRUNCH VEGETABLES	193
CORNY CHICKEN	195
CURRY CHICKEN	194
FRUITY SALAD	194
HAM AND EGG SALAD	195
MANGO SHRIMP	189
NUTTY VEGETABLES	193
PEANUT BUTTER CHICKEN	192
ROYAL PORK CHOPS	193
SALMON BURGERS WITH FRUITY SALSA	191
SPICY CABBAGE	193
SPICY SALSA TILAPIA	190
SPINACH SHRIMP	194
STUFFED POTATO	191
SWEET POTATO FRITTERS	192
TEMPTING DUCK	190
TUNA PITA POCKETS	191

How to Order Additional Copies

Get additional copies of this cookbook by returning an order form and your check or money order to:

Rotarian Flavors of the World Cookbook
P.O. Box 6099
Buffalo Grove, IL 60089 USA
rotarianflavorsworldcookbook@gmail.com

Please send me _____ copies of:
Rotarian Flavors of the World Cookbook
at **$10.00** plus **$2.00** for s/h in the **US and Canada**.
(**$4.00** for s/h in all other countries)
Enclosed is my check or money order for $_____.

Mail Books To:

_____
Name

_____
Address

_____ _____ _____
City   State   Zip

Please send me _____ copies of:
Rotarian Flavors of the World Cookbook
at **$10.00** plus **$2.00** for s/h in the **US and Canada**.
(**$4.00** for s/h in all other countries)
Enclosed is my check or money order for $_____.

Mail Books To:

_____
Name

_____
Address

_____ _____ _____
City   State   Zip

PANTRY BASICS

A WELL-STOCKED PANTRY provides all the makings for a good meal. With the right ingredients, you can quickly create a variety of satisfying, delicious meals for family or guests. Keeping these items in stock also means avoiding extra trips to the grocery store, saving you time and money. Although everyone's pantry is different, there are basic items you should always have. Add other items according to your family's needs. For example, while some families consider chips, cereals and snacks as must-haves, others can't be without feta cheese and imported olives. Use these basic pantry suggestions as a handy reference list when creating your grocery list. Don't forget refrigerated items like milk, eggs, cheese and butter.

STAPLES

- Baker's chocolate
- Baking powder
- Baking soda
- Barbeque sauce
- Bread crumbs (plain or seasoned)
- Chocolate chips
- Cocoa powder
- Cornmeal
- Cornstarch
- Crackers
- Flour
- Honey
- Ketchup
- Lemon juice
- Mayonnaise or salad dressing
- Non-stick cooking spray
- Nuts (almonds, pecans, walnuts)
- Oatmeal
- Oil (olive, vegetable)
- Pancake baking mix
- Pancake syrup
- Peanut butter
- Shortening
- Sugar (granulated, brown, powdered)
- Vinegar

PACKAGED/CANNED FOODS

- Beans (canned, dry)
- Broth (beef, chicken)
- Cake mixes with frosting
- Canned diced tomatoes
- Canned fruit
- Canned mushrooms
- Canned soup
- Canned tomato paste & sauce
- Canned tuna & chicken
- Cereal
- Dried soup mix
- Gelatin (flavored or plain)
- Gravies
- Jarred Salsa
- Milk (evaporated, sweetened condensed)
- Non-fat dry milk
- Pastas
- Rice (brown, white)
- Spaghetti sauce

SPICES/SEASONINGS

- Basil
- Bay leaves
- Black pepper
- Bouillon cubes (beef, chicken)
- Chives
- Chili powder
- Cinnamon
- Mustard (dried, prepared)
- Garlic powder or salt
- Ginger
- Nutmeg
- Onion powder or salt
- Oregano
- Paprika
- Parsley
- Rosemary
- Sage
- Salt
- Soy sauce
- Tarragon
- Thyme
- Vanilla
- Worcestershire sauce
- Yeast

Copyright © 2006
Morris Press Cookbooks
All Rights Reserved.

HERBS & SPICES

DRIED VS. FRESH. While dried herbs are convenient, they don't generally have the same purity of flavor as fresh herbs. Ensure dried herbs are still fresh by checking if they are green and not faded. Crush a few leaves to see if the aroma is still strong. Always store them in an air-tight container away from light and heat.

BASIL — Sweet, warm flavor with an aromatic odor. Use whole or ground. Good with lamb, fish, roast, stews, beef, vegetables, dressing and omelets.

BAY LEAVES — Pungent flavor. Use whole leaf but remove before serving. Good in vegetable dishes, seafood, stews and pickles.

CARAWAY — Spicy taste and aromatic smell. Use in cakes, breads, soups, cheese and sauerkraut.

CELERY SEED — Strong taste which resembles the vegetable. Can be used sparingly in pickles and chutney, meat and fish dishes, salads, bread, marinades, dressings and dips.

CHIVES — Sweet, mild flavor like that of onion. Excellent in salads, fish, soups and potatoes.

CILANTRO — Use fresh. Excellent in salads, fish, chicken, rice, beans and Mexican dishes.

CINNAMON — Sweet, pungent flavor. Widely used in many sweet baked goods, chocolate dishes, cheesecakes, pickles, chutneys and hot drinks.

CORIANDER — Mild, sweet, orangy flavor and available whole or ground. Common in curry powders and pickling spice and also used in chutney, meat dishes, casseroles, Greek-style dishes, apple pies and baked goods.

CURRY POWDER — Spices are combined to proper proportions to give a distinct flavor to meat, poultry, fish and vegetables.

DILL — Both seeds and leaves are flavorful. Leaves may be used as a garnish or cooked with fish, soup, dressings, potatoes and beans. Leaves or the whole plant may be used to flavor pickles.

FENNEL — Sweet, hot flavor. Both seeds and leaves are used. Use in small quantities in pies and baked goods. Leaves can be boiled with fish.

HERBS & SPICES

GINGER — A pungent root, this aromatic spice is sold fresh, dried or ground. Use in pickles, preserves, cakes, cookies, soups and meat dishes.

MARJORAM — May be used both dried or green. Use to flavor fish, poultry, omelets, lamb, stew, stuffing and tomato juice.

MINT — Aromatic with a cool flavor. Excellent in beverages, fish, lamb, cheese, soup, peas, carrots and fruit desserts.

NUTMEG — Whole or ground. Used in chicken and cream soups, cheese dishes, fish cakes, and with chicken and veal. Excellent in custards, milk puddings, pies and cakes.

OREGANO — Strong, aromatic odor. Use whole or ground in tomato juice, fish, eggs, pizza, omelets, chili, stew, gravy, poultry and vegetables.

PAPRIKA — A bright red pepper, this spice is used in meat, vegetables and soups or as a garnish for potatoes, salads or eggs.

PARSLEY — Best when used fresh, but can be used dried as a garnish or as a seasoning. Try in fish, omelets, soup, meat, stuffing and mixed greens.

ROSEMARY — Very aromatic. Can be used fresh or dried. Season fish, stuffing, beef, lamb, poultry, onions, eggs, bread and potatoes. Great in dressings.

SAFFRON — Aromatic, slightly bitter taste. Only a pinch needed to flavor and color dishes such as bouillabaisse, chicken soup, rice, paella, fish sauces, buns and cakes. Very expensive, so where a touch of color is needed, use turmeric instead, but the flavor will not be the same.

SAGE — Use fresh or dried. The flowers are sometimes used in salads. May be used in tomato juice, fish, omelets, beef, poultry, stuffing, cheese spreads and breads.

TARRAGON — Leaves have a pungent, hot taste. Use to flavor sauces, salads, fish, poultry, tomatoes, eggs, green beans, carrots and dressings.

THYME — Sprinkle leaves on fish or poultry before broiling or baking. Throw a few sprigs directly on coals shortly before meat is finished grilling.

TURMERIC — Aromatic, slightly bitter flavor. Should be used sparingly in curry powder and relishes and to color cakes and rice dishes.

Use 3 times more fresh herbs if substituting fresh for dried.

BAKING BREADS

HINTS FOR BAKING BREADS

- Kneading dough for 30 seconds after mixing improves the texture of baking powder biscuits.

- Instead of shortening, use cooking or salad oil in waffles and hot cakes.

- When bread is baking, a small dish of water in the oven will help keep the crust from hardening.

- Dip a spoon in hot water to measure shortening, butter, etc., and the fat will slip out more easily.

- Small amounts of leftover corn may be added to pancake batter for variety.

- To make bread crumbs, use the fine cutter of a food grinder and tie a large paper bag over the spout in order to prevent flying crumbs.

- When you are doing any sort of baking, you get better results if you remember to preheat your cookie sheet, muffin tins or cake pans.

3 RULES FOR USE OF LEAVENING AGENTS

1. In simple flour mixtures, use 2 teaspoons baking powder to leaven 1 cup flour. Reduce this amount 1/2 teaspoon for each egg used.

2. To 1 teaspoon soda, use 2 1/4 teaspoons cream of tartar, 2 cups freshly soured milk or 1 cup molasses.

3. To substitute soda and an acid for baking powder, divide the amount of baking powder by 4. Take that as your measure and add acid according to rule 2.

PROPORTIONS OF BAKING POWDER TO FLOUR

biscuits ....to 1 cup flour use 1 1/4 tsp. baking powder
cake with oil ....to 1 cup flour use 1 tsp. baking powder
muffins ....to 1 cup flour use 1 1/2 tsp. baking powder
popovers ....to 1 cup flour use 1 1/4 tsp. baking powder
waffles ....to 1 cup flour use 1 1/4 tsp. baking powder

PROPORTIONS OF LIQUID TO FLOUR

pour batter ....to 1 cup liquid use 1 cup flour
drop batter ....to 1 cup liquid use 2 to 2 1/2 cups flour
soft dough ....to 1 cup liquid use 3 to 3 1/2 cups flour
stiff dough ....to 1 cup liquid use 4 cups flour

TIME & TEMPERATURE CHART

Breads	Minutes	Temperature
biscuits	12 - 15	400° - 450°
cornbread	25 - 30	400° - 425°
gingerbread	40 - 50	350° - 370°
loaf	50 - 60	350° - 400°
nut bread	50 - 75	350°
popovers	30 - 40	425° - 450°
rolls	20 - 30	400° - 450°

BAKING DESSERTS

PERFECT COOKIES

Cookie dough that must be rolled is much easier to handle after it has been refrigerated for 10 to 30 minutes. This keeps the dough from sticking, even though it may be soft. If not done, the soft dough may require more flour and too much flour makes cookies hard and brittle. Place on a floured board only as much dough as can be easily managed. Flour the rolling pin slightly and roll lightly to desired thickness. Cut shapes close together and add trimmings to dough that needs to be rolled. Place pans or sheets in upper third of oven. Watch cookies carefully while baking in order to avoid burned edges. When sprinkling sugar on cookies, try putting it into a salt shaker in order to save time.

PERFECT PIES

- Pie crust will be better and easier to make if all the ingredients are cool.

- The lower crust should be placed in the pan so that it covers the surface smoothly. Air pockets beneath the surface will push the crust out of shape while baking.

- Folding the top crust over the lower crust before crimping will keep juices in the pie.

- When making custard pie, bake at a high temperature for about 10 minutes to prevent a soggy crust. Then finish baking at a low temperature.

- When making cream pie, sprinkle crust with powdered sugar in order to prevent it from becoming soggy.

PERFECT CAKES

- Fill cake pans two-thirds full and spread batter into corners and sides, leaving a slight hollow in the center.

- Cake is done when it shrinks from the sides of the pan or if it springs back when touched lightly with the finger.

- After removing a cake from the oven, place it on a rack for about 5 minutes. Then, the sides should be loosened and the cake turned out on a rack in order to finish cooling.

- Do not frost cakes until thoroughly cool.

- Icing will remain where you put it if you sprinkle cake with powdered sugar first.

TIME & TEMPERATURE CHART

Dessert	Time	Temperature
butter cake, layer	20-40 min.	380° - 400°
butter cake, loaf	40-60 min.	360° - 400°
cake, angel	50-60 min.	300° - 360°
cake, fruit	3-4 hrs.	275° - 325°
cake, sponge	40-60 min.	300° - 350°
cookies, molasses	18-20 min.	350° - 375°
cookies, thin	10-12 min.	380° - 390°
cream puffs	45-60 min.	300° - 350°
meringue	40-60 min.	250° - 300°
pie crust	20-40 min.	400° - 500°

VEGETABLES & FRUITS

COOKING TIME TABLE

Vegetable	Cooking Method	Time
artichokes	boiled	40 min.
	steamed	45-60 min.
asparagus tips	boiled	10-15 min.
beans, lima	boiled	20-40 min.
	steamed	60 min.
beans, string	boiled	15-35 min.
	steamed	60 min.
beets, old	boiled or steamed	1-2 hours.
beets, young with skin	boiled	30 min.
	steamed	60 min.
	baked	70-90 min.
broccoli, flowerets	boiled	5-10 min.
broccoli, stems	boiled	20-30 min.
brussels sprouts	boiled	20-30 min.
cabbage, chopped	boiled	10-20 min.
	steamed	25 min.
carrots, cut across	boiled	8-10 min.
	steamed	40 min.
cauliflower, flowerets	boiled	8-10 min.
cauliflower, stem down	boiled	20-30 min.
corn, green, tender	boiled	5-10 min.
	steamed	15 min.
	baked	20 min.
corn on the cob	boiled	8-10 min.
	steamed	15 min.
eggplant, whole	boiled	30 min.
	steamed	40 min.
	baked	45 min.
parsnips	boiled	25-40 min.
	steamed	60 min.
	baked	60-75 min.
peas, green	boiled or steamed	5-15 min.
potatoes	boiled	20-40 min.
	steamed	60 min.
	baked	45-60 min.
pumpkin or squash	boiled	20-40 min.
	steamed	45 min.
	baked	60 min.
tomatoes	boiled	5-15 min.
turnips	boiled	25-40 min.

DRYING TIME TABLE

Fruit	Sugar or Honey	Cooking Time
apricots	¼ c. for each cup of fruit	about 40 min.
figs	1 T. for each cup of fruit	about 30 min.
peaches	¼ c. for each cup of fruit	about 45 min.
prunes	2 T. for each cup of fruit	about 45 min.

VEGETABLES & FRUITS

BUYING FRESH VEGETABLES

Artichokes: Look for compact, tightly closed heads with green, clean-looking leaves. Avoid those with leaves that are brown or separated.

Asparagus: Stalks should be tender and firm; tips should be close and compact. Choose the stalks with very little white; they are more tender. Use asparagus soon because it toughens quickly.

Beans, Snap: Those with small seeds inside the pods are best. Avoid beans with dry-looking pods.

Broccoli, Brussels Sprouts and Cauliflower: Flower clusters on broccoli and cauliflower should be tight and close together. Brussels sprouts should be firm and compact. Smudgy, dirty spots may indicate pests or disease.

Cabbage and Head Lettuce: Choose heads that are heavy for their size. Avoid cabbage with worm holes and lettuce with discoloration or soft rot.

Cucumbers: Choose long, slender cucumbers for best quality. May be dark or medium green, but yellow ones are undesirable.

Mushrooms: Caps should be closed around the stems. Avoid black or brown gills.

Peas and Lima Beans: Select pods that are well-filled but not bulging. Avoid dried, spotted, yellow or limp pods.

BUYING FRESH FRUITS

Bananas: Skin should be free of bruises and black or brown spots. Purchase them slightly green and allow them to ripen at room temperature.

Berries: Select plump, solid berries with good color. Avoid stained containers which indicate wet or leaky berries. Berries with clinging caps, such as blackberries and raspberries, may be unripe. Strawberries without caps may be overripe.

Melons: In cantaloupes, thick, close netting on the rind indicates best quality. Cantaloupes are ripe when the stem scar is smooth and the space between the netting is yellow or yellow-green. They are best when fully ripe with fruity odor.

Honeydews are ripe when rind has creamy to yellowish color and velvety texture. Immature honeydews are whitish-green.

Ripe watermelons have some yellow color on one side. If melons are white or pale green on one side, they are not ripe.

Oranges, Grapefruit and Lemons: Choose those heavy for their size. Smoother, thinner skins usually indicate more juice. Most skin markings do not affect quality. Oranges with a slight greenish tinge may be just as ripe as fully colored ones. Light or greenish-yellow lemons are more tart than deep yellow ones. Avoid citrus fruits showing withered, sunken or soft areas.

NAPKIN FOLDING

FOR BEST RESULTS, use well-starched linen napkins if possible. For more complicated folds, 24-inch napkins work best. Practice the folds with newspapers. Children will have fun decorating the table once they learn these attractive folds!

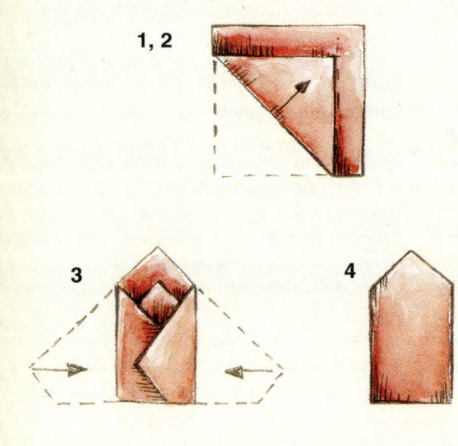

SHIELD

Easy fold. Elegant with monogram in corner.

Instructions:
1. Fold into quarter size. If monogrammed, ornate corner should face down.
2. Turn up folded corner three-quarters.
3. Overlap right side and left side points.
4. Turn over; adjust sides so they are even, single point in center.
5. Place point up or down on plate, or left of plate.

ROSETTE

Elegant on plate.

Instructions:
1. Fold left and right edges to center, leaving 1/2" opening along center.
2. Pleat firmly from top edge to bottom edge. Sharpen edges with hot iron.
3. Pinch center together. If necessary, use small piece of pipe cleaner to secure and top with single flower.
4. Spread out rosette.

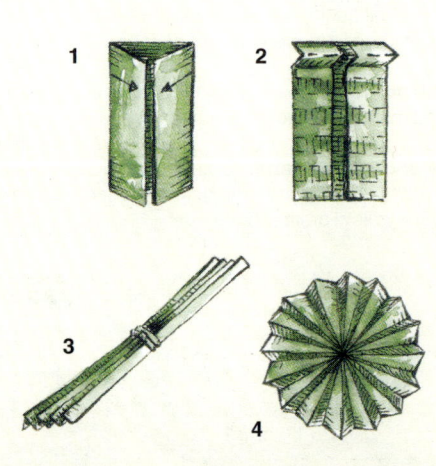

NAPKIN FOLDING

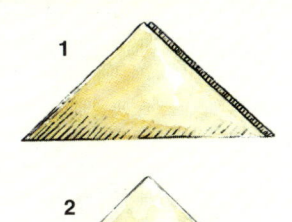

CANDLE

Easy to do; can be decorated.

Instructions:
1. Fold into triangle, point at top.
2. Turn lower edge up 1".
3. Turn over, folded edge down.
4. Roll tightly from left to right.
5. Tuck in corner. Stand upright.

FAN

Pretty in napkin ring or on plate.

Instructions:
1. Fold top and bottom edges to center.
2. Fold top and bottom edges to center a second time.
3. Pleat firmly from the left edge. Sharpen edges with hot iron.
4. Spread out fan. Balance flat folds of each side on table. Well-starched napkins will hold shape.

LILY

Effective and pretty on table.

Instructions:
1. Fold napkin into quarters.
2. Fold into triangle, closed corner to open points.
3. Turn two points over to other side. (Two points are on either side of closed point.)
4. Pleat.
5. Place closed end in glass. Pull down two points on each side and shape.

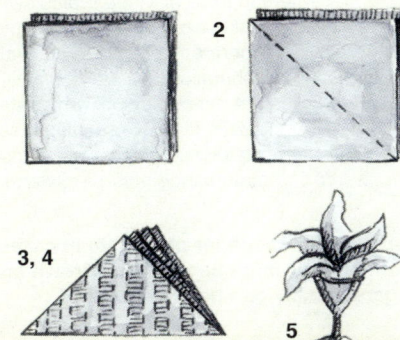

MEASUREMENTS & SUBSTITUTIONS

MEASUREMENTS

a pinch	1/8 teaspoon or less
3 teaspoons	1 tablespoon
4 tablespoons	1/4 cup
8 tablespoons	1/2 cup
12 tablespoons	3/4 cup
16 tablespoons	1 cup
2 cups	1 pint
4 cups	1 quart
4 quarts	1 gallon
8 quarts	1 peck
4 pecks	1 bushel
16 ounces	1 pound
32 ounces	1 quart
1 ounce liquid	2 tablespoons
8 ounces liquid	1 cup

Use standard measuring spoons and cups. All measurements are level.

C° TO F° CONVERSION

120° C	250° F
140° C	275° F
150° C	300° F
160° C	325° F
180° C	350° F
190° C	375° F
200° C	400° F
220° C	425° F
230° C	450° F

Temperature conversions are estimates.

SUBSTITUTIONS

Ingredient	Quantity	Substitute
baking powder	1 teaspoon	1/4 tsp. baking soda plus 1/2 tsp. cream of tartar
chocolate	1 square (1 oz.)	3 or 4 T. cocoa plus 1 T. butter
cornstarch	1 tablespoon	2 T. flour or 2 tsp. quick-cooking tapioca
cracker crumbs	3/4 cup	1 c. bread crumbs
dates	1 lb.	1 1/2 c. dates, pitted and cut
dry mustard	1 teaspoon	1 T. prepared mustard
flour, self-rising	1 cup	1 c. all-purpose flour, 1/2 tsp. salt, and 1 tsp. baking powder
herbs, fresh	1 tablespoon	1 tsp. dried herbs
ketchup or chili sauce	1 cup	1 c. tomato sauce plus 1/2 c. sugar and 2 T. vinegar (for use in cooking)
milk, sour	1 cup	1 T. lemon juice or vinegar plus sweet milk to make 1 c. (let stand 5 minutes)
whole	1 cup	1/2 c. evaporated milk plus 1/2 c. water
min. marshmallows	10	1 lg. marshmallow
onion, fresh	1 small	1 T. instant minced onion, rehydrated
sugar, brown	1/2 cup	2 T. molasses in 1/2 c. granulated sugar
powdered	1 cup	1 c. granulated sugar plus 1 tsp. cornstarch
tomato juice	1 cup	1/2 c. tomato sauce plus 1/2 c. water

When substituting cocoa for chocolate in cakes, the amount of flour must be reduced. Brown and white sugars usually can be interchanged.

EQUIVALENCY CHART

Food	Quantity	Yield
apple	1 medium	1 cup
banana, mashed	1 medium	1/3 cup
bread	1 1/2 slices	1 cup soft crumbs
bread	1 slice	1/4 cup fine, dry crumbs
butter	1 stick or 1/4 pound	1/2 cup
cheese, American, cubed	1 pound	2 2/3 cups
American, grated	1 pound	5 cups
cream cheese	3-ounce package	6 2/3 tablespoons
chocolate, bitter	1 square	1 ounce
cocoa	1 pound	4 cups
coconut	1 1/2 pound package	2 2/3 cups
coffee, ground	1 pound	5 cups
cornmeal	1 pound	3 cups
cornstarch	1 pound	3 cups
crackers, graham	14 squares	1 cup fine crumbs
saltine	28 crackers	1 cup fine crumbs
egg	4-5 whole	1 cup
whites	8-10	1 cup
yolks	10-12	1 cup
evaporated milk	1 cup	3 cups whipped
flour, cake, sifted	1 pound	4 1/2 cups
rye	1 pound	5 cups
white, sifted	1 pound	4 cups
white, unsifted	1 pound	3 3/4 cups
gelatin, flavored	3 1/4 ounces	1/2 cup
unflavored	1/4 ounce	1 tablespoon
lemon	1 medium	3 tablespoon juice
marshmallows	16	1/4 pound
noodles, cooked	8-ounce package	7 cups
uncooked	4 ounces (1 1/2 cups)	2-3 cups cooked
macaroni, cooked	8-ounce package	6 cups
macaroni, uncooked	4 ounces (1 1/4 cups)	2 1/4 cups cooked
spaghetti, uncooked	7 ounces	4 cups cooked
nuts, chopped	1/4 pound	1 cup
almonds	1 pound	3 1/2 cups
walnuts, broken	1 pound	3 cups
walnuts, unshelled	1 pound	1 1/2 to 1 3/4 cups
onion	1 medium	1/2 cup
orange	3-4 medium	1 cup juice
raisins	1 pound	3 1/2 cups
rice, brown	1 cup	4 cups cooked
converted	1 cup	3 1/2 cups cooked
regular	1 cup	3 cups cooked
wild	1 cup	4 cups cooked
sugar, brown	1 pound	2 1/2 cups
powdered	1 pound	3 1/2 cups
white	1 pound	2 cups
vanilla wafers	22	1 cup fine crumbs
zwieback, crumbled	4	1 cup

FOOD QUANTITIES

FOR LARGE SERVINGS

	25 Servings	50 Servings	100 Servings
Beverages:			
coffee	1/2 pound and 1 1/2 gallons water	1 pound and 3 gallons water	2 pounds and 6 gallons water
lemonade	10-15 lemons and 1 1/2 gallons water	20-30 lemons and 3 gallons water	40-60 lemons and 6 gallons water
tea	1/12 pound and 1 1/2 gallons water	1/6 pound and 3 gallons water	1/3 pound and 6 gallons water
Desserts:			
layered cake	1 12" cake	3 10" cakes	6 10" cakes
sheet cake	1 10" x 12" cake	1 12" x 20" cake	2 12" x 20" cakes
watermelon	37 1/2 pounds	75 pounds	150 pounds
whipping cream	3/4 pint	1 1/2 to 2 pints	3-4 pints
Ice cream:			
brick	3 1/4 quarts	6 1/2 quarts	13 quarts
bulk	2 1/4 quarts	4 1/2 quarts or 1 1/4 gallons	9 quarts or 2 1/2 gallons
Meat, poultry or fish:			
fish	13 pounds	25 pounds	50 pounds
fish, fillets or steak	7 1/2 pounds	15 pounds	30 pounds
hamburger	9 pounds	18 pounds	35 pounds
turkey or chicken	13 pounds	25 to 35 pounds	50 to 75 pounds
wieners (beef)	6 1/2 pounds	13 pounds	25 pounds
Salads, casseroles:			
baked beans	3/4 gallon	1 1/4 gallons	2 1/2 gallons
jello salad	3/4 gallon	1 1/4 gallons	2 1/2 gallons
potato salad	4 1/4 quarts	2 1/4 gallons	4 1/2 gallons
scalloped potatoes	4 1/2 quarts or 1 12" x 20" pan	9 quarts or 2 1/4 gallons	18 quarts 4 1/2 gallons
spaghetti	1 1/4 gallons	2 1/2 gallons	5 gallons
Sandwiches:			
bread	50 slices or 3 1-pound loaves	100 slices or 6 1-pound loaves	200 slices or 12 1-pound loaves
butter	1/2 pound	1 pound	2 pounds
lettuce	1 1/2 heads	3 heads	6 heads
mayonnaise	1 cup	2 cups	4 cups
mixed filling			
meat, eggs, fish	1 1/2 quarts	3 quarts	6 quarts
jam, jelly	1 quart	2 quarts	4 quarts

QUICK FIXES

PRACTICALLY EVERYONE has experienced that dreadful moment in the kitchen when a recipe failed and dinner guests have arrived. Perhaps a failed timer, distraction or a missing or mismeasured ingredient is to blame. These handy tips can save the day!

Acidic foods – Sometimes a tomato-based sauce will become too acidic. Add baking soda, one teaspoon at a time, to the sauce. Use sugar as a sweeter alternative.

Burnt food on pots and pans – Allow the pan to cool on its own. Remove as much of the food as possible. Fill with hot water and add a capful of liquid fabric softener to the pot; let it stand for a few hours. You'll have an easier time removing the burnt food.

Chocolate seizes – Chocolate can seize (turn coarse and grainy) when it comes into contact with water. Place seized chocolate in a metal bowl over a large saucepan with an inch of simmering water in it. Over medium heat, slowly whisk in warm heavy cream. Use 1/4 cup cream to 4 ounces of chocolate. The chocolate will melt and become smooth.

Forgot to thaw whipped topping – Thaw in microwave for 1 minute on the defrost setting. Stir to blend well. Do not over thaw!

Hands smell like garlic or onion – Rinse hands under cold water while rubbing them with a large stainless steel spoon.

Hard brown sugar – Place in a paper bag and microwave for a few seconds, or place hard chunks in a food processor.

Jello too hard – Heat on a low microwave power setting for a very short time.

Lumpy gravy or sauce – Use a blender, food processor or simply strain.

No tomato juice – Mix 1/2 cup ketchup with 1/2 cup water.

Out of honey – Substitute 1 1/4 cups sugar dissolved in 1 cup water.

Overcooked sweet potatoes or carrots – Softened sweet potatoes and carrots make a wonderful soufflé with the addition of eggs and sugar. Consult your favorite cookbook for a good soufflé recipe. Overcooked sweet potatoes can also be used as pie filling.

Sandwich bread is stale – Toast or microwave bread briefly. Otherwise, turn it into breadcrumbs. Bread exposed to light and heat will hasten its demise, so consider using a bread box.

Soup, sauce, gravy too thin – Add 1 tablespoon of flour to hot soup, sauce or gravy. Whisk well (to avoid lumps) while the mixture is boiling. Repeat if necessary.

Sticky rice – Rinse rice with warm water.

Stew or soup is greasy – Refrigerate and remove grease once it congeals. Another trick is to lay cold lettuce leaves over the hot stew for about 10 seconds and then remove. Repeat as necessary.

Too salty – Add a little sugar and vinegar. For soups or sauces, add a raw peeled potato.

Too sweet – Add a little vinegar or lemon juice.

Undercooked cakes and cookies – Serve over vanilla ice cream. You can also layer pieces of cake or cookies with whipped cream and fresh fruit to form a dessert parfait. Crumbled cookies also make an excellent ice cream or cream pie topping.

COUNTING CALORIES

BEVERAGES

apple juice, 6 oz.	90
coffee (black)	0
cola, 12 oz.	115
cranberry juice, 6 oz.	115
ginger ale, 12 oz.	115
grape juice, (prepared from frozen concentrate), 6 oz.	142
lemonade, (prepared from frozen concentrate), 6 oz.	85
milk, protein fortified, 1 c.	105
skim, 1 c.	90
whole, 1 c.	160
orange juice, 6 oz.	85
pineapple juice, unsweetened, 6 oz.	95
root beer, 12 oz.	150
tonic (quinine water) 12 oz.	132

BREADS

cornbread, 1 sm. square	130
dumplings, 1 med.	70
French toast, 1 slice	135
melba toast, 1 slice	25
muffins, blueberry, 1 muffin	110
bran, 1 muffin	106
corn, 1 muffin	125
English, 1 muffin	280
pancakes, 1 (4-in.)	60
pumpernickel, 1 slice	75
rye, 1 slice	60
waffle, 1	216
white, 1 slice	60-70
whole wheat, 1 slice	55-65

CEREALS

cornflakes, 1 c.	105
cream of wheat, 1 c.	120
oatmeal, 1 c.	148
rice flakes, 1 c.	105
shredded wheat, 1 biscuit	100
sugar krisps, 3/4 c.	110

CRACKERS

graham, 1 cracker	15-30
rye crisp, 1 cracker	35
saltine, 1 cracker	17-20
wheat thins, 1 cracker	9

DAIRY PRODUCTS

butter or margarine, 1 T.	100
cheese, American, 1 oz.	100
camembert, 1 oz.	85
cheddar, 1 oz.	115
cottage cheese, 1 oz.	30
mozzarella, 1 oz.	90
parmesan, 1 oz.	130
ricotta, 1 oz.	50
roquefort, 1 oz.	105
Swiss, 1 oz.	105
cream, light, 1 T.	30
heavy, 1 T.	55
sour, 1 T.	45
hot chocolate, with milk, 1 c.	277
milk chocolate, 1 oz.	145-155
yogurt	
made w/ whole milk, 1 c.	150-165
made w/ skimmed milk, 1 c.	125

EGGS

fried, 1 lg.	100
poached or boiled, 1 lg.	75-80
scrambled or in omelet, 1 lg.	110-130

FISH AND SEAFOOD

bass, 4 oz.	105
salmon, broiled or baked, 3 oz.	155
sardines, canned in oil, 3 oz.	170
trout, fried, 3 1/2 oz.	220
tuna, in oil, 3 oz.	170
in water, 3 oz.	110

COUNTING CALORIES

FRUITS

- apple, 1 med. 80-100
- applesauce, sweetened, ½ c. 90-115
- unsweetened, ½ c. 50
- banana, 1 med. 85
- blueberries, ½ c. 45
- cantaloupe, ½ c. 24
- cherries (pitted), raw, ½ c. 40
- grapefruit, ½ med. 55
- grapes, ½ c. 35-55
- honeydew, ½ c. 55
- mango, 1 med. 90
- orange, 1 med. 65-75
- peach, 1 med. 35
- pear, 1 med. 60-100
- pineapple, fresh, ½ c. 40
- canned in syrup, ½ c. 95
- plum, 1 med. 30
- strawberries, fresh, ½ c. 30
- frozen and sweetened, ½ c. ..120-140
- tangerine, 1 lg. 39
- watermelon, ½ c. 42

MEAT AND POULTRY

- beef, ground (lean), 3 oz. 185
- roast, 3 oz. 185
- chicken, broiled, 3 oz. 115
- lamb chop (lean), 3 oz. 175-200
- steak, sirloin, 3 oz. 175
- tenderloin, 3 oz. 174
- top round, 3 oz. 162
- turkey, dark meat, 3 oz. 175
- white meat, 3 oz. 150
- veal, cutlet, 3 oz. 156
- roast, 3 oz. 76

NUTS

- almonds, 2 T. 105
- cashews, 2 T. 100
- peanuts, 2 T. 105
- peanut butter, 1 T. 95
- pecans, 2 T. 95
- pistachios, 2 T. 92
- walnuts, 2 T. 80

PASTA

- macaroni or spaghetti, cooked, ¾ c. 115

SALAD DRESSINGS

- blue cheese, 1 T. 70
- French, 1 T. 65
- Italian, 1 T. 80
- mayonnaise, 1 T. 100
- olive oil, 1 T. 124
- Russian, 1 T. 70
- salad oil, 1 T. 120

SOUPS

- bean, 1 c. 130-180
- beef noodle, 1 c. 70
- bouillon and consomme, 1 c. 30
- chicken noodle, 1 c. 65
- chicken with rice, 1 c. 50
- minestrone, 1 c. 80-150
- split pea, 1 c. 145-170
- tomato with milk, 1 c. 170
- vegetable, 1 c. 80-100

VEGETABLES

- asparagus, 1 c. 35
- broccoli, cooked, ½ c. 25
- cabbage, cooked, ½ c. 15-20
- carrots, cooked, ½ c. 25-30
- cauliflower, ½ c. 10-15
- corn (kernels), ½ c. 70
- green beans, 1 c. 30
- lettuce, shredded, ½ c. 5
- mushrooms, canned, ½ c. 20
- onions, cooked, ½ c. 30
- peas, cooked, ½ c. 60
- potato, baked, 1 med. 90
- chips, 8-10 100
- mashed, w/milk & butter, 1 c. ..200-300
- spinach, 1 c. 40
- tomato, raw, 1 med. 25
- cooked, ½ c. 30

COOKING TERMS

Au gratin: Topped with crumbs and/or cheese and browned in oven or under broiler.

Au jus: Served in its own juices.

Baste: To moisten foods during cooking with pan drippings or special sauce in order to add flavor and prevent drying.

Bisque: A thick cream soup.

Blanch: To immerse in rapidly boiling water and allow to cook slightly.

Cream: To soften a fat, especially butter, by beating it at room temperature. Butter and sugar are often creamed together, making a smooth, soft paste.

Crimp: To seal the edges of a two-crust pie either by pinching them at intervals with the fingers or by pressing them together with the tines of a fork.

Crudites: An assortment of raw vegetables (i.e. carrots, broccoli, celery, mushrooms) that is served as an hors d'oeuvre, often accompanied by a dip.

Degrease: To remove fat from the surface of stews, soups or stock. Usually cooled in the refrigerator so that fat hardens and is easily removed.

Dredge: To coat lightly with flour, cornmeal, etc.

Entree: The main course.

Fold: To incorporate a delicate substance, such as whipped cream or beaten egg whites, into another substance without releasing air bubbles. A spatula is used to gently bring part of the mixture from the bottom of the bowl to the top. The process is repeated, while slowly rotating the bowl, until the ingredients are thoroughly blended.

Glaze: To cover with a glossy coating, such as a melted and somewhat diluted jelly for fruit desserts.

Julienne: To cut or slice vegetables, fruits or cheeses into match-shaped slivers.

Marinate: To allow food to stand in a liquid in order to tenderize or to add flavor.

Meuniére: Dredged with flour and sautéed in butter.

Mince: To chop food into very small pieces.

Parboil: To boil until partially cooked; to blanch. Usually final cooking in a seasoned sauce follows this procedure.

Pare: To remove the outermost skin of a fruit or vegetable.

Poach: To cook gently in hot liquid kept just below the boiling point.

Purée: To mash foods by hand by rubbing through a sieve or food mill, or by whirling in a blender or food processor until perfectly smooth.

Refresh: To run cold water over food that has been parboiled in order to stop the cooking process quickly.

Sauté: To cook and/or brown food in a small quantity of hot shortening.

Scald: To heat to just below the boiling point, when tiny bubbles appear at the edge of the saucepan.

Simmer: To cook in liquid just below the boiling point. The surface of the liquid should be barely moving, broken from time to time by slowly rising bubbles.

Steep: To let food stand in hot liquid in order to extract or to enhance flavor, like tea in hot water or poached fruit in syrup.

Toss: To combine ingredients with a repeated lifting motion.

Whip: To beat rapidly in order to incorporate air and produce expansion, as in heavy cream or egg whites.